TO

The Pharmaceutical corporate
presence in developing
countries

THE PHARMACEUTICAL CORPORATE PRESENCE
IN
DEVELOPING COUNTRIES

MULTINATIONAL MANAGERS AND
DEVELOPING COUNTRY CONCERNS

Lee A. Tavis, series editor

*Multinational Managers and Poverty
in the Third World,* Volume I, 1982

*Multinational Managers and Host
Government Interactions,* Volume II, 1988

*Rekindling Development: Multinational
Firms and World Debt,* Volume III, 1988

The Pharmaceutical Corporate Presence in Developing Countries

LEE A. TAVIS
AND
OLIVER F. WILLIAMS, C.S.C.
EDITORS

University of Notre Dame Press
Notre Dame, Indiana

Copyright © 1993 by
University of Notre Dame Press
Notre Dame, Indiana 46556
All Rights Reserved

Manufactured in the United States of America

Library of Congress Cataloging-in-Publication Data

The Pharmaceutical corporate presence in developing
countries / Lee A. Tavis and Oliver F. Williams, editors.
    p.   cm. — (Multinational managers and devel-
oping country concerns ; v. 4)
    ISBN 0-268-01511-2
    1. Pharmaceutical industry—Developing countries—
Moral and ethical aspects—Congresses.   2. International business enterprises—Developing countries—
Moral and ethical aspects—Congresses.   I. Tavis,
Lee A.   II. Williams, Oliver F., 1939- .   III. Series.
HD9674.D442P48   1993
338.8′8716151′091724—dc20   92-56864
                                              CIP

* The paper used in this publication meets the minimum requirements*
of the American National Standard for Information Sciences—Permanence of Paper
for Printed Library Materials, ANSI Z39.48-1984.

TO
REGINA ROWAN, S.C.M.M.

the challenging yet collaborative voice in
the intersection of religious networks and
multinational pharmaceutical corporations

Contents

Contents

Foreword

From the beginning of these seminars in 1978 my overwhelming sense has been how very interdependent we are in this world. We all truly depend upon each other, belong to each other, and help or hurt each other. We can do either one. We are not mandated by some necessity to help rather than hurt, that must come from us.

My sense of interdependence draws its image from the most important photograph of all time: the picture of earth taken from outer space which shows our world, planet earth, our habitat from afar. It shows us against the darkness of space a beautiful green and blue and brown jewel, flecked with white clouds, something like a three-layered opal. It takes your breath away.

We are the only planet in our solar system to have air we can breathe, water we can drink, and land we can cultivate. We are the only planet, to our knowledge, that sustains life, both plant and animal. There is a wonderful symbiosis here—we breathe in oxygen and breathe out carbon dioxide while the plants breathe in carbon dioxide and produce oxygen. We have above us an ozone layer that cuts out the ultraviolet rays that would give us skin cancer and burn our retinas. We have a Van Allen belt that picks up all of the noxious, highly energized cosmic rays from outer space that would fry us if we were exposed to them all of the time. Instead, they are trapped in the two Van Allen belts, discovered by the first space ship we sent—Explorer I. The conditions on this habitat earth are not only beautiful in concept as we see in the picture, but really beautiful in the symmetry of science that allows life to grow on this planet.

As you look at that picture from a philosophical point of view, you see that there are no boundaries—no political boundaries or separations because of ideology, no boundaries of color, no religious boundaries, no technical boundaries, no economical boundaries. It is a human habitat and human in the broadest sense of that word.

Yet, close up, the earth is full of boundaries; it is full of divisions. It has deep within it prejudices against people of other colors, of other religions, of other political systems, even of other cultures. Too often the things that should unite us, like religion, drive us apart and make us kill and maim and torture each other.

Think of the earth, beautiful without but divided within, as the space ship from which the picture was taken. Think of that human habitat not with 5.2 billion people but with five astronauts aboard the enclosed spacecraft. If the spaceship were organized as we are on earth, only one out of the five astronauts, representing the First World, would have access to what Jefferson so beautifully called "the pursuit of happiness." What is needed for the pursuit of happiness? Certainly there are spiritual needs—mostly freedom, which we have, and intelligence, which we have. But other goods are necessary as well: food, shelter from the rain and the cold and the sun, and education, one of the most fundamental needs of all, where all of our human talents are explored and unleashed and enlarged to a point where we can have a meaningful life. Education is not just a matter of knowledge but also of values. Moreover, there is a need for access to health or health care. Can you imagine much peace in that spacecraft if one of those five people had 80 percent of the food, the air, the water, the communications, the renewable environment needed aboard a spacecraft?

In the northern part of our globe we have the well-supported astronaut. In the south there is comparable misery. Humanity on this earth cannot honestly be said to pursue happiness when eighty percent of these human goods necessary for the pursuit of happiness are possessed by only one fifth of the population. Remember the old Latin adage, *opus ustetia pax*—Peace is the work of justice.

The challenge given by our globe seen from afar is the challenge of humanity. We are the first generation of human beings to have seen our habitat from this distant view. From this perspective it no longer matters what the provenance of each person happens to be; whether one is a corporate person or a person who represents an agency of the United Nations or a consumers advocacy group. What really matters is that each of us signs on to this vision of our earth from afar, that indeed we are one humanity, that indeed we inherit one earth, that indeed we are endowed as no other planet in our solar system.

Participants in this seminar come together, each bringing certain connections, with strong ideas, with economical, social, or political drives. They come here to a place which is unique on earth. A university is one of the few places on earth where we can disagree without being disagreeable. No one of us is infallible. Many of us are wrong in many of the things we hold most dear. The world will never become united and intellectually truly interdependent unless we learn to share and respect our differences. We are each bound to emerge somewhat differently because we shared our ideas and listened to someone from a different background or point of view. In all of these seminars, since 1978, no one comes to accuse someone else. We come here for understanding, for enlightenment in an honest search.

Multinationals have the ability to do what even governments cannot do: they can develop a product which is lying fallow whether it is the earth, a mind, or the capacity of a people. A multinational can be first of all an educator; it can be a financier to raise money from sources not available to local people; it can certainly be great at development and merchandising products that otherwise are not being developed or merchandised. In the best of all worlds, it can be an engine of development rather than just an engine of exploitation as so many colonial powers were.

In closing, remember the view of the earth as seen from space. We need to make it look like that close up. We may disagree on how to do it — we all have ideas of doing it better. None of us is as effective as we could be; we are all at fault certainly in some of our ideas. By working together in this place we can take that dream of the earth from afar and make it a little more beautiful up close.

Rev. Theodore M. Hesburgh, C.S.C.
The University of Notre Dame

Acknowledgments

Four people have contributed greatly to this volume. Paul Belford and Sister Regina Rowan have been the counselors for the pharmaceutical study group since the first workshop in April 1985 — Paul for industry as the assistant vice president, international, of the Pharmaceutical Manufacturers Association, and Regina as a change agent in her role as the chairperson of the pharmaceutical workgroup of the Interfaith Center on Corporate Responsibility — together ensuring all views would be aired.

The third key contributor is Jule Poirier. As the executive coordinator for the Program, she sponsored each participant from workshop registration through biographical sketches to accommodations; from typing the transcripts of their papers, responses, and discussions through editing, to clearing all comments so no one would be surprised upon publication. With four workshops and the size of this volume that's a whole lot.

Finally, Sparky Tavis has worked with the Program since its very beginning. She enthusiastically volunteered for the Kenya field work, serving as secretary for the team.

Beyond these individuals, the contribution of the participants is amply demonstrated in the following pages. Each is painfully aware of the desperation among the poor and sick in the developing world. Each shares the vision where health care is accessible to all, knowing that the strategies to get there are what sparks the debate. Each has spent long hours describing and modifying dearly held positions.

Funding for this work was provided by a grant from the Rockefeller Foundation and twenty-five multinational corporations.

Aluminum Company of America
Castle & Cooke, Inc.
Caterpillar Tractor Company
CIBA-GEIGY Corporation
The Coca-Cola Company
CPC International Inc.
Eli Lilly and Company
General Mills, Inc.
W. R. Grace & Co.

H. J. Heinz Company
Johnson & Johnson
Marion Merrell Dow Inc.
Merck & Co., Inc.
Mobil Oil Corporation
Mine Safety Appliances
  Company
Pfizer International Inc.
Ralston Purina International

Schering-Plough International
SmithKline Beechman
  Pharmaceuticals
Sterling Drug Inc.
Syntex Corporation
Texaco Inc.
The Upjohn Company
Warner-Lambert Company
Wyeth-Ayerst International Inc.

This funding reflects the broad base of concern in the United States for poverty in the developing countries. While the funding is necessary, and appreciated, it is the personal commitment of the participating managers in a process and outcome which they do not control that sets our work apart.

Introduction

This book is about the activities of multinational corporations in the production, distribution, and use of pharmaceuticals in the poor countries of Africa, Asia, and Latin America. "What is the appropriate role of multinational pharmaceutical companies in these countries, and how can that role best be implemented?" The question can be asked in terms of responsibility: What are the responsibilities of a pharmaceutical corporation in that part of our world where up to two billion people do not have informed access to quality drugs at a price they can afford? What are the limits to this responsibility? Are there possibilities for collaborative action between multinational pharmaceutical companies and the plethora of national and international groups, institutions, and governments concerned with Third World health care delivery?

As part of the Notre Dame Program on Multinational Managers and Developing Country Concerns a pharmaceutical study group has been debating these issues since 1985. This volume is a mid-stream recounting of that discussion. Given the diversity of the participants — pharmaceutical corporate managers, religious activists, consumer advocates, officials of nongovernmental organizations, representatives from the World Health Organization, academics from across the university, and missionaries — the discussion has been far-reaching. Intense at times, we have debated the macro issues such as the appropriateness of private sector firms in health care delivery, all the way to how drugs can be made available to private mission hospitals in Kenya. Across this broad range of issues and problems, no viewpoint has gone unrepresented.

The Notre Dame Program on Multinational Managers and Developing Country Concerns has been dealing with the issues of multinational corporations and Third World development since 1978. The goal of this program is to help multinational managers direct the resources of their firms toward the amelioration of poverty in the Third World, while maintaining the economic viability of their firms. The pharmaceutical study group is the fourth of its kind organized in the program seminar.

Previous study groups have focused on issues such as Third World debt, the interaction between multinational managers and host governmental officials, the joint venture managerial balance between U.S. multinational managers and their counterparts in the Chinese bureaucracy and enterprises, and the overall role of multinationals in Third World development.

Study groups meet in a workshop setting (two-day sessions of about fifty participants) debating the issues on a conceptual basis. Field studies are undertaken in a Third World location where the specific issue has been confronted. Following the field work, the participants reassemble to assess the field findings from their diverse worldviews. The final step is to share our insight in the form of a published volume.

The pharmaceutical study group held its first meeting in April 1985. Initially structured as a broad study of multinational corporate and activist interactions, South Africa disinvestment was discussed along with the pharmaceutical issue. That first meeting convinced us that the South African issue had become too politicized to find a common pathway for collaboration. A following workshop dedicated to pharmaceuticals was held in December of that year. At that time, Kenya was selected as the research site. The Kenya study was initiated when Sister Regina Rowan visited Nairobi in March 1987 to attend the Fourth International Commonwealth Pharmaceutical Meetings. In June and July of that year four researchers from Notre Dame undertook field interviews in Kenya in conjunction with local academics and missionaries. In October 1987, the study group reassembled to evaluate and generalize the Kenya findings.

In our 1987 workshop, we sensed that the interaction among multinational pharmaceutical corporations, the World Health Organization, activists, and Third World governments was undergoing a fundamental transition. In 1990, we held a fourth workshop to monitor that change.

Volume IV is thus being published mid-stream in the pharmaceutical study group's work. The participants are currently discussing activities for the next phase, to be reported in a later volume.

The pharmaceutical study group deliberations are reported in four parts. PART I analyzes the overall issue of multinational pharmaceutical corporate involvement in Third World locations. The initial section of this part deals with the broad issue of conflict and collaboration between multinational corporations and activists. The second section deals with the role of pharmaceuticals in developing country health, the third with the role of multinational corporations in that process.

PART II addresses what were judged to be the three most significant current issues in the multinational corporate involvement: essential drugs, counterfeit drugs, and intellectual property rights. These issues are examined from the group's diverse perspectives.

PART III reports on the Kenya field research and the evaluation of those findings by the workshop participants. The use of pharmaceutical products in Kenya is traced from traditional healing to First World scientific medical systems; from the poverty-stricken rural areas to urban production facilities; from small local entrepreneurs to large multinational corporations. The Kenya situation is analyzed by the World Health Organization official who established the essential drugs network for the Kenya government, by a Kenyan sociologist working to incorporate traditional healing into the Kenyan medical community, and by Kenyan missionaries, as well as the research team.

PART IV summarizes the interaction between religious networks and multinational pharmaceutical corporations as it has evolved to the present time in our seminar, and in the broader society. Sister Regina Rowan presents the activist voice while Albert Angel poses the fundamental questions to be faced by multinational corporate managers.

The book format follows that of the workshops—the presentation of papers or field findings on specific topics, followed by a formal response from a panel representing the range of institutions involved in Third World health care, concluding with a summary of the ensuing discussion.

Participants are introduced briefly throughout the volume as they present papers or respond to current issues. These brief biographies will give the reader a sense of the wealth of diverse experience struggling with the Third World pharmaceutical problem.

At this point, it is appropriate to remind ourselves of the fundamental issue that drives the work of the Notre Dame Program as well as the pharmaceutical study group. It is the concept of "developmental responsibility." As reported in Volume I, developmental responsibility has been the driving force behind the work since its inception in 1978.

Developmental responsibility is based on the principle that "when a person is in need and unable to help himself or herself, others in a position to assist incur the responsibility to help." Developmental responsibility is tied to needs — to people trapped in a situation from which they cannot extricate themselves without help from someone else. It does not arise from complicity in the circumstances which created the need, but from the need itself.

Developmental responsibility is well established in secular ethics and is a construct of all major religions. It applies to all individuals and institutions across the world. It applies to multinational managers and multinational corporations in their multiple national and international activities. It applies particularly to multinational pharmaceutical corporations where the needs of sick people in the developing world are so desperately unserved.

Set against the health needs in the Third World is the requirement to assure the short-term survivability and the long-term viability of the multinational corporation itself and the specific responsibility to all of its various constituents — owners, employees, suppliers, consumers, and communities.

The translation of developmental responsibility to the determination of who makes what decision in a market economy depends upon the efficiency of the markets and the effectiveness of the regulation of those markets. The underlying concept is the productivity/social separation principle. Briefly put, a multinational corporation, as any business enterprise, is drawn to a market for long-term profit opportunities. When it works as it is supposed to, the multinational enhances its own and the country's productivity. The firm is rewarded with returns commensurate with the risk undertaken while governments gain from the firm's presence through jobs, taxes, and the other accoutrements of increased productivity. The government, of course, has goals other than economic ones and will regulate or constrain the business sector to ensure that they are met. Child labor restrictions and safety requirements are examples of regulations to meet these social minimums. Pharmaceutical corporations, as part of the society's objective to make quality health care available at a cost the people can bear, are subjected to more regulation than, say, clothing producers. In this view, corporations are responsible for productivity while governments are responsible for representing the social objectives of society through effective regulation.

Separation of responsibilities is possible only when markets are efficient enough to force the optimization of productivity and regulation is effective enough to constrain and direct the activities of productivity and profit-maximizing business firms toward social objectives.

Regulation is effective when requirements are clearly signaled and enforced by a government that represents a consensus of the society.

No country fits the perfect model of efficient markets and effective regulation, least of all these that are characterized as less developed. Markets are thin, restricted, dominated by a few (often public) suppliers with governments directly involved in the markets through mechanisms such as price controls or the existence of government-owned enterprises; information is seldom sufficient or uniformly available and, when adequate, flows to buyers and sellers who do not know how to use it. Too often the regulating government does not reflect a consensus in the society or has a bureaucracy incapable of effective regulation. Indeed, the lack of efficient markets and effective regulation is one of the fundamental barriers to economic and social development. Thus, in all countries, but especially in the Third World, managers face desperate needs among the poor combined with governments that are unable or unwilling to adequately serve them.

The gap between what is possible and the reality of what is available drives our passion. Religious networks step into this void, attempting to draw pharmaceutical manufacturers along, or to push them. Nongovernmental organizations and other activists push and pull as well.

The gap is particularly difficult for multinational pharmaceutical companies. Third World drug needs are great. Multinationals have the products that will serve many of them. These products, however, represent the most advanced and complex technology available today, introduced into societies and regions where there is no medical sophistication. Drugs find their way to sick people through distribution networks where the multinational has little control over the product or its related information. An apt analogy is the sale of the latest super computer in an Iranian bazaar.

Over the five-year span of this study group, and the attempts on the part of the religious networks and the corporations to fill the gap, there has been a noticeable transition from push to pull, from confrontation to collaboration. The debate has gradually evolved from "who's right and who's wrong" to a search for common ground.

At this point in our deliberations, the appropriateness of the attempt by religious networks to bring Third World pharmaceutical problems to the attention of the industry is, to our surprise, accepted by the participating managers. This acceptance now places a greater responsibility on the shoulders of the religious health care networks, the health-related nongovernmental organizations, and the World Health

Organization to raise problems that are capable of being solved by multinational corporations and to seek realistic ways through which industry and activists can collaborate. The shift is detectable on both sides.

The openness to collaboration reflected in the study group interaction has contributed to, and been the beneficiary of, a growing sense on both sides (industry and activist) that collaboration serves the needs of the sick poor better than confrontation. This is not to suggest that there has been any diminution of determination or a change in worldview on the part of any participant, only to recognize that we together have a responsibility and together can maximize our impact. The person most singly responsible for this transition to be "the challenging yet collaborative voice in the intersection of religious networks and multinational pharmaceutical corporations" is Regina Rowan, S.C.M.M.

PART 1

The Role of Multinational Pharmaceutical Corporations

Part one of this volume addresses the proper role of multinational pharmaceutical corporations in developing countries. In the first section, "Theological Ethics and the Multinational: A Changing Relationship," Oliver Williams builds on the work published in earlier volumes of the series. He draws on the broad range of participants' backgrounds and world views to contrast the macro view of the radical position with the more micro view of the reformist.

The papers by Louis Lasagna and Klaus Leisinger along with their respondents address the proper role of multinational pharmaceutical companies as seen from these diverse viewpoints.

Louis Lasagna, often referred to as the father of clinical pharmacology, presents his perception of the realities of Third World pharmaceutical use. Beginning with nine postulates that should inform the discussion of developing country pharmaceutical issues, he discusses pharmaceuticals in the overall health care environment. He reviews the accusations commonly leveled at the pharmaceutical industry and suggests guidelines for host governmental policy.

The response by Jean Halloran of Consumers Union crisply states an activist view while David Collins, speaking from an extended career in the pharmaceutical industry, calls for collaboration with religious groups. Discussion of the Lasagna paper and responses was initiated with comments about drug distribution and hazardous materials. Typical of our seminar interaction, however, the participants soon moved to a debate on the multinational corporate responsibility in a market system.[1]

As with Lasagna, Klaus Leisinger also stresses pharmaceutical use as one component of health care, based on his experience as a professor of sociology and an executive for CIBA-GEIGY. Detailing health

1

care delivery problems of the developing countries, he analyzes the role of pharmaceuticals and the responsibility for their rational use. Leisinger presents what he calls a "pragmatic approach to corporate ethics."

In response, Ingar Bruggemann from the World Health Organization (WHO) stresses the need for collaborative action and the potential role of the WHO in that process. James Russo, the director of government and public policy for SmithKline Beecham, calls the pharmaceutical industry to its highest standards.

The discussion for this session focuses on the dialogue between activists and industry, and how it has evolved.

NOTE

1. This discussion took place in April 1985 during the first pharmaceutical workshop of the seminar on "Multinational Managers and Developing Country Concerns." The reader may be interested in comparing the confrontational nature of this discussion with that following the Leisinger paper which took place at the fourth pharmaceutical workshop in November 1990.

Theological Ethics and the Multinational: A Changing Relationship

OLIVER F. WILLIAMS, C.S.C.

CAN MULTINATIONAL BUSINESSES ALLEVIATE POVERTY IN THE THIRD WORLD?

Academics, multinational business managers, and religious activists began discussing multinationals and poverty in the Third World under the auspices of a special seminar at the University of Notre Dame in October 1978. After six sessions it was clear that at least one theme persisted: There is no common agreement on *what* actions will actually be helpful to the truly needy of the Third World. While all would agree that no one ought to be hungry or illiterate or die before their time, the *means* of achieving these important goods for the poor of the Third World are in dispute.

At root, there are dichotomous perspectives from theological ethics on the multinational corporation (MNC), some seeing it as primarily an instrument of dependence, others envisioning it as an instrument of development. For example, Father Arthur McCormack, M.H.M., describes the multinational as "an institution which has shown outstanding capabilities in the past" and which must play a major part in solving the "vast problems that face the world for the rest of the century."[1]

Oliver F. Williams, C.S.C., is the associate provost and co-director of the Center for Ethics and Religious Values in Business at the University of Notre Dame. His doctorate is in theology and was followed by post-doctoral work at Stanford University Graduate School of Business. He has published extensively and is actively involved in a broad range of issues relating the Catholic church and multinational corporate ethics.

3

Father Peter Henriot, S.J., on the other hand, is much less sanguine: "I personally am not yet convinced that the multinationals as now constituted and operating can in fact be a major force in meeting the challenge of Third World poverty."[2] He would advocate at least a partial adoption of the U.N. plan, a New International Economic Order (NIEO).

Considering multinationals as part of a global economic system, three major criticisms emerged: (1) Although most would agree that MNCs do contribute to economic growth in the Third World, critics focus on the inequitable distribution of resources which often leaves the poor without basic needs while an elite group lives in luxury. (2) Regulation, both local and national, was criticized as inadequate. Multinational advocates generally saw present regulation as inefficient while critics argued for more governmental intervention. (3) An issue considered important by critics is that the poor of the Third World have no voice in the decision-making process. Participation by those who will be affected by decisions is considered crucial.[3]

A key insight from the Proceedings of the first three years of the seminar is that "a person's observation about the proper role of the multinationals may well differ depending upon the level of analysis one chooses." Three levels of analysis are evident: (1) The examination of the individual firm or enterprise (microeconomic level); (2) an analysis of multinationals as a group (categorical level); and (3) the consideration of the multinational in the context of a global economy (systemic level).[4] The level of analysis tends to shape one's thinking. Most participants tend to see multinational corporate activity from one dominant point of view, and this point of view influences the level at which analysis takes place as well as the sort of remedies that seem appropriate to correct perceived deficiencies.

For example, consider a multinational manager who views the firm primarily from the micro point of view. This manager will perceive his world in terms of the constituencies for whom and to whom he is accountable. He comes to see things from the various stakeholders' perspectives and assumes that he has ample flexibility for responding on the local level to most problems.

Consider another person, a religious activist, for example, who views the significant unit of analysis to be the global system. This person would see problems as solved primarily through systemic change—national regulations, codes of conduct, NIEO, and so on. The firm is seen as relatively powerless to deal adequately with perceived deficiences, and efforts are directed to broader structural change. Although direct pressure may be applied to a multinational business in some dramatic form, this strategy may be only a means of raising public consciousness so that new public policy might finally be enacted.

The experience of the seminar has been that discussion most often reaches an impasse at the point of assessing the "success" of multinational corporate activity in Third World countries. There are at least two distinct sets of criteria employed for evaluating multinationals, one set from the micro point of view, and one from the macro or systemic level of analysis.

An example from my experience independent of the seminar may illustrate how the horizon or context for judgment influences the criteria for judgment and hence the judgment itself. After spending a week visiting a number of sites at a multinational agricultural operation in a Third World country, I was impressed with the remarkable efforts being made to improve the lot of the black employees, most of whom were very poor. This MNC employed almost 30,000 workers and had made dramatic strides in housing, health care, nutrition, and wages. While there was still much to be done, I judged that relative to others in the country, the MNC's employees were living adequately. Basic needs were being met.

While in the country, I also visited some missionaries from the U.S.-based churches and was most impressed with their dedication to helping the poor. In relating the facts about the MNC's social programs, I had anticipated a positive response. However, I was told by a long-time missionary that she could not share my enthusiasm, for while the MNC's efforts were indeed helping some of the poor, in the long run they did more harm than good, for they only delayed the inevitable socialist revolution that would finally meet the needs of *all* the poor.

What became clear was that I was speaking from a micro point of view in one theory of political economy and she was speaking from quite another theory. From a systemic perspective, she had already decided that the only hope for the Third World nation was to break the economic dependence on the United States and begin to form a new socialist society. The facts that I was enthusiastically relating about the MNC's social programs served as a sad reminder for her that the key instrument of dependence was still in the land. In our discussions, we passed like ships in the night, generating more heat than light. I argued that my "micro" analysis was in the context of a development theory of political economy. Must one always begin with a systemic analysis? How bad must things be before moving from a micro point of view to a systemic analysis? Can revolutionary socialism really deliver all that it promises? Is there really any quick fix for Third World poverty?

It is a safe assumption that in any cross-section of academics and multinational managers there will be some who see things primarily from a micro point of view and others from a macro or systemic point of view. It is also true that even if all perceive an issue from a systemic point of view, they may not all be seeing it from the same system. The two dominant theories of political economy of our time, Smithian and Marxian, both are likely to have adherents. Each of these theory-laden perspectives offers divergent interpretations of the same facts. Before reflecting on the import of perspectives on several important issues, it may be helpful to review the crucial role of theologies in shaping interpretive schemes.

THE SORT OF WORLD MANDATED BY THE CHRISTIAN GOSPEL

Whether a person looks at the MNC from a micro or macro point of view, it is helpful to call to mind that often for managers and activists alike a religious outlook shapes their vision of how the world ought to be. The Roman Catholic church and mainline Protestant churches see their congregations as being called by God to transform the world. In his classic *Christ and Culture,* H. Richard Niebuhr calls this appropriation of the Gospel the "Christ the transformer of culture" model.[5] This vision sees individuals as being called by God to transform the world and shape it along the lines of the way of life of Christ. The theological conviction is that God's incarnate Son is present in creation sustaining it and drawing it to its fulfillment, as well as being present in redemption as the one who died and rose again. History is not the area to form a new counterculture as the Amish might hold, or the encounter with the spirit in nature as in Hegelian philosophy, or simply a period of preparation for the final glory in heaven. Rather history is the area where the drama of God's great deeds and people's response are played out. One encounters Christ in the challenge of the situation, in history, as well as in the church and the quiet of one's own conscience.

Augustine and John Calvin stress that the Gospel must influence the whole fabric of life, and in this sense they are pioneers in the transformationist mentality. The twentieth-century Roman Catholic theologian Karl Rahner, S.J., writes in this transformationist vein when he sees the redemptive work of Christ actually present in individuals, cultures, and society where persons are following their best lights in leading a moral life. For Rahner, Christ is present, and God's intentions are discerned, through human reason; this knowledge is deepened and broadened with the life of the Gospels. Salvation in this view is not a completely other-worldly transaction but rather Christ (or grace) is active in converting the person in the present culture and society.

Mainline Protestant churches and the Catholic church see their mission as both ministering to the individual—nurturing, developing character and virtue—as well as transforming the world by improving social structures to enhance social, political, and economic life.[6] This mission is achieved primarily through teaching, preaching, and the liturgy, although direct social action strategies are sometimes employed. For the churches to be effective in speaking about questions of justice in Third World countries, it is crucial that they maintain unity in the moral advice offered. This, unfortunately, has not been the case in regard to Christian social teaching. There are two quite different approaches to change advocated by theologians and activists today: a gradual or evolutionary approach and a revolutionary approach.[7]

Theologian Gregory Baum employs the terms "radical" and "reformed" to refer to the two broad categories of activists in the churches. According to Baum, the radical envisions "a repudiation of capitalism and a struggle for a radical reconstruction of society."[8] Radical Christians "experience themselves as strangers in their own country. Faithful to Jesus and His message of justice and grace, they form spiritual countercultures. . . . They are willing to live on the fringes of society, waiting for the moment when America will be more profoundly shaken and workers will organize this movement for socialism."[9]

When this sort of person is involved in the various strategies to apply pressure to corporations, managers might just as well face up to the fact that "no good deed will go unpunished." With the "radical" type, it is difficult to imagine how a manager could "win"; for if the ultimate goal is the downfall of the free enterprise system, no reform of that system, no matter how drastic, is likely to be satisfactory.

In contrast to the radical approach, the reformist critic will work in whatever ways possible to promote and protect human dignity, for "as disciples of Jesus they want to incarnate their spiritual vision in some concrete action."[10] To the radical, the reformist seems to have sold out to the establishment, for he or she is willing to work with the system and cooperate with its managers to advance a vision.

It may be helpful to explore some of the theological roots of the radical approach by examining the work of one of the most popular liberation theologians, Gustavo Gutierrez.[11] Father Gutierrez, writing in the context of Latin America, has been profoundly influenced by the widespread misery of his people. On a continent where military tyranny, torture, and manifold violations of human rights are common-place, he calls for a new movement of social justice, liberation.

In reading the work of a religious social ethicist, the key feature to discern is how he or she relates the ultimate concepts to the real world that is being addressed, that is, what sort of world is advocated as the vision for faithful Christians. In the technical language of ethics, "middle axioms" mediate between ultimate concepts (liberation, salva-tion) and present empirical realities. What are the middle axioms of Gutierrez?

Several quotes from Gutierrez lay bare his vision of the sort of world that Christians should be striving for.

> Paradoxically, what the groups in power call "advocating" class struggle is really an expression of a will to abolish its causes, to abolish them, not cover them over, to eliminate the appropriation by a few of the wealth created by the work of the many and not to make lyrical calls to social harmony. It is a will to build a socialist society, more just, free, and human, and not a society of superficial and false reconciliation and equality.[12]

> To participate in class struggle not only is not opposed to universal love; this commitment is today the necessary and inescapable means of making this love concrete. For this participation is what leads to a classless society without owners and dispossessed, without oppressors and oppressed.[13]

Focusing on the biblical mandate to build a just society that is truly human, that is, in accord with the Creator's intentions, Gutierrez singles out private property as the basic impediment. The structural reform advocated by Gutierrez might be summarized by the following middle axioms:

1. Abolish private ownership of the means of production;
2. Redistribute wealth according to needs;
3. Fashion a socialist society;
4. Champion class struggle.

It should be noted that, although a Roman Catholic, Gutierrez advocates a social vision that, in my judgment, is out of step with the teaching of the social encyclicals of the Catholic church and most mainline Protestant thinking as well. The sort of world suggested by Catholic social teaching is most often discussed under the rubric of the common good. Rather than identifying the common good with a socialist society, its middle axioms stress achieving a society where freedom and creativity flourish. Catholic social teaching portrays a vision of society that might be captured with the following axioms:

1. Private property is an important means for ensuring human development, but private property always has a social dimension which requires owners to consider the best interests of the community.
2. Society ought to be structured so that those who are able might provide for themselves and their loved ones by freely employing their talents. Those who are unable to provide for their own basic needs are to be treated with full dignity and cared for by appropriate groupings of society determined by public policy.

These sort of middle axioms do not endorse any particular system of government but allow for a wide variety of applications in different contexts and historical situations.[14]

THE REVELANCE OF THE VISION OF MIDDLE AXIOMS

A set of middle axioms provides the social goal, the vision of the sort of world we should try to create. This vision also provides the backdrop or context for particular judgments. For instance, the missionary I encountered in the earlier example evaluated the facts on the multinationals' improvement of health care, housing, and salary in light of her social goal of transforming the society to a socialist one. She quite correctly perceived that raising the standard of living, even for a distinct minority of the population, would alleviate some of the pressure for revolution. In fact, our moral disagreement in that example was not so much on the level of an ethical assessment of the particular situation as on the level of the context for the judgment. All ethical judgments are made presupposing some context.

It may be interesting to reflect on how a religious activist's middle axioms influence the approach to concrete problems. For example, consider the issue of the role of pharmaceuticals in Third World countries. Even if most activists today are reformists, it may be helpful to see another perspective.

THIRD WORLD HEALTH PROBLEMS AND
THE ROLE OF PHARMACEUTICALS

Experience from past conflict on health-related issues between industry and religious activists would seem to indicate two sorts of serious errors. On the one hand, industry should not assume all critics are Marxists seeking a revolutionary socialistic system. Critics should be listened to and their remarks carefully assessed. On the other hand, critics should be straightforward with the goals they are seeking. No matter how good the end, a less than forthright means is beneath the dignity of church representatives. The church as a moral leader ought to ensure that its representatives are beyond reproach. In this light, consider the strategy on infant formula summarized by James Post in a recent article.

> Societies often have difficulties in shaping "sensible" policy solutions to complex policy issues. The reason that children die in developing nations is not because infant formula is a bad product. Rather, there is an environment of poverty, illiteracy, inadequate sanitation, unhealthy water, and limited health services that create dangerous conditions for the use of formula. Marketing did not create these conditions, but marketing was a more actionable aspect of the problem than poverty, water, or education. . . . Because business corporations are responsive to external pressure, action targeted at them has a better chance of producing change than actions aimed at such underlying conditions as poverty and illiteracy. A marketing code will not alleviate the problems of poverty, illiteracy, and poor sanitation, but it can help to insure that companies do not exploit such conditions to their own advantage.[15]

While this may be acceptable strategy for some consumer groups, is it the most appropriate one for the church, the model of what human community ought to be like? The church must indeed be concerned to better the lot of the poor, but are not straightforward attempts to influence public policy much more fruitful? Should not the churches' major effort be directed at securing public policy aimed at improving the underlying conditions of poverty, illiteracy, and so on. Is settling for a marketing code, settling for too little?

Again, the radical and the reformist would have different responses to the query. The radical, already convinced that the status quo is evil, would see any strategy likely to diminish the influence of multinationals as the lesser of evils. The radical would see no utility in trying to reform the present system.

The reformist, however, would likely take quite another tack. Trying not only to reform the system, but also to be a model of integrity in the process, the reformer would actively pursue all avenues to bring justice to the oppressed.

The radical and the reformist positions are usually represented whenever religious activists from around the globe are involved with multinational business corporations. If it be true that multinational leaders and the critics speak from different levels of analysis and systems that are unlikely to converge, what is a reasonable goal at this stage? My contention is that a reasonable goal is *not* to form a consensus on fundamental perspectives and consequent decisions. At this point, probably the only way that sort of consensus could be achieved is by artificially suppressing differences. Rather, a more realistic objective of the dialogue is *to clarify the consequences of our different perspectives and interpretations.* Much more serious discussions, supported by empirical research, must focus on the likely consequences of the various scenarios.

THE STATE OF THE DIALOGUE TODAY

Since the Notre Dame seminar began in 1978, there has been a remarkable shift in activists' thinking on the question of Third World development. The shift is clearly evident in this volume where, for example, in the discussion of intellectual property rights, there is a consensus on the part of the activists that market solutions, e.g., patent protections, are appropriate in developing countries. There is little talk of "a repudiation of capitalism and a struggle for a radical reconstruction of society" but rather a focus on how markets and incentives can be made to work for the poor in the Third World.

Although there are still some religious critics who long for the downfall of market economies, these are a dying breed. Events of recent years have dramatically demonstrated that, although Marxist theory might be intellectually appealing, its practice is a dismal failure. Only the most strident ideologue could fail to learn the lesson of the collapse of socialism in Eastern Europe. On the positive side, the amazing growth of the Asian market economies, especially Singapore, South Korea, and Taiwan, has not gone unnoticed by activists interested in increasing the standard of living of the least advantaged.

Today's activist has a sound appreciation of the market economy while also being convinced that all those who wield power have corresponding responsibilities. This is seen, for example, in the plea by activists that those who hold intellectual property rights also exercise an appropriate level of responsibility in developing countries, for all rights entail responsibilities. While the market is accepted as appropriate for the economy, it is not accepted as *the mechanism* to solve all problems. There are some goods, for example, human health, which may require an appropriate level of responsibility by those who hold property rights and therefore power. Pope John Paul II, in the 1991 encyclical *Centesimus Annus,* makes a point similar to the activists in this volume:

> Certainly the mechanics of the market offer secure advantages: They help to utilize resources better; they promote the exchange of products; above all they give central place to the person's desires and preferences, which in a contract meet the desires and preferences of another person. Nevertheless, these mechanisms carry the risk of an "idolatry" of the market, an idolatry which ignores the existence of goods which by their nature are not and cannot be mere commodities. (Para. 40)

The dilemma is in determining just what constitutes an "idolatry" of the market. People of good will often disagree on what level of intervention in the market is actually in the best interest of the poor. The essays which follow offer several perspectives on the question and finally outline some suggested directions for the future of the dialogue.

NOTES

Part of this article appeared in an earlier version in Oliver F. Williams, "Theological Ethics and the Multinational," in *Ethics and the Multinational Enterprise,* ed.

W. Michael Hoffman, Ann E. Lange, and David A. Fredo (New York: University Press of America, 1986), 175–185.

1. Arthur McCormack, M.H.M., "Poverty and Population," in *Multinational Managers and Poverty in the Third World*, ed. Lee Tavis (Notre Dame, Ind.: University of Notre Dame Press, 1982), 25.

2. Peter J. Henriot, S.J., "Restructuring the International Economic Order," in *Multinational Managers*, 49. For the economic perspectives, a good summary is presented in Karen Paul and Robert Barbato, "The Multinational Corporation in the Less Developed Country: The Economic Development Model Versus the North-South Model," *Academy of Management Review* 10 (January 1985): 8–14.

3. Donald McNeill, C.S.C., and Lee Tavis, "The Nature of the Debate," in *Multinational Managers*, 258–259.

4. William P. Glade, "Multinational Firms and National Economies," in *Multinational Managers*, 102–112.

5. H. Richard Niebuhr, *Christ and Culture* (New York: Harper & Row, 1951).

6. For an elaboration of the social dimensions of the mission of the church, see O. Williams, "Introduction," *The Judeo-Christian Vision and the Modern Corporation*, ed. O. F. Williams, C.S.C., and J. W. Houck (Notre Dame, Ind.: University of Notre Dame Press, 1982), 1–21. See also O. Williams, "Being a Christian in the Business World," *Horizons* 11, no. 2 (1984): 383–392.

7. Peter Drucker argues against the "revolutionary" approach to business ethics in "What Is 'Business Ethics'?" *Public Interest* 63 (1981): 18–36. For my response to Drucker, see O. Williams, "Business Ethics: A Trojan Horse?" *California Management Review* 24, no. 4 (1982): 14–24.

8. Gregory Baum, *The Priority of Labor* (New York: Paulist Press, 1982), 44.

9. Ibid., 87.

10. Ibid.

11. For further discussion of this theme, see O. Williams, "Religion: The Spirit or Enemy of Capitalism?" *Business Horizons* 26, no. 6 (1983): 6–13; and O. Williams, "Who Cast the First Stone?" *Harvard Business Review* 62, no. 5 (1984): 151–160.

12. Gustavo Gutierrez, *A Theology of Liberation*, trans. Sister Caridad Inda and John Eagleston (Maryknoll, N.Y.: Orbis Books, 1973), 174.

13. Ibid.

14. For extended discussions of the middle axioms appropriate for the United States, see *Catholic Social Teaching and the U.S. Economy: Working Papers for a Bishop's Pastoral*, ed. J. W. Houck and O. F. Williams, C.S.C. (Washington, D.C.: University Press of America, 1984).

15. James E. Post, "Assessing the Nestle Boycott: Corporate Accountability and Human Rights," *California Management Review* 27 (1985): 128.

Pharmaceuticals and Developing Countries

LOUIS LASAGNA, M.D.

If it is true, as has been proposed, that there are only two ways to be free of bias — either being completely ignorant or completely uninterested — then I confess to bias about this topic. Let me start, therefore, by expounding on my orientation so that you may have a better insight into the values and constraints that afflict my own intellectual options. I presume that your own prejudices will go on display during the discussion, and I will be disappointed if we do not disagree vigorously on some points. As an editor once pointed out to me, "If two intelligent people are conversing and do not disagree about anything, it means that at least one of them isn't listening." And, if I may quote a delicious footnote of George J. Stigler: ". . . a lecturer denoucing cannibalism naturally must view the applause of vegetarians as equivocal evidence of his eloquence." (Incidentally, I owe a debt of gratitude to Stigler for a lot of other things, which will be obvious to Stigler fans as I proceed.)

PHARMACEUTICAL POSTULATES

Now for Lasagna's Postulates:
1. Pharmaceuticals by and large do far more good than harm.

Louis Lasagna, M.D., is dean of the Sackler School of Graduate Biomedical Sciences of Tufts University. An author of over four hundred publications, he has extended his work on the problems that keep drug development from being optimally beneficial to the public through centers that he has established at the Johns Hopkins and Rochester Schools of Medicine.

2. We have undergone a pharmaceutical revolution in the last half-century, but the world continues to need more and better drugs. There is not one major disease for which I do not desire medicines that are either safer or more effective, and for some diseases we lack any truly effective remedies.

This is not to say that we need all the drugs we now have.[1] Countries like France, Germany, Sweden, the United States, and the United Kingdom, for instance, differ remarkably in the number of medicines available on prescription. The United Kingdom, the United States, and France are similar with regard to the number of active substances on the market (1,000 to 2,000), but Sweden has 750 and Germany has 2,500. If one looks at all *formulations* for these countries, the range is about 2,500 to 12,000.

Norway has nine so-called beta-blockers (drugs used primarily to treat cardiovascular disorders); the United Kingdom has seventeen. The Dutch have twenty-two prescription anti-inflammatory drugs; the average Dutch physician tends to use only seven of these, but one doctor's favorite seven will be different from another's. In Norway, a survey showed that physicians used only four to six of the available drugs in this class, but 40 percent of Norwegian doctors use drugs not on the country's approved list (i.e., drugs marketed in other countries but nevertheless available on special request in Norway).

3. It is better to prevent illness than to treat it, but despite a few exceptions like vaccines and antihypertensive drugs, medicine today is not terribly good at preventing most diseases.

4. New drugs are developed primarily by industrial application of basic scientific information, but new drugs sometimes lead in turn to important advances in basic science.

5. Support of basic science has predominantly depended on government support, and only to a minor degree on private foundations and industries; most progress in basic and applied science has occurred, up to the present, in capitalist countries, and most new drugs have come from the innovative segment of the pharmaceutical industry, not manufacturers of generic drugs.

6. The pharmaceutical industry can only survive if it is profitable. While the industry does its share of "good works," it is silly to expect it to play Lady Bountiful, as if philanthropy were its business. Industry should stop apologizing for making profits. The corollary to this is that the marketplace cannot take care of *all* social problems, which is why we also need government and private charity.

7. I am more interested in results than in motives; results are not only more important, but are easier to measure. I suppose it would be more romantic if all medical progress were achieved by scientists with a selfless commitment to humankind, but the desire for fame or for creature comforts can be a powerful motivating force, and scientific genius is not strongly correlated with spirituality.

8. Business is not a zero-sum game, where winners are always coupled with losers, unless the product being sold is useless trash. Consumers of needed and effective pharmaceuticals gain in health at the same time the drug manufacturer gains in dollars.

9. To be anti-business is not synonymous with being pro-society.

HEALTH NEEDS OF DEVELOPING COUNTRIES

Let me now discuss the health needs of the developing countries, since drugs cannot be discussed rationally out of context. Many Third World countries have needs in regard to the following: nutrition (and therefore, agriculture), sanitary engineering, housing, clothing, pest control, vaccination programs, treatment of infectious (including parasitic) diseases, and population planning and control, as well as treatment for most of the diseases that afflict developed countries. Poverty is not protection against schizophrenia or cancer, although dreadful socio-economic conditions may kill a person before he has a chance to develop a chronic illness.

In evaluating health needs, we must not use models inappropriate to the Third World. Let us consider, for example, a poor country with a very limited health budget and many different kinds of bacterial diseases. For such a country, it might be most cost-effective to treat the majority of infected patients with chloramphenicol, a drug whose usage in the United States is greatly restricted because of a very rare but serious side effect—aplastic anemia. Chloramphenicol is cheap, easy to produce, does not disturb the gastrointestinal tract or produce skin rashes or allergic reactions, and can be taken by mouth. For every patient who might die from chloramphenicol-related aplastic anemia, thousands will be saved from dying of infections treatable with this antibiotic. For a few countries, it might be most cost-effective for them to spend most of their health budget on food, mosquito-spraying, or contraception rather than on drugs, a policy that would be insane in the United States, and indeed in most countries.

What are some of the major barriers to achieving the health goals of the Third World?

1. Poverty. Wealth is not synonymous with liberty or health, but it is difficult to move significantly toward good health if you are too poor to eat properly or to consult a physician. Freedom of action is impossible if one is limited by crushing and dehumanizing poverty.

2. Lack of adequate health care professional infrastructure. Third World countries tend to have shortages of doctors, nurses, dentists, pharmacists, clinics, hospitals, chemists, biologists, toxicologists, pharmacologists, etc.

3. Ignorance. A population with misplaced faith in folk pseudo-remedies and a pathetic infatuation with modern antibiotics will be difficult to enlist in planning and executing a rational drug program.

4. National pride. Third World physicians and laypersons alike may resent being told what "luxury drugs" they should do without, even if the drugs are in fact medically unnecessary, because of the implications that the poor are not entitled to the same medical options as the privileged.

5. Greed and venality. Romantics still adhere to the notion that primitive cultures are innocent and noble, until perverted by wicked capitalists. Sad to say, there is no need for the West or multinational drug firms to teach the Third World about theft and corruption. Stealing and reselling drugs is not rare in the Third World, nor is bribery.

6. Incompetence and inefficiency. Stupidity is more common than evil, in all societies. Even if theft and diversion of drugs were not a problem, ordering a year's supply of drugs at one time, when adequate storage is impossible and distribution facilities almost nonexistent, can only waste money. Making one's own drugs or getting samples from competitive bidders is pointless if one lacks the know-how to test the quality of drugs and predict their biologic performance. Lall, a former enthusiast for local production, has characterized the Indian industry "as the most severely regulated of all manufacturing industry," and gone on to point out that the Indian pharmaceutical industry turns out an unacceptably high number of substandard drugs.

7. Lack of political will. Why have so few countries adopted some version of the WHO Essential Drug List if it is, in fact, in their best interest to implement some minimal formulary?

8. Absence of first-rate remedies. Some of the diseases that afflict the Third World cannot be treated or prevented today because of the

lack of drugs and biologicals of proven and high-level efficacy for these diseases.

9. Economic threats to the pharmaceutical industry. The innovative sector of industry is being squeezed by a variety of factors: the increasing cost and duration of the drug development process, decreasing effective patent life, increasing costs of litigation and court-awarded damages, cost-containment policies by governments and other third-party players, and decreasing support of basic research by government. An economically uneasy industry is not likely to have as much interest in "good works" and in providing help to the Third World as would an economically vigorous one.

PHARMACEUTICALS IN DEVELOPING COUNTRIES

What about the accusations commonly leveled at the pharmaceutical industry? Does industry manufacture and promote pharmaceutical rubbish? This has certainly been true to some extent in the past, but has become less and less of a problem at least among the large multinationals, for the last decade or two.

Are products labeled differently in different countries? Yes, but less so than used to be the case. Criticism along these lines had prodded multinational corporations to move toward uniformity of labels except where local laws dictate different approaches. (I predict that unconscionable misrepresentation will be seen in the future less from multinationals than from indigenous pharmaceutical firms. In Spain, for example, I have found that a popular anti-inflammatory drug made by its original manufacturer contains a list of warnings, contraindications, etc., that is identical to that seen in any other country, but if one consults the label for another version of the same drug made by a Spanish generic manufacturer, no such warnings or constraints can be found.)

Do multinationals "dump" drugs on developing countries, i.e., sell drugs that they would not sell at home? This practice is, I think, rapidly disappearing, although one must distinguish between "dumping" and the sale of drugs that really represent differences in national value judgments. Take Depo-Provera, for example. This drug has been marketed all over the world, including the United States, but in our country alone it is not yet approved for use as a long-lasting parenteral contraceptive. Is it "dumping" for the American manufacturer of this drug to promote it abroad for the purpose of contraception? I would submit not.

Do multinationals spend enough money on research and development for Third World diseases? This is a difficult question to answer, since "enough" is not an easy word on which to achieve agreement. In regard to infectious diseases as an example, multinationals have a reasonably good track record. Vaccines against smallpox, polio, yellow fever, cholera, and typhoid fever have certainly provided remarkable benefits throughout the Third World, and valuable new drugs have come along in recent years for treating such parasitic diseases as amebiasis, malaria, and schistosomiasis. Research continues on new remedies for tropical diseases targeted for special attention, including filariasis, leishmaniasis, trypanosomiasis, and leprosy.

(It should also be remembered that *every* country has an "orphan drug" or "orphan disease" problem, i.e., drugs or diseases that are not pursued because such remedies would be economically unprofitable. This explains why our own country has developed orphan drug legislation and why there is an industrial task force in the United States to address these needs.)

Are drug prices for the Third World too high? Difficult to say. Prices differ not only from country to country, but from customer to customer within a country. In the United States, for example, deals are cut all the time between manufacturers and purchasers, provided that there is competition. In a competitive and free market, fraud and coercion are much less likely than in a market that is not free. (The same is true for ideas.) Some of the national differences in the prices of drugs are also due to government subsidy so that relatively poor populations can afford to buy medicines. I do not believe that we can demand that drugs be shipped below cost to a poor country unless we simultaneously face up to who will foot the bill for this largesse.

Are multinational companies unwilling to help the Third World? Industry has in recent years mounted efforts to supply basic drugs at low cost to the Third World. There is other evidence of increasing attempts on the part of industry to accommodate the Third World's special needs and to respond to some of their complaints. I would submit as examples the development of an Infant Formula Code, the Code of Pharmaceutical Manufacturing Practices of the International Federation of Pharmaceutical Manufacturers Association (IFPMA), and joint projects between pharmaceutical companies from the West and such countries in Africa as Somalia, Burundi, Gambia, Malawi, and Senegal.

What should a developing country do about its drug needs?

1. Establish its own priorities in regard to drugs vis-à-vis other health or social needs and develop national policy accordingly.

2. Reevaluate its national drug policy periodically, since neither society nor science remains static. We have already seen three versions of the WHO Essential Drug List, and we shall need new ones in the years ahead. An unchanging health policy is a bad health policy.

3. Drugs should be produced locally only if that makes economic, political, and scientific sense. At certain stages in a country's development, it should import all drugs, while at other times some local manufacturing would be sensible. Only when a scientifically sophisticated and reasonably well-to-do society exists should a country think of native research and development.

4. Drugs should be purchased efficiently, with bids being requested from multiple sources and quantities being ordered that are optimal from the standpoint of storage and distribution.

5. Manufacturers' promotion of drugs should be monitored and deficiences or excesses prevented or corrected.

6. If a certain drug or device or food product is deemed unacceptable, it should be banned. (Why were not baby food products regulated, for example, when Third World countries identified problems with infant health as a result of their use? I refer to the famous Nestle case.)

7. Educate the lay public and physicians about drugs, the need for compliance with directions for taking drugs, etc. The blandishments of unscrupulous advertisers and the irrational demands of patients will be equally difficult to resist so long as one is dealing with a poorly educated public and medical profession.

8. Developing countries should avoid being seduced by euphoric slogans such as "Health for All in the Year 2000." Setting unachievable goals is often counterproductive and usually engenders cynicism. (Such puffery is, of course, not unique to WHO and the Third World. I remember years ago when one leader in American cancer research promised that with enough money, the cure for cancer would be available "in five years." After several repetitions of this promise, the scientist lost credibility, as he deserved to.)

What should the developing world keep in mind when thinking about the Third World's drug needs?

1. They should not lose track of long-term goals in the desire to cope with short-term ones. Drug development is not static, so the

approach to pharmaceutical research and development, pricing, etc., should not be based on the erroneous assumption that our challenge is simply how to produce and distribute the drugs we already have. Overall planning must also worry about the drugs we *do not have* but desperately *need*. This means putting money into innovative research.

2. A good many years ago, I proposed that the developed countries could help developing countries by providing expert advice in regard to how to match pharmaceutical acquisition problems with the developing countries' own resources. I still think that this is a good idea, and it is obviously now being attempted in isolated instances. Considerable progress would be made by combining realism with efficient planning and management.

3. I believe that the IFPMA Code should be open to scrutiny by people outside of the industry. The idea of the Code is a good one, but without a chance to see how valid the submitted complaints are, and how they are dealt with, I am afraid that the Code's existence will not effectively answer criticisms of the industry. Industry is simply not trusted to police itself, just as our society is increasingly reluctant to trust physicians or lawyers (or policemen!) to police themselves.

4. The industry should seek special tax benefits in their home countries for research on "unprofitable" Third World diseases and should negotiate for tax benefits in the Third World in return for moving technology there. Partnership is most effective when the partners both benefit.

5. The developed countries should avoid galloping paternalism. In December 1982, for example, a resolution was adopted by the United Nations General Assembly entitled "Protection Against Products Harmful to Health and the Environment." This resolution proposed that unapproved products could indeed be exported "when a request for such products is received from an importing country." Some in the West would deny developing countries the right to import such unapproved products, but if I read the resolution correctly, the Third World is saying: "Let us be the judges of what is good for us. Give us information and advice, and then stand back out of our way."

6. The public both in the West and in the Third World should be educated about the realities of research and development, the heterogeneity of the drug industry, and the cost-effectiveness of drugs (especially where there are few physicians or other health professionals).

7. Finally, I believe that the pharmaceutical industry should keep pointing out that it alone cannot possibly solve the health problems

of the Third World. Kicking the industry may give pleasure to those who dislike successful capitalist entrepreneurs, but it is a disservice to developing countries to delude them with solutions that do not exist and with fairy-tale scenarios.

NOTE

1. The next two paragraphs contain data that were accurate for 1985. The proportions remain more or less the same today.

Response

JEAN HALLORAN

If one has never been to a Third World country, it is difficult to comprehend the total absence of a drug distribution system, something
on which those in the United States are dependent. In many developing countries, there is no such thing as a prescription drug. Every drug
is an over-the-counter drug. In many cases, there is not even a pharmacist to assist the consumer. The person who owns the pharmacy is
the primary health care delivery person in many areas.

For example, a person from a remote Thai village gets ill. That
person goes to a nearby village where there is an equivalent of a general store and says, "I have a stomach ache. What should I take?" The
owner of the general store pulls a product off the shelf and sells it to
the villager. If the store owner's choice is based on anything, it probably will be the advertising provided by the pharmaceutical company.
So the pharmaceutical firms have, at the very least, an enormous responsibility in those countries. They cannot rely, as in the United States,
on the responsibility of physicians and health care providers. That is
simply not the way the health care system works in developing countries.

In effect, the regulatory systems in most of the developing countries are as they were in the United States in the 1930s. The abuses
of that time — the marketing of hazardous products, the making of excessive claims — are prevalent in Third World countries today. For example, one of the most horrendous misuses of drugs regularly marketed in Third World countries is anabolic steroid products which are

Jean Halloran is director of the Institute for Consumers' Policy Development,
a division of Consumers Union of the United States, with a principal responsibility
for international consumer issues. As a staff member of the President's Council on
Environmental Quality, she was one of the principal drafters of President Carter's executive order on trade-banned products.

sold as a cure for malnutrition in children. Even though anabolic steroids build the body, the cure for a child's malnutrition is food, not a drug that will induce muscle growth and that will also, in the process, induce various premature sexual developments or sex changes.

In terms of some of the self-policing methods mentioned by Louis Lasagna, Health Action International filed a complaint with the International Federation of Pharmaceutical Manufacturers Association under its code regarding the marketing of anabolic steriods for malnutrition in the Third World. When, months later, the IFPMA responded, it was a cursory statement saying that the organization had looked into the problem and it really was "not very serious."

Another important issue that needs to be addressed is how corporations deal with the questions of basic human rights. The traditional answer to that issue has been that there is no relationship. Corporations are in the business of making money. They will operate in whatever human rights climate exists in the country. Human rights is not their business.

This ignores the facts. Corporations employ people. As a result of the fact that they employ people, they somehow have to deal with questions of equality in the workplace. Either they segregate or they do not. Companies that sell health products invariably are involved in a person's right to decent health. They are impacting on basic human rights whether they like it or not. It is important for corporations to face human rights issues, not only for ethical reasons, but because it is in a company's long-term business interest to acknowledge that there are such things as basic human rights and that it is imperative for a corporation to deal with them.

Following is an example of how some pharmaceutical companies have failed to recognize the basic rights of Third World consumers to be informed, and their right to adequate health care and honest treatment. During 1980, I held a job in the Carter administration that involved an effort to deal with the problem of the dumping of hazardous products. The result of that effort was an executive order which was signed by President Carter in the closing days of his administration. The order called for an annual report listing all products which were banned or severely restricted in the United States, including pesticides, pharmaceuticals, and consumer products. The order also created a mechanism for preventing the export of such products except in very restricted circumstances; it outlined a long review process of the necessary steps prior to the exporting of such products. It was designed only to be able to restrict export of things that are dangerous. Throughout the process of developing that executive order, pharmaceutical firms, led by the Pharmaceutical Manufacturers Association (PMA), lobbied heavily against it. And, after Carter lost his reelection bid and Ronald Reagan was inaugurated, the PMA asked for the revocation of that executive order. They were successful. The Reagan administration revoked this order in February 1981, on the grounds that this was part of the over-regulation of the pharmaceutical industry.

It is worthwhile to emphasize that the primary function of this order would have been to create a hazardous products list. It would have made it easier for developing nations to discover what products were restricted in the United States and which ones were not. Interestingly, a resolution was submitted to the United Nations in 1982 which sought to accomplish a similar goal. It called for creation of a United Nations worldwide list of banned and restricted products. There was a distinct similarity between these two measures. In questioning one of the sponsors of the resolution as to why it had been introduced, his response related how heartened he had been by the Carter executive order and his anger at its revocation.

The Pharmaceutical Manufacturers Association opposed passage of the creation of that U.N. consolidated list and passage of the resolution in the United Nations in 1982 and again in 1984. In addition, the PMA has lobbied the State Department of the United States not to provide any information to this resource and was successful in persuading the State Department to boycott this U.N. effort. Obviously developing countries are aware of the role of the Pharmaceutical Manufacturers Association and the International Chamber of Commerce in business lobbies in opposing these resolutions. What has that opposition accomplished? It has put the United States government and U.S. industry on record as favoring free trade to an ignorant and uninformed consumer. It has not succeeded in preventing the dissemination of information that the Third World consumers were seeking.

This is just one example of the kind of ways pharmaceutical firms need to look at their responsibilities in dealing with the Third World. There are also questions regarding double standards in labeling of products. Lasagna believes this is disappearing as a problem, but other people working in the Third World would disagree.

Pharmaceutical corporations can do a number of things. They can work to control the conditions of sale in countries where they operate. They can work to educate the public. They can work to educate people who dispense drugs. They can label their products abroad in exactly the same way as they are labeled in the United States. They can avoid selling hazardous products. They can avoid selling products like combination antibiotics which the medical profession universally agrees are therapeutically ill-advised. They can urge strict Third World regulation of the pharmaceutical industry, along the United States model.

Response

DAVID E. COLLINS

People who work in the pharmaceutical industry are human beings. They have children, they live in communities, they send their children to school, they live by what they perceive to be sound, moral values; and they are sensitive when they feel others look on them as unethical, immoral, or unprincipled. And, they react where that has happened. Activists who are interacting with the pharmaceutical industry must input that to their evaluations and must recognize the human response involved. My first encounter with activists was in 1970 when a religious group brought a shareholder resolution to Johnson & Johnson. My initial reaction was one of shock. Today it is clear, unquestionable, and accepted by most of the principled people in industry that there is a definite role and a contribution to be made by the activist organizations.

There is a process by which many actors are contributing to the common goal of making pharmaceuticals available to those who need them. Business is one of the actors. It seems to be the one receiving the most attention. However, there are other actors — religious activists, consumer protection groups, consumer unions throughout the world — all having a legitimate role to play.

Each role carries with it certain obligations. These obligations cannot be discharged lightly. In the process of evolving toward our common goals, activists and pharmaceutical corporate managers need to be jointly challenged by the obligations. First, human understanding

David E. Collins is president of HealthCare Products for Schering-Plough International. An executive with Johnson & Johnson for twenty-three years at the time of the workshop, he served as general counsel, vice president, member of the Johnson & Johnson board of directors, president of McNeil Pharmaceuticals, vice chairman of the Executive Committee, and chairman of the Consumer Division Europe/Africa/ Middle East sector.

is very important. There is a myth that portrays a business executive as a highly efficient robot-like individual who has a computer for a head and hordes of assistants poised to effectively execute every order. In actuality, business is an inefficient organization. Corporate executives are unable to respond to activists by return mail. Time is equally important to all actors in these roles. All are busy people. All are imperfect people. Human understanding is imperative.

Second, an activist and a pharmaceutical corporate manager need to understand the role of one another. We executives would like activists to understand what business is all about. What are some of the issues faced as we attempt to develop and market good drugs, bring them to the developing world, and make them available to those who need them? Too often corporate executives are faced with activists who know little or nothing about the business world and the pressures of the actual day-to-day activities of a multinational pharmaceutical firm. The corporate world cannot be held responsible for all the existing health problems in the Third World. There are many gray areas. In many areas of the developing world, there are no pharmacists. How are drugs to be delivered to those people not served by a pharmacist? If the way it is elected to be done is without a prescription and without a label and without a doctor and without a nurse to save the life of a human being, is that bad? It seems the pharmaceutical industry is being held responsible for the solving of most of the problems that exist in the Third World today.

Third, and most important, is goodwill. We in the pharmaceutical industry have goodwill. We do not want to kill people. We do not want people to die from taking our drugs. We want people to live. That is why we are in business. We want all people to have a quality of life equivalent to the highest possible standards. We have goodwill. I challenge activists and pharmaceutical managers to formulate a set of objectives. What do we really want in the delivery of drugs to the Third World? Do we want no profits? Do we want affordable drugs, adequately available, safe, and effective? Do we want educated, literate consumers who can adequately care for self and family? Do we want new drugs for new conditions? Dr. Louis Lasagna made an excellent point. He said, "Not only do we want drugs that we now have distributed to the Third World, we want drugs that we do not yet have distributed to the Third World. We want them available." They are going to originate from only one place. A record of drugs developed in this world reveals that most have come out of private industry. If steps are taken to discourage private industry, then, by that very step, the future of new drugs will be terminated.

We want freedom. We want freedom for those who buy our products. We want them to be able to make a choice. We want the consumer to be able to make a choice because the bottom line is that we will deliver health to the lowest poverty level in this world when those people have available to them the drugs and the information necessary to make their own decisions. That is health for all by the year 2000.

Discussion Summary

Paul Belford addressed some of the issues raised by Jean Halloran.

The industry accepts the role of criticism. In a world of imperfect human beings, the critic is absolutely essential.

Still, common sense dictates, "If it ain't broke, don't fix it." The complaints relative to anabolic steroids have been addressed effectively. This means the company has been notified through the Pharmaceutical Manufacturers Association about the complaint and has taken corrective action.

Indeed, there are problems with the distribution of pharmaceuticals in the hinterlands. Developing countries have regulations requiring a prescription for the sale of certain products. They know most of these products are not sold by prescription because most of the towns where the products are sold do not have doctors, and those who sell them are seldom practicing pharmacists. In our search for solutions, we must remember that the least-developed countries account for less than 2 percent of the total world pharmaceutical market. The question is, "Should a country like Bolivia be denied access to antibiotics, antimalarials, and antiparasitics because it lacks a distribution system like the one in the United States?" Denial would be insane and inhuman.

The list of harmful products mentioned by Jean Halloran poses an especially difficult issue. The World Health Organization, the United Nations Environmental Program, the United Nations Commission on Drugs with Narcotics, and the Single Convention of Psychotropic Drugs have all produced lists that are distributed to all member countries of the United Nations. The Pharmaceutical Manufacturers Association opposed the United Nations' list on the grounds that it was redundant, it involved nonscientifically competent people in its preparation, and it was being assembled in a politically charged atmosphere. The list consisted primarily of products that were submitted by the organizations who were already producing and distributing these lists. Initially, the small secretariat at the United Nations assembled a list of ninety-four drugs of which twenty were approved by the Food and Drug Administration. It is a reasonable estimate that as many as forty-five or fifty products on this list are approved and available in either Germany, France, the United Kingdom, or the United States. Currently, the United Nations Secretariat in New York is attempting to involve more closely the World Health Organization in a process that will hopefully allow comment by groups such as the International Pharmaceutical Manufacturers Association.

Louis Lasagna discussed some of the problems with a hazardous materials list.

There have been serious problems with pharmaceutical use in the Third World in the past, but there is improvement. The critics deserve a good deal of credit for this. No industry likes to be criticized. If someone says your kid has big ears, you hate it whether the kid has big ears or not. If you put a rat in a Skinner box, you can shape its behavior by either punishment or reward. And, with rats, it works better if you reward them than if you punish them. Critics have not applauded industry enough when it has done something right.

The developing countries are full of characters distributing drugs who know nothing about pharmaceuticals. In these cases, even if the industry were to act together in an enlightened manner, there still would be no solution to the distribution problem. And, in the light of dismal distribution systems, the problem of pharmaceutical use cannot be adequately handled with proper labeling or proper advertising. As for anabolic steroids, when they are being grossly misused in developing countries, the countries should ban the steroids. It would not be a great disservice to a country to have that happen.

Finally, what is a hazardous substance, and what is something that is severely restricted? A drug such as chloramphenicol is classified as hazardous and severely restricted in the United States. In certain countries and under certain conditions, however, it would be a drug of choice. To stigmatize that drug as hazardous or unexportable is to make a mistake. The same argument could apply to dichlorodiphenyltrichloroethane (DDT). In Sri Lanka hospitals are now loaded with patients who have malaria, a disease that has returned to the country through restrictions on the use of DDT in their mosquito-spraying programs. The restrictions have led to a decrease in life expectancy far greater than any damage the DDT would cause.

John Houck raised questions concerning the proper role of church groups.

There is an elaborate religious network battling the pharmaceutical industry. Should its focus be extended to include more than the problem of dumping dangerous drugs overseas? This network seems to be moving toward a proposition that the American pharmaceutical industry, by its marketing practices, its economics, and its profitablity is not serving either the American public or those in more difficult straits in the Third World. Is that a correct interpretation of the religious network's aim? Is one of its purposes to move to a more coherent critique of the industry?

Regina Rowan responded:

The American industry has served us well. There are abuses, but its constituents have been well served. Rather than waste valuable time in critiquing, I would like to see the churches, the groups, and the industry form collaborative stances to address needed issues. For instance, in a developing country, it is useless to treat hookworm infestation if the sanitation system is not improved. So, I challenge the pharmaceutical industry, in this scenario, to get involved in infrastructures. The Gambia project undertaken by the Pharmaceutical Manufacturers Association sets a good example. The pharmaceutical industry cannot do everything in the world, but in this situation it could supply the expertise or the money to get the expertise as the developing country supplied onsite personnel who knew the issues, spoke the language, and understood the culture so education about the need for good sanitation could begin and infrastructure could be implemented. Other examples might include working with health officials on the infrastructure of developing a list of essential drugs or improving a distribution system or teaching people how to make intelligent bids.

John Houck expanded the view of this role.

The role of an international organization like the Catholic church or any large religious network is to report on the Third World conditions. Those in First World countries must be aware of Third World situations. If the drug industry is developing sophisticated drugs for the well-to-do countries, drugs that are not essential and will not help the Third World poor, there must be feedback to that effect. Where there is that kind of feedback, there is a radical critique of the way the industry is organized; if it is organized on the profit motive, it is going to pursue the research of drugs that have a good payback. If this situation exists, the religious networks should emphasize it instead of the dumping problem.

James Russo described a project in Gambia.

Attack yields defensiveness. Disease does not have economic boundaries, and developing, say, hypertension medications is not an elitist project. Hypertension is a fairly general condition. The kind of thing I am hearing is just what the industry, in its worst sense, wants to hear. The industry wants its critics to try to push radical reform so it can draw the wagons into a circle and defend its policies. Please be more creative than the attack mode; communicate needs instead of criticizing irrationally.

For example, the penicillin G drug would be beneficial in The Gambia. The Gambians do not know how to buy penicillin G. They need to be educated. Belford was instrumental in the development of a project that has demonstrated goodwill on behalf of the industry despite opposition from member firms of the PMA. The project taught people how to buy, store, and distribute medication. The project could be adopted and repeated in a multitude of creative forms. Projects of this kind have the potential of restructuring the pharmaceutical industry's attitude toward the Third World and toward the involvement with constituents. However, attempts to restructure the industry will incur defensiveness and a tremendous waste of time for all involved.

David Collins countered criticism of the system.

Any discussion of alternatives must begin with a supportable hypothesis. The hypothesis that the disease problem in the Third World, which is not now currently being addressed, can be solved by eliminating the profit system, the free-enterprise system currently in place in the drug development area of the pharmaceutical industry, is totally unsupportable. It is not worth discussing; there is no empirical evidence to support it. Why should we discuss radical changes in the system that are based upon hypotheses which have no empirical support?

John Houck pointed out that the job of the religious network was to gather that empirical data.

Peter Henriot explained the view of the religious health care community.

Houck's point can be seen in the context of a wider debate that is alive in the religious health care community. The key issue of the religious networks' concerns about pharmaceuticals is a current debate about its overall relationship to health care. The debate in the Catholic Health Association has been around two models of health care: health care ministry and health care industry. Historically, health care was ministry. Health care was a form of service to the community before it was a business. Today, because of economic constraints, technology, government regulations, and reasons too numerous to list, one of the fastest growing sectors of the economy has been born: the health care industry. Within that context, religiously affiliated groups who sponsor health care facilities are asking, "How can we keep health care as ministry, first and foremost?" In order to survive there must be an industry connection, but how can the priority be ministry? It is here the debate begins.

Are pharmaceutical corporations part of this health care ministry? If so, a different set of questions must be raised than if they are simply part of the health care industry. How could managers in the pharmaceutical industry even get into a discussion about being part of ministry? However, it would be helpful for them to understand the following facets of ministry: the concern about sick people whose health needs demand attention; the uneasiness toward a profit motive; questions concerning the ethics involved in the decision-making process surrounding new drug development, marketing procedures, and the justice of code implementation. That kind of debate within the religious community has serious implications for the future of international church-related health care over the next several years.

David Collins responded:

I am aware of the uncomfortable feeling associated with making a profit on a pharmaceutical that has the potential of saving someone's life, particularly when that person cannot afford to purchase the drug.

The feeling is very much a part of the pharmaceutical industry. One of the reasons the health care system in the United States is so advanced today is because drugs are sold for a profit. Profits feed back into the system to create incentive to develop new drugs, to pursue scientific breakthroughs for application in the drug field, and to maintain the potential for addressing more challenges. Profit, the free-enterprise system, drives the whole process. Ministry versus industry is an understandable way to present the dilemma.

Rosemary Sabino gave examples of a good working relation.

There is a tension between ministry and business, but also a long history of working together. Religious congregations of women have depended on a working relationship with pharmaceutical companies over the years. If it were not for that relationship, we could not have progressed in foreign countries. We have been the grateful recipients of expired drugs, or drugs nearing their expiration dates. But it is the relationship that allowed the necessary dialogue on ways to use a drug nearing its expiration date.

Packaging is another problem in tropical climates. By the time a nearly expired drug would reach its destination, deterioration would have begun. However, due to a working relationship, methods for retarding drug deterioration have been exchanged.

The relationship between religious congregations and pharmaceutical companies needs to be explored further in the areas of marketing, labeling, and packaging for the tropical areas.

Jean Halloran pointed out the difficulty of systemic critique.

There is a definite distinction between the two levels of discussion in which the drug industry and its critics normally engage. One has proved to be constructive, the other has met abysmal failure. There can be constructive discussion about marketing, labeling, distribution, and advertising practices. Perhaps many activists would like to see a different social organization in the world that eliminates the need for profits. That level of discourse is on another plane, one that involves issues unlikely to be resolved in dialogue between companies and critics.

Prakash Sethi made a point on profits.

We have discussed the industry's part of the solution, and we have talked about the profit motive. No one seems to disagree with either. However, there is another dimension. Profit can be made from both effective and noneffective products. Profit is not the price of doing business, profit is a reward for doing the right kind of business.

Denis Goulet expanded this point.

The question was posed officially in 1973 by the United Nations' Group of Eminent Persons: "Are multinational corporations good or bad for development?" There is a basic qualitative difference between a maximizing and an optimizing pattern of profit seeking. When "optimizing" is in force, the quest for profit is relativized to accommodate other goals. In the past, however, these other goals have largely remained outside decision making in corporations. Only through public pressure leading to legislation or other forms of constraint have companies found themselves obliged to "internalize the externalities."

Under the old pattern of operation, a corporate charter was simply a grant from the government to a corporation giving it a hunting license to make profit provided it met a few requirements such as obeying the laws of the land or behaving as a good citizen. It no longer seems to be acceptable to issue a license solely to make profit. In other words, many values formerly treated as external considerations, e.g., racial justice, sexually fair treatment, ecological responsibility, safety, priority for human basic needs, and development concerns have now risen to prominence and demand treatment as internalities in the benefit-cost calculation, rather than maximum profit seeking in a kind of isolated, nonsystemic view. The terrain upon which issues are engaged goes beyond profit seeking. It concerns new modalities of decision making where substantative representatives of these other interests have an early voice in the shaping of decisions.

The central question in development is: "Whom does it benefit and on what terms and at what cost is the package of goods and services provided?" For all multinationals, including the pharmaceutical industry, the relevant question is: "Is it basically good or bad for development?" What pattern of profit seeking then becomes compatible with a more comprehensive view of human development?

Prakash Sethi asked how the industry viewed the pharmaceutical problems of the Third World.

David Collins responded.

There is no question that there is a lack of adequate drugs available at reasonable prices in the Third World. Further, industry does have a responsibility in that situation. I doubt industry caused the problem, but it is imperative for it to be instrumental in forming solutions.

There is also clear evidence that ineffective and unsafe drugs are being distributed for profit in some areas of the world today. In the Third World, where the recording of adverse side effects is virtually nonexistent, it is difficult to identify the scope of the problem. The pharmaceutical industry has a duty to recognize the issues. For the individual company, the first step is to ensure it is not part of the problem. The second step is for the industry to address this problem.

The third issue is one of cost. The cost of health care in the world today is too high. The pharmaceutical industry is responsible for contributing to this cost, although the cost of pharmaceuticals in relation to the cost of total health care in the world is very small. Nevertheless, it does contribute and industry bears a responsibility to reduce costs to the consumer for its products and for overall health care. The multinational pharmaceutical industry must adopt the objective of the World Health Organization—Health for All in the Year 2000. Even though it may not be reached, it must be the goal.

However, the major global health problem is the absence of drugs to cure certain disease. There are drugs that will ameliorate cancer, there is no cure for cancer. Given the spectrum of disease, there are too few drugs for prevention and fewer still for cure. Pharmaceutical firms have the major role to play in this issue.

Multinational Pharmaceutical Corporations and Developing Countries

KLAUS M. LEISINGER

HEALTH PROBLEMS IN THE THIRD WORLD

Health and economic development are mutually interdependent. Although economic growth does not guarantee an improvement in the state of health of the poor segments of a population, the health of this segment will clearly be most at risk in case of an economic stagnation or recession. However, health is not only an end to itself, but also an essential prerequisite in order to reach economic development. Without health there can be no economic progress, and consequently no social progress. This in turn implies no improvement in the health status, or at least not on a large scale and not at a sustainable level.

Poor people are trapped in a vicious circle where poverty breeds disease, and disease results in poverty. This self-perpetuating plight deprives the poor segments of a population of any social and economic progress which has taken place elsewhere in their countries. And it prevents a change for the better: poor health impairs productivity and leads to loss of income, which again makes it impossible to break out of the vicious circle.

> Men and women were sick because they were poor, they became poorer because they were sick, and sicker because they were poorer.[1]

Klaus M. Leisinger is a vice president of CIBA-GEIGY Limited, a delegate of the advisory board for its Foundation for Cooperation with Developing Countries, and a professor of sociology at the University of Basel. He spent four years with CIBA-GEIGY in sub-Saharan Africa and three as staff relations to the Third World.

Figure 1

The Poverty–Morbidity–Mortality System

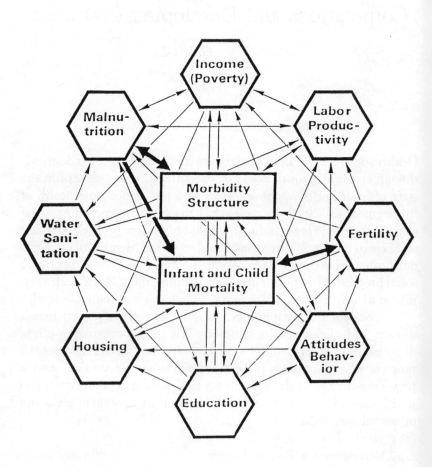

It is obvious that current morbidity and mortality problems cannot be solved without tackling the other issues that are an integral part of underdevelopment at the same time. However this endeavor requires an appropriate development strategy which in turn needs political will to initiate and finance the necessary changes, and it needs time.

But hundreds of millions of people in the Third World are sick now. This condition is primarily reflected in high infant and child mortality rates, widespread disability, and low life expectancy. Human beings living under such circumstances cannot be expected to lean back and wait until "development" takes its course and solves all problems. High infant and child mortality have highly detrimental effects: since parents want "surviving progeny" and not just "born babies," high mortality tends to be over-compensated by high birth rates.

From an individual point of view this is understandable, but from a public health perspective it is disastrous: the shorter the time interval between two births, the greater the number of births per woman, and the higher the age of the woman,[2] the more these additional children and their mothers die.[3] For example, according to UNDP figures, in Somalia 1,100 mothers die for every 100,000 live births. The corresponding figure in Bhutan is 1,710 and in Ghana 1,000, whereas that for the United States and Norway is only 9 and 2 respectively. Mortality in childbirth is also a result of inadequate prenatal and post-maternity health care. Although there have generally been significant improvements in life expectancy and infant mortality during the past twenty years, they still illustrate the "North-South conflict" (see Table 1).

TABLE 1

Health Indicators in Selected Countries

	Life Expectancy (1987)	Infant Mortality per 1,000 (1988)
Sierra Leone	42	153
Ethiopia	42	153
Afghanistan	42	171
Guinea	43	146
Mali	45	168
Angola	45	172
USA	76	10
Switzerland	77	7
Japan	78	5

Source: UNDP, *Human Development Report* 1990 (New York, 1990).

The Disease Pattern in the Third World

The disease pattern of the poor in Third World countries is totally different from that in industrialized countries. The poverty system with its elements of malnutrition, poor hygiene, lack of clean drinking water, etc., is particularly conducive to infectious and parasitic diseases. The World Bank model highlights the difference as shown in Table 2.

Reliable statistics on the incidence of specific diseases are difficult to obtain. This is a result of inadequate trained staff and diagnostic facilities as well as the "poverty-undercount." In remote rural areas poverty and related health problems are predominant. These areas are often inaccessible, particularly at certain times of year, which makes it difficult to obtain reliable health statistics.[4]

Contrary to public perception, that poor countries of the Third World only have to cope with tropical diseases, diseases which prevail in industrial countries (e.g., cardiovascular diseases, rheumatism, and cancer) are also causing increasing problems in the Third World. These diseases emerge primarily in those segments of the population which can be considered as atypical for the majority of people in most Third World countries with regard to their social status and economic situation, their life-style, and their purchasing power. They represent a special case in the sense that a solution for their specific problems has to be found outside the public health-care sector.

Public Health Care in the Third World

In spite of their enormous health problems only very limited financial resources, few doctors and hospital beds are available to the

TABLE 2

Disease Pattern in Industrialized and Developing Countries
(in percent)

	Industrialized Countries	Developing Countries
Infectious, parasitic, and diseases of the respiratory tract	10.8	43.7
Cancer	15.2	3.7
Circulatory disorders	32.2	14.8
Accidents	6.8	3.5
Other Illnesses	35.0	34.3
Total	100	100

Source: World Bank, 1981.

population of the Third World (Table 3). Even today the large majority of the rural population has hardly any access to modern medical care due to cultural, geographical and financial reasons. Eight out of ten patients in the Third World are treated by traditional healers, medicine men, and witch doctors. Where medical problems are greatest, non-traditional health care is most meagerly provided.

Public health programs—although of high economic and social benefit—have a disturbingly low priority for most governments in Third World countries. Public health policies often have an ad hoc nature and are implemented in an unsystematic manner.[5] The efficiency and effectiveness of the measures and administrative provisions to reach the public health objectives are rarely investigated.

The practical policies followed by many governments in the Third World fail to give sufficent attention to the fact that development and an efficient public health infrastructure go hand in hand. Instead of ensuring that priority is given to public health care, the lion's share of government funds is used for military expenditure (Table 4).

Most governments fail to translate public policy statements (e.g., "health for all by the year 2000") into appropriate action, i.e., they do not allocate enough resources for public health care and if they do, urban areas are given preferential treatment. The poorest and most vulnerable segment of a population lives primarily in rural areas and is seriously threatened by disease and premature death. They are hardly

TABLE 3

Health Infrastructure in Selected Countries

Country	Population per Physician (1984)	Population per Nursing Person (1984)	Percentage of Population with access to health services (1985–1987)
Burkina Faso	57,000	1,700	49
Chad	38,000	3,400	30
Guinea	57,400	6,400	32
Burundi	21,000	3,000	61
Pakistan	2,900	4,900	55
Ethiopia	77,400	5,300	46
Zaire			26
USA	500	100	100
Japan	700	200	100

Source: UNDP, 1990.

reached at all, not by doctors nor hospital facilities nor pharmaceutical products.

THE ROLE OF PHARMACEUTICALS IN THE THIRD WORLD

Particularly in those countries where the medical infrastructure is limited and where well-trained personnel are scarce, pharmaceuticals are especially important. They can help:

- prevent premature death,
- expedite recovery,
- prevent disability,
- alleviate the symptoms of diseases for which no cure exists to date.

But many people in the Third World, particularly in rural areas, still have insufficient or no access to drugs. If no drugs, or not the right drugs, are available at the basic health centers, then an essential prerequisite for their functioning is lacking. People lose confidence in the public health system.

The selection of the essential drugs poses a problem for the health authorities in many developing countries. For this reason in 1977 the World Health Organization, in cooperation with an international group of experts, compiled the so-called "Essential Drugs List." This list includes approximately 270 indispensable drugs required for the basic

TABLE 4

Central Government Expenditure in Selected Countries
Percentage of Total Expenditure

Country	Defense	Education	Health
Burkina Faso	17.9	14.0	5.2
Uganda	26.3	15.0	2.4
India	19.3	2.9	1.8
Pakistan	29.5	2.6	0.9
Yemen, Arab Rep.	31.2	17.6	3.6
El Salvador	27.7	17.1	7.1
Peru	20.0	15.3	5.8
Malawi	5.6	10.0	5.9
Nepal	5.6	10.9	4.3
Ghana	3.2	25.7	9.0
Costa Rica	2.2	16.2	19.3

Source: World Bank, 1990.

medical care of the majority of the population. The list is reviewed regularly; the last edition was issued in 1988.

The Essential Drugs List can serve only as a model list because of the diverse disease patterns and heterogeneous genetic and social conditions in various countries. Developing countries can use this list as a basis to compile a national drug list adapted to their local conditions. WHO-experts stress that their selection for the Essential Drugs List does not constitute a value judgment with regard to the usefulness of preparations not included in the list. However, the essential drugs should be available in sufficient quantities and in all necessary forms of administration.

Drugs can be of high therapeutic value. But the therapeutic efficacy is determined by their rational use. In order to guarantee this to the largest possible extent, cooperation among all parties carrying responsibility in the health sector, namely patients, doctors, pharmacists, wholesalers, the pharmaceutical industry, the legislator, and in certain cases other partners (e.g., non-governmental organizations and churches), is essential.

Two parties have a special responsibility: the government, i.e., regulatory authorities in a country, and the drug manufacturer. It is assumed that the medical profession (doctors, pharmacists, and other qualified personnel) act in line with their training and professional ethical standards and that patients are given the proper information and the possibility to make an informed choice.

RESPONSIBILITIES FOR A RATIONAL USE OF DRUGS

The National Political Responsibility

Governments carry the primary responsibility for their health policies—which also include drug policies. The factors influencing public health can differ widely from country to country, particularly with respect to:

- the general level of development,
- public health objectives and priorities,
- available resources,
- the efficient use of the available resources,
- morbidity and mortality patterns as well as
- historical factors.

Nevertheless, the government of any country has the political responsibility for ensuring the necessary framework:

(1) To develop and implement a drug policy that takes into consideration the needs of the entire population. Different segments of the population have distinct disease patterns, whose treatment requires a diverse range of drugs. It is important that the state-financed services of the public health sector are available to the poor segments of the population.

Experience shows that a certain "freedom of choice" with regard to doctors, hospitals, laboratories, and drugs, along with private cost sharing, raises the standard of medical services.

(2) To ensure that all health personnel (from the "bare-foot doctor" to the specialist, from the nurse to the pharmacist) have access to the drug information they require.

(3) To use central purchasing through tenders or by making use of particularly advantageous, reliable supply sources for the drugs needed by the country, in order to ensure that good quality drugs are purchased at the lowest possible price.

(4) To restrict the dispensing (sale) of pharmaceutical products to trained staff (such as pharmacists, also "bare-foot pharmacists" in the remote rural areas). The likelihood of the inappropriate use of drugs can be significantly reduced if those dispensing drugs can be sufficiently informed about indications, contraindications, side-effects, duration of treatment, etc.

(5) To enforce and monitor compliance with prescription requirements. This creates considerable difficulties in practice. However, there are many examples showing that it can be achieved.

(6) To establish an effective drug distribution network to ensure regular availability of the essential drugs on a national level.

(7) To set up quality control laboratories.

The authorities of many countries have committed themselves to use all available means to achieve the ambitious objective of "Health for all by the year 2000." Once the regulatory framework exists and the ensuing laws and decrees have been passed, an important prerequisite for a rational use of drugs has been fulfilled.

However, in many Third World countries one often encounters what Gunnar Myrdal described as the "dichotomy between the ideal and the reality, between laws which have been issued and their enforcement."[6] Thus the law cannot remain the only point of reference. The drug manufacturer must accept additional responsibilities.

Responsibility of the Pharmaceutical Manufacturer

The pharmaceutical industry is heterogeneous, including both multinational corporations that invest billions in research and small companies headquartered in the industrial areas of Third World capitals. In this paper, "pharmaceutical companies" or "the drug manufacturers," refers primarily to the large research-based multinational corporations.

The responsibilities of pharmaceutical companies comprise:

- research to identify active substances for treatment or prevention of sickness;
- development of these active substances into pharmaceutical preparations;
- testing of their safety and efficacy;
- registration with the competent authorities;
- production of high quality pharmaceuticals in suitable delivery forms;
- sales within the framework of the registered indications, and with the necessary product information;
- post marketing surveillance to improve drug safety.

In market-oriented systems this investment must provide an adequate return, in both the short term and the long term.

Some of the Third World activities of multinational pharmaceutical companies have led to criticism. For example, it has been claimed that they apply different standards in their home markets and in the Third World with regard to drug information (indications, contraindications, possible side-effects, etc.), that they use overly aggressive marketing methods and charge exorbitant prices. This criticism created the impression that the drugs sold by profit-seeking manufacturers do more harm than good to the people of developing countries.[7]

The activities that led to this criticism are deplorable. Such behavior must be condemned for it is unethical and illegal. It is also bad for business. Today's multinational corporations are subject to public scrutiny through individuals, interest groups, and the media. The discovery of misconduct by a company leads to public debate, which hurts the reputation of the company, and consequently its sales and the motivation of its employees.

My experience leads me to believe that intentional misconduct is rare and not the tip of an iceberg it is often claimed to be. Generalized criticism of "bitter pills" is just as inappropriate as exaggerated expectations from "wonder pills." In any case, the mainstream of criticism has shifted away from multinational drug companies. The *Interim Report* of the 1987–89 *Third World Drug Study* noted "impressive improvements" in multinational drug corporations' marketing practices:

> During the past five years or so, there has been a striking improvement in the promotion of their products by multinational drug companies. Most of them, though certainly not all, have tempered their claims in developing countries to conform to scientific evidence, and they are more willing to disclose hazards. In short, they are more likely to tell the truth, to tell the same story in the Third World that they tell in industrialized countries.[8]

At the same time the practices of domestic manufacturers in the Third World have attracted more criticism:

> But while the multinationals have made obvious improvements in their Third World drug promotion, many of the domestics are now presenting claims which cannot be justified by scientific evidence, and they are reluctant to disclose hazards.[9]

There will always be room for improvement because knowledge and the understanding of drug safety increase constantly. It therefore is possible for multinational drug companies to improve the quality and presentation of the information they provide. Research-based multinational pharmaceutical companies must display leadership in their endeavors to ensure drug safety on an international basis.[10] They must act in search of excellence and according to ethical requirements, even if, or even more so, if respective regulations do not exist.

ETHICS AND THIRD WORLD BUSINESS

To many people the phrase "business ethics" constitutes a contradiction in terms. For them, high profits and high moral principles are incompatible. Yet the growing number of institutions, publications,[11] and university courses dealing with the subject suggests that it is highly fashionable. Over the last ten years, people from business and academia have come together in dozens of conferences, seminars, and meetings to discuss this intellectually appealing subject. However, corporate ethics continues to be a source of confusion and sometimes cynical humor among academicians and practitioners alike. The task of defining and implementing business ethics has been likened to nailing jello to a wall.[12]

"Business ethics," as Thomas Donaldson and Patricia Werhane put it, looks "at corporate profits not for their own sake, but with respect to the achievement of some basic human good."[13] What has to be understood by "human good," at what expense a specific goal is to be achieved, or how a conflict of aims is to be resolved are influenced by subjective value premises.

Corporate, or business, ethics is *applied ethics*. And this is exactly the problem: it is intellectually fun and morally edifying to read books about ethics and to give lectures on the subject, but the devil is in the nuts and bolts of the application of moral reasoning in daily practice, especially under economic pressure and time stress. In a 1977 study, Brenner and Molander found that 43 percent of the executives interviewed were forced to resort to practices that they considered ethically questionable, but that they apparently found necessary for their companies' survival, and hence for their own careers.[14] The authors of the study traced this conflict to the fact that many executives are appraised almost exclusively according to their short-term financial results, and incentive systems were too often geared to rewarding lower costs, increased turnover, and higher profits regardless of social consequences.

Public discontent about the state of business ethics is rising. Much of the U.S. public seems to believe that corporate ethics are in decline and that most companies would sacrifice the environment, public safety, or consumer health for the sake of higher profits.[15] Publications in Europe suggest that executives increasingly perceive a moral conflict between the expediency of business decisions and the moral imperatives suggested by their personal value judgments.[16] In some cases blatant corporate misconduct has discredited whole trades and industries.

Tocqueville's words have undiminished relevance:

> when an immense field for competition is thrown open to all, when wealth is amassed or dissipated in the shortest possible space of time . . . visions of sudden and easy fortunes, of great possessions easily won and lost, of chance under all its forms haunt the mind. The instability of society itself fosters the natural instability of man's desires. . . . [T]he present looms large upon his mind; it hides the future . . . and men seek only to think about tomorrow.[17]

Therefore, he writes, "At all times it is important that those who govern nations [or, for that matter, those who are in charge of corporations] should act with a view to the future."

Although there is no need for a special "pharmaceutical ethics," there are some important ethical differences between the pharmaceutical industry and others. Drugs are not commodities in the same sense as other consumer or investment goods. They are used because people are sick or in pain, because they have physical or mental disorders, or because they are dying. "Consumer sovereignty," the freedom to choose or refuse a product, is limited in this market.

Similarly, the industry's drug safety and risk/benefit assessments have particularly fateful properties. If their specialists or managers err, it is not only their companies that suffer, but sick people. Even when the pharmaceutical industry is governed by comprehensive laws it must be conscious of the special position it holds due to its involvement in public health.

A Pragmatic Approach to Corporate Ethics

Although many assume otherwise, there is no contradiction between ethical corporate conduct and profit, neither for pharmaceutical companies nor for most others. The pure pursuit of ethical objectives runs a high risk of jeopardizing the financial viability of a company. Likewise, the singular pursuit of profit can end in ethical disaster. However, neither of the two extremes is an issue in most businesses.

Corporate policies and ethical codes of conduct, supported by sound personnel and management development practices, are pragmatic responses to the challenge of corporate ethics. What is needed first, though, is common sense.

The following rules of thumb, which Goodpaster refers to as "moral common sense," may appear unsophisticated, but they reflect sound and prudent basic principles:[18]

- Avoid harming others.
- Respect the rights of others.
- Do not lie or cheat.
- Keep promises and contracts.
- Obey the law.
- Prevent harm to others.
- Help those in need.

- Be fair.
- Reinforce these imperatives in others.

Yet life is not so simple, of course. These basic rules do not provide moral guidelines for every case. The rule "obey the law," for example, might not suffice to prevent harm. Many Third World countries do not have state-of-the-art legislation in product safety or environmental protection; or they are "soft states," where existing laws are not enforced. These and other circumstances require that we take a deeper look at our moral obligations.

Even when the quality of law and its enforcement is high, there is room for ethical reflection. At best, civil and criminal law reflect a common denominator of acceptable behavior. And because law does not encompass all moral judgments (and in fact can sometimes be wrong), ethical behavior goes beyond law. Technological innovation in particular often runs far ahead of the legislative framework. Thus, acting legally is at best the ethical minimum, and should not be taken as acting morally.

Transnational corporations can face even further complexities. Anthropologists and experts in jurisprudence have shown that moral and legal codes may vary from country to country and from culture to culture. Practices legally and morally frowned on in one place may comply with the letter and spirit of the law or even be seen as virtues elsewhere. Nevertheless, issues that concern the basic well-being of people and environment cannot be dismissed by invoking ethical relativism; in some cases there are preferable values that can and should be determined and applied.

Better information or insight can impose a responsibility that must lead to action, even if local law does not compel it. Particularly in areas like product, industrial, and environmental safety, standards that embody state-of-the-art knowledge and the highest morality must be brought to bear consistently throughout the world, regardless of local requirements.

The health problems in developing countries require more than pharmaceutical products. They require solutions to complex health care problems. Extreme poverty and lack of public health services are obstacles to adequate treatment for much of the population of the Third World. Illiteracy renders printed information of little use, increasing the risk that products will not be properly used. The pharmaceutical industry should cooperate with other health care organizations to create the preconditions of the rational use of drugs by developing reliable distribution channels and communication methods and improving access to medical care.

The obvious necessity to follow the rule "help those in need" has no appeal for those who take the bottom line as the guiding beacon. The school of thought associated with Peter Drucker[19] and Milton Friedman,[20] for example, argues that the only social responsibility of business is to increase profit, as long as it stays within the rules of the game, engaging in free and open competition without deception or fraud. These thinkers maintain that the free and competitive market automatically moralizes corporate behavior, quite independently of any explicit action. Morality, responsibility, and conscience reside, according to this school of thought, in the "invisible hands" of the free market system, not in the hands of particular organizations, and even less in the hands of their managers.

Drucker's and Friedman's thinking is based on that of Adam Smith, and deserves serious consideration. I share Adam Smith's view that "It is not from the benevolence of the butcher, the brewer, or the baker, that we expect our dinner, but from their regard to their own interest."[21] It should be kept in mind, though, that Adam Smith was a moral philosopher first and an economist second, a background that few executives can match. More importantly, we should remember that our economies do not demonstrate the perfect market conditions, the complete transparency and rational consumption patterns, that economic models may assume. Thus, the "invisible hands" of the system, I believe, need support by explicitly considered moral commonsense rules.

Corporate Policies and Codes of Conduct

Again, not everything legal is legitimate, and better knowledge and deeper insight should lead to appropriate measures regardless of existing regulations. A multinational corporation, which must function in varied legal and social frameworks and yet strive for uniform ethical standards, is well advised to develop explicit corporate policies for its sensitive activities, including marketing, environmental protection, activities in the Third World, animal rights, and research policy. These policies must be enforced by internal codes of conduct.

Both policies and codes of conduct must be comprehensive and specific. They must embody state-of-the-art knowledge, and be realistic with regard to their implementation. They should reflect not only the philosophy of corporate management, but also the results of discussions with the best expert minds inside and outside the corporation, even if relations have been adversarial in the past. Before adoption they should be seriously challenged by external, independent reviewers.

Company guidelines on sensitive matters are obviously not standardized "instructions on dealing ethically" that can always clearly determine what is ethically acceptable. No code of conduct can possibly cover every ethical dilemma encountered in daily business practice. Rich points out that an ethical question is one to which there is no clear, soothing, and harmonious answer — no answer that will leave a totally clear conscience.[22] There are diverse and sometimes conflicting determinants for ethical decisions, stemming from individual, social, professional, and organizational norms. However, reasonable guidelines give employees a clear basis for setting some priorities, and, when necessary, for weighing commercial interests against moral concerns, especially for decisions that must be made under time pressure and financial constraints.

The guidelines must contain meaningful and clearly stated provisions, and sanctions must be enforced for noncompliance. It must be made clear within the organization that a person can be demoted or discharged for violating codes of conduct, even if the result was beneficial in economic terms, and that ethical behavior may lead to a promotion even if its short-term economic effect was negative. Codes are more useful if they are complemented by complaint review procedures, ombudsman services, and education and certification programs.[23]

Yet the best policies and codes of conduct are only as good as the executives who implement them. The decisive element is the *human* element.

Personnel Policy

Max Weber, the eminent German sociologist, once observed that people who must decide on matters that affect many people's lives will, unless they have lost all reason, find themselves forced to evaluate their ethical motivations and the likely consequences of their decisions based on their knowledge and conscience. Moral rules for business people are not significantly different from those for others, but responsibilities certainly increase with increasing knowledge, abilities, and complexity of technology. We need executives who are fully aware that they are accountable for the consequences of their actions (or omissions), people who try to live in keeping with fundamental ethical ideas.

Personnel policy must therefore aim at recruiting people who are more than just expert in special fields. Expertise in conventional business disciplines, marketing, economics, or general management in no way guarantees moral proficiency. Yet responsiveness to the values, convictions, and needs of others is the foundation for sustainable business and should be reflected in the criteria for hiring personnel.

Sound personnel policy also can improve leadership and human relations within the company. Here as elsewhere the "Golden Rule" is appropriate: "Act in the way you hope others act toward you." If we apply this "Golden Rule" to our professional lives, it implies a full sharing of information, involvement of those concerned in decision making, and serious consideration of conflicting points of view to build consensus. A participatory style of management is thus indispensable and we will have to refrain from elitist authoritarian decisions.

Management Development

All major corporations have sophisticated management development programs to continually upgrade their executives' skills. Yet only a few programs cover "ethics," and those that do are directed at top management, not middle and lower management, where ethical pressures (perceived or real) are higher.[24] Admittedly, the subject of ethical reasoning is difficult; and virtues like modesty, sensitivity, social responsibility, and the ability to take a larger view of life are not as easily taught as marketing or finance. Moral philosophy, the discussion of case studies dealing with ethical issues,[25] and other disciplines can help us find a reasonable approach. But such disciplines do not supply mechanical solutions or procedures, so practical wisdom, experience, and ethically sensitive judgment continue to be indispensable.

Management development must include holistic training in ethics as well as traditional management disciplines, and must be sustained. A "quick bleach job" in ethics will not do justice to the subject's complexity. Nor will it change attitudes. Sustained endeavors are worth the effort, since they raise the value of decision making and the ease of group efforts, and the effectiveness of the company.

Such an investment in people can improve the ethical quality of a firm. A corporate environment that supports higher ethical standards in individual decisions is likely to make them contagious. Every manager can encourage ethical behavior in his or her sphere of activity, first of all by setting a good example.

Broader Measurement and Reward Systems

A serious treatment of business ethics requires not only selecting and training executives properly, we must also revise performance appraisals. Executives faced with ethical dilemmas tend to opt for the profitable rather than the ethical, where these options are not the same.[26] This bias is partly due to the prevailing incentive and appraisal systems. As long as we measure employees by short-term financial results only, we risk forcing them to choose between self-esteem and clear consciences on the one hand and careers and financial benefits on the other. Performance appraisal criteria must increasingly incorporate social and ecological goals and strive to include ethical objectives in addition to economic and technical ones, regardless of how hard they are to quantify. Improvements in product safety, environmental protection, truth and accuracy in information, and fairness in hiring, firing, and promotion, to name a few areas that are not immediately related to economic efficiency, must be visibly rewarded.

The measurement of ethical performance is a difficult task. It could, of course, be elevated to the philosophical heights of the Kantian categorical imperative: Did we act in such a way that the action could be taken as a universal law or rule of right behavior? In most cases, however, a much simpler test will suffice: Would we feel comfortable explaining why we made this decision to a national television audience?

An important virtue to be considered in appraisal and reward systems is the courage to stand up for one's beliefs. The analysis of several great disasters of recent years shows that long before the Challenger tragedy, the Chernobyl disaster, and the Exxon-Valdez accident, critical voices had pointed to the problems that later triggered off the tragedies. But these warnings were ignored or swept aside. We need to keep in mind the ultimate truth of President Andrew Jackson's dictum, "One man with courage makes a majority."

Companies should employ people who are aware of their responsibilities and sensitive in their judgment. Employee training and performance appraisal should encompass ethical as well as technical content. Managers in such companies will be well-balanced personalities rather than performing robots who do not care what happens to the rest of the world as long as they feather their own and their company's nests.

Ethics Makes Good Business

Why should a company consider ethics in their decision-making process, in addition to law, self-interest, and convention? First of all, to prevent harm to people. Profits to companies are like food to people: absolutely necessary. But few people consider eating the central purpose of life. Companies, similarly, have broader purposes.

Second, the reputation of a company is one of its most valuable assets, even though it does not appear on the balance sheet. That reputation depends increasingly on the company's contribution to socially valued ends. The public is increasingly well informed about corporate activities, and many are skeptical of the inherent legitimacy and value of private corporate dealings. Simply doing business efficiently is no longer enough. A growing proportion of our customers and employees are convinced that greater corporate responsibility is necessary to save present and future generations from harm. These convictions influence many consumers' choices.

Applied business ethics is also increasingly important to employees and investors. Employees who regard themselves as one with their company in spirit, outlook, and principles have greater motivation to work. Serious investors, too, do not want to be shareholders in a suspect company. Applied business ethics is a matter of enlightened self-interest: frictions within a company can be avoided or diminished, cooperation encouraged, and the corporate image improved.

Ethical conduct in business is additionally important in protecting entrepreneurial freedom. If business ethics are perceived to be low, politicians and government agencies will have to respond. Disclosures of unethical behavior, of carelessness, or of gross negligence will lead to more and more stringent legislation. Corporate leadership must take the initiative to practice ethical responsibility, or their choices in the matter may be severely curtailed.

Business ethics are likely to provide a solid new basis of competition, beyond the standard forces of classical markets. A more affluent society, better informed about the opportunities and problems of today's technology, may see company ethics as decisive in consumer choice. We are already witnessing the first stirrings of this movement. It will become a business problem for those who ignore it, but an opportunity for corporations that take ethics seriously.

Ethical business conduct of pharmaceutical corporations is an important precondition for a positive impact on health issues in Third World countries—but real improvement cannot be achieved by one party alone.

IN SEARCH OF NEW PARTNERSHIPS

The dimension and the complexity of today's health problems in the Third World are immense. They pose one of the twentieth century's biggest social challenges—one that cannot be met by any single party or by non-integrated approaches. Whatever the governments in the Third World or the pharmaceutical industry or charitable organizations do on their own is bound to have a limited impact. Whatever a single actor can contribute is often limited and less effective than the result of synergistic cooperation of many partners.

Appropriate solutions with regard to meeting the development challenge in the health sector require the formation of new coalitions that include not only governments and pharmaceutical companies, but also nongovernmental organizations (NGOs) whose grassroots experience is not available to the other parties. Project-related and solution-oriented dialogues with medical and social scientists, governmental officials, industry experts, and patient, consumer, and public interest groups can help us to reach a shared understanding of the issues involved and lead to new perspectives.

The process of wrestling with problems that have no simple solutions and the willingness to be challenged by people who have different experiences and who base their judgments on different values increase the quality of all kinds of decisions. All who can contribute in some way to solutions should be accepted as a partner, even if there have been adversarial relationships in the past. Ideological lines of demarcation or fundamentalistic rejections are not attitudes that promote problem solving.

In many countries, for example, the church has established a functional health care infrastructure with highly trained and charity-oriented personnel. Such church organizations, but also other NGOs involved in health care might

- assume responsibility for health education of the public,
- educate medical and paramedic personnel,
- expand rural health services,
- distribute drugs and ensure their rational use,
- develop *social marketing* programs for stigmatized diseases (e.g., leprosy, epilepsy, depression, or AIDs),
- develop programs to overcome the social isolation of humans resulting from stigmatized diseases.

The pharmaceutical industry, for its part, has a broad experience in a number of areas beyond research and production of drugs. Particularly in the following areas, useful contributions could be made:

- logistics and distribution systems,
- health education and health information,
- management,
- production,
- quality control,
- marketing.

These complementary strengths can form the basis for a partnership bringing together governments, international organizations, and other experienced partners in the public health sector. The goal is to find the most effective way to tackle health problems. Anybody who can contribute should feel called upon to do so.

Conclusions

Commercial success is no longer simply determined by annual profits. Society expects considerably more: companies should be socially responsible, use energy and other resources wisely, protect the environment, and contribute to solutions of the problems of those societies which represent a majority on our earth, the people in the Third World.

Instead of succumbing to the temptation to concentrate scarce and expensive research, marketing, and information exclusively on markets that produce higher returns, pharmaceutical corporations should embark on sustainable actions for human health and welfare all over the world. And so should other institutions, organizations, or individuals who share the concerns for the social problems of our times. The costs involved are still rather modest for the non-poor in North and South, so one should not wait until the problems become even more complex than they already are.

Underdevelopment and global problems are caused by a multitude of factors, and all these factors together exercise a powerful influence upon the political, social, economic, and ecological conditions in which people live.

Single actions are too quickly soaked up by this huge dry sponge, underdevelopment. This is also true if external interventions are not backed by the political will of the recipient nations. To avert the bitter prospects for the world's most vulnerable societies and to make development sustainable, new coalitions should be built, thus melting the potential of each of the partners to a unified whole. Only concerted efforts can bring about relief for the wretched and deprived.

NOTES

1. See C. E. A. Winslow, *The Cost of Sickness and the Price of Health* (Geneva: WHO, 1951), 9.

2. Over 35 (but also under 18).

3. See K. M. Leisinger, *Project Hope: Analyses and Theses on Population Growth* (Zurich: UNICEF, 1989).

4. See R. Chambers, "Rural Poverty Imperceived: Problems and Remedies," *World Development* 9 (1981): 1–19.

5. For a comprehensive analysis of the issues see K. M. Leisinger, *Health Policy for Least Developed Countries* (Basel: Social Strategies Publishers Cooperative Society).

6. G. Myrdal, *Asian Drama*, vol. 1 (Harmondsworth: Penguin Books, 1968), 277.

7. As examples, see R. Hartog and H. Schulte-Sasse, *Das Bundesdeutsche Arzneimittelangebot in Der Dritten Welt*, ed. Buko Pharma-Kampagne, Bielefeld, June 1990, and the literature quoted there; Milton Silverman, *The Drugging of the Americas* (Berkeley: University of California Press, 1976); and Dianne Melrose, *Bitter Pills* (Oxford: Oxfam, 1982).

8. M. Silverman, P. Lee, and M. Lydecker, *Interim Report* mimeo, San Francisco, November 8, 1988, p. 4.

9. Ibid., 6.

10. See, for example, *The Perception and Management of Drug Safety Risks,* ed. D. Horisberger and R. Dinkel (Berlin, Heidelberg, and New York: Springer Verlag, 1989).

11. See, for example, *Ethical Theory and Business,* ed. T. L. Beauchamp and N. E. Bowie (Englewood Cliffs: Prentice Hall, 1988); *Ethics, Free Enterprise, and Public Policy,* ed. R. T. De George and J. Pichler (Englewood Cliffs: Prentice Hall, 1982);

62   The Role of Multinational Pharmaceutical Corporations

and *Ethical Issues in Business,* ed. T. Donaldson and P. Werhane (Englewood Cliffs: Prentice Hall, 1982).

12. P. V. Lewis, "Defining 'Business Ethics': Like Nailing Jello to a Wall," *Journal of Business Ethics* 4 (1985): 377–383.

13. Donaldson and Werhane, *Ethical Issues in Business,* 2.

14. See *Harvard Business Review* (January-February 1977): 57–71.

15. See *Business Week,* May 29, 1989, p. 29.

16. See *Management Wissen* 12 (December 1988): 52–65.

17. Alexis de Tocqueville, *Democracy in America,* vol. 2, chap. 27.

18. K. E. Goodpaster, *Ethics in Management* (Boston: Harvard Business School, 1984).

19. P. Drucker, "What is 'Business Ethics'?" *Public Interest* 63 (1981): 18–36.

20. M. Friedman, "The Social Responsibility of Business Is To Increase Its Profits," *New York Times Magazine,* September 13, 1970, p. 32f.

21. Adam Smith, *The Wealth of Nations* (New York: Modern Library, 1937), 14.

22. A. Rich, *Wirtschaftsethik* (Gütersloher Verlagshaus, 1985).

23. W. W. Lowrance, *Modern Science and Human* (New York: Oxford University Press, 1985).

24. G. Laczniak, "Business Ethics: A Manager's Primer," *Business Atlanta* 33 (1983): 23–29.

25. Bowen H. McCoy, "The Parable of the Sadhu," *Harvard Business Review* (Sept.–Oct. 1983): 103–108.

26. S. J. Vitell and T. A. Festervand, "Business Ethics: Conflicts, Practices, and Beliefs of Industrial Executives," *Journal of Business Ethics* 8 (1987): 111–122.

Response

INGAR G. F. BRUGGEMANN

The matters under discussion have been the subject of heated polemic for at least the past fifteen years. Klaus Leisinger raised some issues on which I will concentrate from the perspective of the World Health Organization as a neutral broker, in keeping with its international as opposed to supranational status. WHO has tackled many of these thorny issues by first identifying the questions, and then bringing together different ideas from across the world in an attempt to answer them.

This forum allows different ways of thinking about the challenges facing society. It is important for us not to be compartmentalized just because we work in a particular compartment of society. We all share being human, having feelings, and owning a sense of morality. Although we have different obligations to society, we all are people who care and are concerned.

Leisinger's analysis of the health and related socioeconomic problems facing the developing countries is in line with WHO policy. This analysis led the WHO to adopt its well-known policy, "Health for All by the Year 2000." The goal of the policy is a level of health that will permit people all over the world to lead economically productive and socially satisfying lives.

Two billion people in the world have little or no access to the most essential drugs. These people live in the developing countries. They represent 50 percent of the population. We must remember this stark reality when we discuss challenges. These are not challenges for the

Ingar G. F. Bruggemann is director of the World Health Organization office at the United Nations, New York, where she represents the director-general of the WHO to the United Nations system and other intergovernmental organizations. She joined the WHO in 1966 and in the course of her career has been closely involved in the development of health program evaluation both by member states and by the WHO itself as part of a broader managerial process for health development.

multinational pharmaceutical corporations alone, they are challenges for all of us.

Unfortunately, the response to this situation does not lie simply in unloading medicinal drugs on the Third World. Medicines cannot act on their own. They form part of health technology in general, and that in turn is only one element of a health system. Technology implies not only methods, equipment, and supplies; it also implies the people who use them. Technology must be not only scientifically sound, but affordable and acceptable to those on whom it is used, not merely to those who use it. Appropriate health systems do not develop on their own. If the developing countries allow them to sprout haphazardly, as happened in many industrialized countries, they will certainly not be appropriate. The richer countries learned the hard way; the poor ones cannot afford to do that. They require a health policy to guide them—a set of guidelines that provides clear understanding of ultimate health goals.

The "Health for All" policy was adopted by WHO's member states. Health systems based on primary health care are the key to attaining the goals of that policy. The member states agreed on a worldwide strategy to put the policy into effect. That strategy includes action to be taken not only by governments, but also by nongovernmental organizations, universities, industry, and many other partners. I shall address one component of an appropriate health system—the medicinal drug component—and in particular, the rational use of such medicines.

Leisinger emphasized business ethics as the challenge for multinational pharmaceutical firms in the Third World. I challenge that. Ethics is a means—an important one in itself—but not an end. The "end" for all of us is to get needed drugs to people and to ensure they are used in a rational way. If forming appropriate health systems requires a clear health policy, so does ensuring the rational use of medicines as part of that broad policy. In other words, a clear medicinal drug policy is required. My plea to pharmaceutical corporations is for them to become a strong ally in a common effort to support developing countries in defining and implementing drug policies as part of their health policies.

At the WHO Conference on the Rational Use of Drugs in Nairobi in 1985, it was generally accepted that to ensure rational use, a national drug policy is necessary. WHO subsequently issued guidelines for the preparation of such policies. These guidelines clarify the requirements regarding information on medicinal drugs, not only for prescribers, but also for users. Rational drug use requires an informed public. There should not be a barrier between health personnel and the public. This jointness in providing relevant and unbiased information has obvious ethical overtones.

Another important component of the guidelines is the education and training of health personnel in the correct use of drugs. Most personnel in developing countries are not qualified doctors, nurses, or pharmacists in the area of primary health care. However, it is possible to train them how to use a specific list of essential drugs.

A third component of a national drug policy is the choice of drugs to be used — the selection of those most required in the light of the particular country's health situation. There are approximately 260 essential drugs. That number makes no sense for developing countries. Quite apart from the problems in training in the use of so many products, there are the roadblocks of supply and cost. Management is not the strong suit of health systems. Therefore there is a need for carefully planned supply systems which are easier to ensure when there are only a few dosage forms for each of the 260 drugs. Leisinger discussed how little is being spent on health altogether in many developing countries, and of that only a small proportion goes to drugs. The WHO has shown that in many of these countries, essential drugs for primary health care can be ensured for as little as one dollar per person per year. That seems ridiculously small, but for these countries it remains out of reach in terms of covering the whole country's population, and is likely to be unreachable for many years to come. This is an ethical issue of paramount importance.

According to Leisinger, ethical responsibility starts where juridical responsibility ends. However, drug legislation and regulation are essential components of national drug policies. People are entitled to know not only that the medicines they take are effective, but also that they are safe and of good quality. Since most drugs in developing countries are imported, ensuring the quality of those drugs is of great importance. The use of the WHO's "Voluntary Certification Scheme on the Quality of Pharmaceutical Products Moving in International Commerce" goes a long way toward ensuring this.

The rational use of drugs goes far beyond the acts of prescribing and using. Their subsequent effects must be monitored and evaluated. This implies surveillance of how drug products are being used, and their effects. It also implies monitoring adverse reactions to drugs and taking any corrective measure required. To this end, the WHO as part of its neutral international role, disseminates to all countries information on such adverse reactions submitted to it by any country.

As Leisinger stressed, policies never suffice. They must be enforced and this requires the human element. I agree with Leisinger's outline of the respective responsibilities of governments and the pharmaceutical industry. To that should be added input from the Nairobi conference which delineated the responsibilities of the WHO, governments, prescribers, universities, the public, consumer groups, the mass media, and the pharmaceutical industry. Following are added responsibilities of industry that seem to go beyond those in Leisinger's paper: developing new drugs in neglected fields, particularly to solve the health problems of developing countries; responding to the need of developing countries for low-cost drugs of acceptable quality; providing complete and unbiased information on pharmaceutical products to all concerned; and complying with established drug promotional procedures to avoid double standards in different countries.

The issues of information and drug promotion have been the most contentious at the national and international levels over the past fifteen years. I support Leisinger's statement that issues concerning the basic well-being of people cannot be dismissed by invoking ethical relativism. He rightly maintains that ethics is good business, and that the reputation of a company is one of its most valuable assets. The right kind of promotion of the right kind of drugs for the developing countries at affordable prices will lead to the sale of more drugs, not less. No one expects the pharmaceutical industry to be Santa Claus. Hopefully it will help make essential drugs available to the other two billion people in the developing countries who do not have access to them today. Industry can devise ways of doing that at prices these people can bear and still make a reasonable profit considering the immense size of the market.

What, then, is the "right" kind of promotion? Leisinger described it as behaving so that the action could be taken as a universal law or rule of right behavior. He referred to a list of what has been called "moral common sense." The WHO went a step further. It defined universal ethical criteria for medicinal drug promotion as general principles, not as legal obligations. Here are some of the highlights of these criteria: All promotional claims should be reliable, accurate, truthful, informative, balanced, up-to-date, capable of substantiation, and in good taste. The wording and illustrations in advertisements to health personnel should be fully consistent with the approved source of scientific information. Adequate information on the use of medicines should be made available to patients. Any advertisements to the general public should help people make rational decisions on the use of drugs legally available to them without a prescription. Ethical criteria for the promotion of exported drugs should be identical to drugs used domestically

In the field of health, there is only one world. The provision to all concerned of reliable information and the ethical promotion of preventive measures with drugs reputed to be curative or palliative assume outstanding importance for people everywhere, rich and poor, inhabitants of an underdeveloped or a more developed country alike.

The challenge for multinational pharmaceutical corporations in developing countries is to support them to ensure the availability of medicinal drugs for all their people at prices they can afford, as well as to ensure their rational use. Corporations can make substantial contributions by helping developing countries establish or strengthen their national drug policies as part of their national health policies, and to implement these policies by providing them with necessary information. Corporations can also promote the drugs that are essential for the people in less-developed countries in compliance with international ethical critera. This is enlightened self-interest.

Response

JAMES B. RUSSO

I agree with much of Klaus Leisinger's paper. One statement, however, must be challenged — his assertion that industrial misconduct is a rare deviation in the pharmaceutical business. Let us be loving enough to be honest. With thirty years of experience in this industry, an industry I love and which has achieved more good than many others and employed more decent people than most others, I must honestly disagree. Misconduct in the pharmaceutical industry is unfortunately not rare, although not commonplace. We are in danger of many things in this industry, but general canonization is not one of them. Assertions of saintliness, particularly from our own mouths, offend not only the facts but our credibility. In a peculiar way, they seem to be equally effective in luring our managements to the brink of hibernation while at the same time stimulating the bile of our critics. I suggest that we give self-congratulatory speeches a well-deserved rest.

When a product is innocuous or misused, the perception — right, wrong, or indifferent — is that the industry producing that product is questionable. Whether or not this reputation is deserved, it exists. The answer to that perception is not for the industry to say simply, "We never make mistakes." It is a matter of credibility. It is not wise for any of us to brag. It is not seemly. Most importantly, it is not convincing.

Many of us here know and admire Milton Silverman and Mia Liedecker. It is certainly true they have seen marked improvements in recent years in the quality of drug promotion by multinationals in the Third World. It is also true as noted in the book, *Bad Medicine,*[1] that exceptions to the trend are not particularly difficult to find, nor

---

James B. Russo is currently the director of government and public policy for SmithKline Beecham. He joined SmithKline after serving with the Pharmaceutical Manufacturers Association for eighteen years.

are they confined to firms of ill repute. Some of the firms with whom they still found difficulty are among the most admired and the most profitable in the world. Well acquainted with the concept of what is usually called the Judeo-Christian morality, these firms are sufficiently financially secure that they have little excuse not to practice that morality.

Thus, I would add to Leisinger's list of responsibilities of multinational drug firms the obligation to conduct marketing efforts not only within the framework of approved labeling as he suggests, but in the context of prudent economy. We have all seen the remarkable film documentaries of immodest medical meetings in nations of modest means sponsored by multinational drug companies. Who among us while watching those films has not felt a pang of conscience. We humans have to blunt the shame that comes from seeing something we would hate to try to explain to anyone we really respect, or whose respect we need, such as our children. It is probably inevitable that reconsideration of these practices will come. Indeed, physician groups in the United States, at least, have already begun that process. This will mark the end of a practice that has offended all of us and interferes with the achievement of the higher ethic that got us into this business in the first place.

What a wonderful, powerful notion Leisinger advances about applied ethics, the notion not only that we can identify the principles of right conduct, but that we can apply them in a very practical way. This brings me to the function of the churches. In addition to all that Leisinger lists we should add "pressure." In my experience, nothing is more efficacious in raising the sense of decency which lies, sometimes asleep, in all of us than the prospect of approval for doing the right thing from a company's most senior management; even if prompted to a small degree by the prospect of a visit from Sister Regina Rowan.

But of course, the central point Leisinger makes is something we must, and I hope will, embrace: the promise of partnership. We need to pay closer attention to the very pragmatic concept that says, "Our shareholders' interests and those of the poorest and most vulnerable of the world closely coincide." How many industries can say that? And what does that mean in pragmatic terms? One of the rules of moral common sense, as Leisinger uses it, comes to mind: Help those in need. The idea of helping those in need should not be abstract, it should take very specific forms—like joining with our colleagues in medicine and all of health care to urge the United States Congress to change the emphasis in foreign aid away from guns toward health. That may seem radical but it is an ethical imperative. We need to work together with consumer activists to deal with the need for drugs and vaccines around the world. We need to get on with the job of providing not only the products but the infrastructures and the information in a world sometimes, unfortunately, dominated by illiteracy and corruption.

In all of this, we must not lose sight of the need to keep our feet on the ground. That is a rule of behavior in the business environment that must be demonstrably grounded in economics, not simply in morality. The 1990 elections in the United States provide instructive evidence on this point. In almost every instance where voters were asked to spend money on protection or improving the environment, they refused to vote affirmatively. The reason, analysts say, is that people are worried about the economy, most particularly, their personal economies. They want clean air, but they see it as a bit of a luxury to be purchased by people whose jobs are secure. Their jobs are not secure and they do not feel secure. So clean air will have to wait. This is a complex matter of human behavior, albeit one of exquisite importance.

Leisinger has illuminated the issues well. Our chances of addressing those issues responsibly depend perhaps too much on how grounded our colleagues in the church, the consumer movement, and the government are in helping us keep our eyes on the right prize. Left to our own devices, history suggests, we will not do quite as well. Leisinger mentioned the Exxon incident; it all comes down to things like that. Captain Joseph Haywood of the Exxon-Valdez might not have left the bridge if he had known he would have to explain his actions to Sister Regina Rowan.

NOTE

1. Milton Silverman, Mia Lydecker, and Philip R. Lee, *Bad Medicine: The Prescription Drug Industry in the Third World* (Stanford, Calif.: Stanford University Press, 1992).

Discussion Summary

Klaus Leisinger discussed the economic constraints of drug distribution in the Third World.

To say that the main contribution of the pharmaceutical industry is just "getting drugs to people" is rather simplistic. It is, more precisely, the provision of drugs that *meet the needs of public health*, the complete and true information on those drugs to physicians, pharmacists, health care personnel, and patients, and the monitoring of adverse reactions.

Whatever it is termed, the problem is in another orbit: Important drugs and vaccines needed against endemic diseases are available. However, they are not accessible in sufficient quantities and their cost is beyond the means of those who are in dire need. Mainly responsible for this situation are the geographical, economic, and political circumstances in developing countries.

- The larger portion of the population is remote from free and private distribution centers.
- Most patients' purchasing power is dramatically weak, so that any price for a given drug to treat any condition would be too high.
- Resources are insufficiently allocated to the health care sector.

While private pharmaceutical corporations can extend their services beyond the provision of products, as in helping solve logistic problems and establishing distribution channels, it has no influence on governmental and expenditure priorities. Where resources are absorbed by militaristically asserted ambitions of the elite, or by prestigious projects designed for the benefit of the privileged, socioeconomic and health problems as well as inequitable distribution of drugs among the great majority of the population are pronounced. It is the responsibility of the local government to formulate and implement a health policy according to the needs of its entire population, both in the public and

73

in the private sector—the pharmaceutical industry can play a support-ing role only.

Pharmaceutical industries cannot operate without generating ade-quate profits, even in developing countries. CIBA-GEIGY spends about 1.8 billion Swiss Francs yearly on research. In 1990, the company had a return on investment of about 6 percent. Compared to international standards, this is low. To make affordability of drugs a criteria for drug development is an interesting proposal, but this is easier said than done given the fact that the purchasing power of the people living in ab-solute poverty, for example those in sub-Saharan Africa, is zero! Con-stant drug donations would not solve their immense health problems as long as socioeconomic underdevelopment and political negligence of the wretched pave the way for ever more diseases. Also, under such conditions, programs sponsored by the World Bank or the World Health Organization cannot be successful.

Profits make companies tick. But commercial interests alone are not an adequate guide, not only from a humanitarian point of view, but also for the long-term prosperity of a company which, of course, depends on the well-being of society at large. As Bruggemann said, the first company to discover a cure for AIDS patients has an enormous moral responsibility: It could allow conditions in the marketplace to be the deciding factor between life and death. But the pursuit of a commercial short-term opportunity could backfire.

Hospitals I recently visited in Tanzania, Uganda, and Kenya are filled with children whose parents have both died of AIDS. In the se-verely AIDS-afflicted countries of the African continent, people are either over 65 years of age or under 20. The age category in between is missing due to AIDS. Of course, the company with the AIDS cure will have to be compensated for its research and development efforts, but one cannot select the minority of patients with liquid assets for cure, and let AIDS wipe out whole generations of poorer segments.

Conferences like this, where ideas and opinions are honestly shared and exchanged should be held more frequently. Solutions are like a mosaic. We all have stones that belong to that mosaic, but none of the individual stones alone forms the entire picture. CIBA-GEIGY is ready to contribute its share for the completion of the picture.

Paul Belford underscored improvements within the industry.

The pharmaceutical industry has changed dramatically in the eleven years I have been involved with it. One of our first charges, in the early 1980s, was to be certain senior management was aware of its critics. An interesting trail has brought us to where we are.

Every major corporation is included in this seminar. They do not see the industry as exploitative. All the great shifts in the post-war era, such as India's independence, were the result of people determining to act against evil. Ghandi obtained independence for India not in India, but in London, because the English people basically said, "This is wrong." Pharmaceutical corporations agree with the principle of moral behavior, and sincerely believe, "We are not exploiting anyone. We are making our product available in the Third World. We are working with infrastructure development. We are taking the extra steps." The industry has made and will continue to take realistic steps to "clean up its act." It has already done a lot of that. With this interest and willingness, the industry has remedied many of the wrongs brought to its attention. How can the industry participate more?

Regina Rowan offered a direction for the future.

The challenge for multinational pharmaceutical managers goes beyond the provision of funds or drugs. The time has come for multinational pharmaceutical corporations to be an active part of the solution to the problem associated with pharmaceuticals in developing countries. The call is for them to give the expertise only they can give — management skills. These firms know how to get drugs out there. They are the only ones who do. The experts in corporations know how to make good informational packages with all the necessary graphics. Others know the content but not the communication techniques. All health care givers and others working toward health for all by 2000 need help. They need the multinational pharmaceutical companies as partners in getting aid, expertise, and medicines where they are needed. They do not need help that stops at, "Here is medicine, here is money." We are all in this together.

PART 2

Global Pharmaceutical Issues

Three specific issues relative to pharmaceutical delivery in developing countries were selected as foci for the study group: essential drugs, counterfeit drugs, and intellectual property rights. These are issues with the potential for great conflict among multinational corporations, religious networks, consumer representatives, and other health-related nongovernmental organizations. They are also problems where collaboration among these groups has great potential to improve the access of the poor in the Third World to quality drugs at the lowest possible cost.

Essential drugs have been an agenda item for the World Health Organization and a source of concern for multinational corporations since 1975. By 1981, the Health Action International (HAI) had been formed as a network of consumer and public interest organizations to promote the implementation of the WHO Essential Drugs Programme, and the International Federation of Pharmaceutical Manufacturers Associations had reacted with a proposed Code of Pharmaceutical Marketing Practices. During the early 1980s, as developing countries adopted essential drugs programs and pharmaceutical companies saw these markets increasingly constrained with the strong possibility of regulation feeding back to the First World, the industry bulwarked against these programs.

In recent years, as evidence — problems as well as the potential — on essential drugs programs accumulated, industry and activists have reached a more nuanced understanding of each other's position. The conflict has muted.

The reaction on the part of the pharmaceutical industry has been dramatic, as reflected in the comments at the November 1990 workshop. Those responses and the discussion summary all call for further collaboration. The managers are now asking nongovernmental organizations and religious networks to be more specific in what they need

77

and want and are encouraging the World Health Organization to be more assertive in initiating programs where the industry can collaborate.

The problem of counterfeit drugs grows out of the inefficiency and ineffectiveness of Third World drug delivery systems, the same problems that led to the efforts on essential drug programs. As a specific issue, however, counterfeit drugs has only recently emerged.

Counterfeiting covers a broad range of activities from a completely fake drug where there is no active ingredient, packaged in a way that makes it indiscernable from the real product; to drugs where the amount of the active ingredient is a small fraction of that in the original product; to some cases where one active ingredient is replaced with another. The sophistication of the counterfeiters has rapidly outpaced the ability of multinational pharmaceutical corporations and host governments to deal with it. Drug counterfeiting is despicable in that it directly counters the intended purpose and threatens the life of the patient.

The counterfeit drug problem is one with strong congruence of interest among multinational manufacturers, host governments, the World Health Organization, religious networks, nongovernmental organizations, local Third World channels of distribution, and all who are concerned or are involved in the delivery of health care to the poor. Unfortunately, there has been little information or public discussion about counterfeit drugs, and to date only minimal cooperative action among the concerned parties. Multinational pharmaceutical manufacturers have not even shared information among themselves. The reticence of producers and host governments is understandable. The manufacturer does not want it known there are indistinguishable, substandard copies of its drugs in the marketplace. For their part, governments do not want to be perceived as being incapable of controlling the problem, and do not want the populus to question every drug available to them or to avoid the use of drugs altogether. For developing country governments, the serious lack of quality control and quality assessing facilities encourages the existence of counterfeit drugs as well as inhibits their detection.

As the presentors and respondents uniformly agree, counterfeiting is a major, now internationally syndicated problem calling for strong coordinated response from all organizations concerned with pharmaceutical delivery to Third World peoples.

There is at least one matter about which the pharmaceutical industry has a common mind and that is the question of patent protection or what is called intellectual property rights. The third section of Part II presented the industry position and its rationale as well as some challenges to that position by consumer activists. From the corporate view, the economics of the industry demands patent protection and a system of sanctions for offenders. This is the strong position of the United States government. It is also argued that patents are in the best interest of Third World countries.

If intellectual property rights are valid, however, just what responsibilities on the part of the companies should be correlated with these rights? The activists have some suggestions and these, as well as industry response, are reported in the discussion summary.

Essential Drugs

Three presentors introduced the issue of essential drugs from the development of the concept, to the views of the World Health Organization (the WHO has been the central institution involved in its development), to the experience of a UNICEF primary health program of which essential drugs are a key component.

Drawing from his work on the various approaches for evaluating national essential drugs programs, Michael Reich outlines how this approach was nurtured by the WHO as a single solution to the multiple problems caused by the limited capabilities of health systems in poor countries in the early 1970s. At that point, essential drugs promised to "extend access, reduce costs, and improve treatment . . . all at the same time." Reich addresses the tension that exists between the public and private sectors. Noting the great progress that has been made in the relationship between multinational pharmaceutical companies and the WHO over essential drugs, he argues that three areas of conflict remain: the extent of regulation, the role of the market, and local production.

Speaking from his experience as the program manager of the WHO Action Programme on Essential Drugs, Fernando Antezana stresses the importance of getting drugs to those who need them in the Third World: "A vast number of people — perhaps as many as two billion — still lack regular access to the most needed essential drugs." Reviewing the findings of various WHO studies, Antezana stresses the barriers in production and distribution that contribute to this tragic situation. Against this background, the purposes and procedures of the Action Programme are discussed, concluding with suggestions for action on the part of the international pharmaceutical industry.

The third paper in this section presents essential drugs as a key component of an ongoing primary health care delivery program — UNICEF's Bamako Initiative. In his presentation, Agostino Paganini, the manager of the Initiative, stated that the solution to the present danger arising from the lack of control in drug availability and use lies in the accessibility for the poor of public health care facilities "with a constant supply of a limited range of appropriate cheap drugs administered by trained personnel." He stressed the need for international solidarity, local empowerment, more emphasis on training, and financial strategies to reach the half of the population in sub-Saharan Africa who do not currently have access to public health.

Two respondents addressed the essential drugs issue from the perspective of multinational pharmaceutical corporations. Robert McDonough, the manager for public policy planning of Upjohn, calls us to work together, "to get out there and break the barriers that keep us from finding ways to help the people who need it." He argued that, even though industry may not like the activist challenge, managers need to accept it and use it beneficially.

Paul Belford, speaking from a decade of experience on developing country issues facing the PMA as the organizer of three Third World projects for the PMA, and as an active participant in all of the workshops of the pharmaceutical study group, makes the point that multinational pharmaceutical firms are not experts in Third World development. He notes how difficult it is for the multinational pharmaceutical industry to be pro-active on development issues. They can and do respond to problems that are brought to them by activists but are not particularly good at identifying problems themselves. In these activities, multinational managers need and seek the guidance of the religious networks.

A third respondent, Linda Pfeiffer, reflected on the experience of her organization, International Medical Services for Health (INMED), that works on building bridges between multinational corporations and nonprofit agencies. She outlines the nature of this relationship and how both multinationals and nonprofit agencies relate to the basic principles involved in providing pharmaceuticals to the poor in the Third World.

The discussion reported in this section took place in November 1990. Interestingly, it did not focus on the conflict among activists, the WHO, and industry over the limitations of essential drugs lists and national essential drugs programs. Rather, the group was looking for collaborative possibilities and was concerned on where to draw the limits on the corporate commitment to the poor. They asked, "What can be expected?" and "How can nongovernmental organizations and religious networks help in that definition?"

Essential Drugs:
Economics and Politics
in International Health

MICHAEL R. REICH

BACKGROUND ON WHO'S ACTION PROGRAMME
ON ESSENTIAL DRUGS

In 1975, the WHO's Director-General, Halfdan Mahler, issued a report to the annual meeting of the World Health Assembly that identified national drug policies as a top priority for developing countries. The report called for drug policies that would meet health needs and economic priorities, and stressed the essential drugs approach as an effective means to improve health conditions in poor countries [1]. That document built on a history of concern at the WHO with various aspects of pharmaceuticals, expressed as early as the first World Health Assembly in 1948 [2]. But the report in 1975 marked a clear step toward creating a new campaign on pharmaceuticals, focusing on the concept of essential drugs, with the goal of influencing domestic policy in poor countries.

This concept of essential drugs emerged from a growing realization of the gap between the potential of modern drugs to control basic diseases and the limited capability of health systems in poor countries.

Michael R. Reich is the director of the Takemi Program in International Health of the Harvard School of Public Health, an advanced research and training program on problems of allocating resources for health, especially in poor countries.

This paper was presented to the seminar in December 1985, and later published in *Health Policy* 8 (1987): 39–57. The article is reproduced here with the permission of Elsevier Science Publishers.

At all levels of the health system—from the national to the hospital to the patient—many poor countries lack modern drugs in sufficient quantities [3]. But limited resources alone do not explain the gap between what can be done and what is done. The gap results from multiple problems in the interaction of pharmaceutical companies with the social organization of poor countries. Some companies, both domestic and international, have engaged in irresponsible business practices, including product dumping, misleading advertisements, and aggressive product promotion and gift-giving to physicians and pharmacists [4,5]. Inadequate social infrastructure has exacerbated the problems of procurement, distribution and prescription, due to a lack of government policy, implementation difficulties, poor training of physicians and pharmacists, and ineffective management capacity [6–8]. As a result, available drugs often are not appropriately prescribed or used [4]. The practice of selling prescription drugs over the counter, the problems of assuring patient compliance, and the lack of laboratory facilities to assess drug quality contribute to the complex web of pharmaceutical problems in poor countries.

Many of these problems relate to difficulties of resource allocation in conditions of scarcity. Who should receive existing supplies of drugs? Which drugs should be purchased with a limited budget? How can drugs best be provided to the periphery and to the urban poor? How can a nation reduce its expenditures of limited foreign exchange on imported drugs? How can the training of health personnel be improved? The concept of essential drugs sought to address these questions, as a single solution to multiple problems, and promised to extend access, reduce costs, and improve treatment—all at the same time.

The WHO defined essential drugs in 1975 as 'those considered to be of the utmost importance and hence basic, indispensable, and necessary for the health needs of the population. They should be available at all times, in the proper dosage forms, to all segments of society' [9]. In 1977, to make this concept more specific, the WHO prepared and published a Model List of Essential Drugs, including about 200 drugs and vaccines, by generic name. Most products on the list were known to be therapeutically effective and were no longer protected by patent rights [10]. That step, according to the current WHO Programme Manager of essential drugs, marked the start of 'a peaceful revolution in international public health' [11].

The concept of essential drugs has introduced major changes in the ways of thinking about pharmaceuticals in poor countries. Indeed, the concept represents an innovative and effective strategy by the WHO for mobilizing opinion and resources. How could one oppose 'essential' drugs, especially for the poorest of the poor? The changes, however, have not always been entirely peaceful. The concept has carried with it complex economic, political, and ethical implications, which have not always been directly addressed by the WHO. The crux of the problem, and one ambiguously approached in WHO materials on essential drugs, is the relationship between the public and private sectors to achieve the stated goals. This issue, in turn, touches on fundamental value judgments and material interests of individuals, organizations, and societies.

In the late 1970s, the WHO took additional steps to integrate the concept of essential drugs into broader ideas about health care in poor countries. The WHO's goal of 'Health for All by the Year 2000' included the regular supply of certain essential drugs as a key indicator to evaluate progress. The Declaration of Alma Ata on primary health care in 1978 identified the provision of essential drugs as a basic element [12]. Then, in 1978 and 1979 the WHO took formal steps to establish an Action Programme on Essential Drugs and Vaccines, which began operation in February 1981.

A brief review of WHO's major activities on essential drugs (in Table 1) indicates a continuously expanding scope. The initial emphasis on the selection of appropriate drugs changed in the late 1970s to stress the use of essential drugs, reflected in a title change of the WHO's basic document [13]. Following the establishment of the Action Pro-

TABLE 1

Chronology of Major WHO Actions on Essential Drugs

1975	**28th World Health Assembly:** Director-General's Report reviewed main drug problems in poor countries, presented possible new drug policies, and noted experiences of some countries with approaches using basic or essential drugs to improve access to appropriate drugs.
1975	**28th World Health Assembly:** Resolution WHA28.66 (2) requested WHO Director-General 'to develop means by which the Organization can be of greater direct assistance to Member States in advising on the selection and procurement, at reasonable cost, of essential drugs of established quality corresponding to their national health needs'.
1975–76	**World Health Organization:** Two consultants prepared a working document that: (a) described how lists of drugs are used; (b) defined terms related to basic or essential drugs and drug policy, economics and evaluation; (c) proposed criteria of drug selection; and (d) provided a preliminary list of drugs. The report was then circulated for comment and revised.

TABLE 1 *continued*

1977   **Meeting of First Expert Committee on the Selection of Essential Drugs:**
Publication of WHO Technical Report Series No. 615, 'The Selection of Essential Drugs', 1977. A WHO bestseller, the Report included a model list for adaptation by each country and guidelines on the process for preparing a list of essential drugs. The Report also stressed the need for additional information about drugs to prescribers and patients.

1978   **WHO/UNICEF:**
Declaration of Alma Ata, which included the provision of essential drugs and vaccines as one of the basic components of primary health care.

1978   **WHO Executive Board:**
Resolution EB61.R17 proposed the establishment of an 'action programme of technical cooperation on essential drugs', and noted the need for cooperation with the pharmaceutical industry.

1978   **31st World Health Assembly:**
Resolution WHA31.32 urged Member States to establish drug lists and adequate pharmaceutical supply systems, enact legislation, and collaborate with WHO and aid agencies to achieve these objectives. The Resolution authorized the WHO to study strategies for reducing the prices of pharmaceuticals, 'including the development of a code of marketing practices'. WHO's Director-General was asked to study ways of supporting Member States and of collaborating with the pharmaceutical industry to improve the health status of poor populations.

1979   **Meeting of Second Expert Committee on the Selection of Essential Drugs:**
The Committee reviewed and updated the model list in the first report, making 13 deletions, 42 additions, and 66 amendments (mostly explanatory notes). The Committee also suggested that seminars be held in developing countries on the selection and use of essential drugs, and emphasized the importance of exchanging information on essential drugs with the pharmaceutical industry.

1979   **World Health Assembly:**
Resolution WHA32.41 called for the establishment of an Action Programme on Essential Drugs, with initial funding from WHO, if necessary.

1981   **WHO:**
Establishment of the Action Programme on Essential Drugs and Vaccines in February 1981.

1981   **International Federation of Pharmaceutical Manufacturers Associations (IFPMA):**
Proposed a Code of Pharmaceutical Marketing Practices in Spring 1981, in an effort to promote self-regulation by the industry rather than WHO action.

1981   **Health Action International (HAI):**
Formation of HAI as a network of consumer and public interest organizations, 'to promote the safe, rational and economic use of pharmaceuticals worldwide,' to promote full implementation of WHO's Essential Drugs Programme, and to seek 'non-drug solutions' to health and nutrition problems.

1981   **WHO/UNICEF:**
Collaborative agreement on essential drugs, to promote methods for low-cost procurement.

1982   **WHO Executive Board Meeting, January:**
International Federation of Pharmaceutical Manufacturers Associations (IFPMA) stated that its member firms are ready to supply essential drugs at favorable prices for underserved populations in developing countries, and to assist the WHO in other ways.

TABLE 1 *continued*

1982 **Meeting of Third Expert Committee:**
The model list was revised again, with fewer additions and deletions, and a greater emphasis on clearer explanatory notes. The published report in 1983 stressed usage more than selection, reflected in the title, 'The Use of Essential Drugs'.

1982 **Action Programme:**
Initiated a cooperative programme with the International Federation of Pharmaceutical Manufacturers Associations (IFPMA) for training in quality control for persons from developing countries, with tuition and living expenses provided by IFPMA.

1982 **35th World Health Assembly:**
Endorsed the principles of the WHO Action Programme on Essential Drugs and adopted a plan of action for the Programme which included the major components of a national drugs policy.

1982–83 **Action Programme:**
Organized three demonstration workshops in collaboration with the Government of Kenya to illustrate the use of ration kits to improve the distribution of essential drugs to dispensaries and health centers. Participants included government officials from 30 countries and representatives of other UN organizations and bilateral donors.

1983 **36th World Health Assembly:**
IFPMA requested WHO Member States to submit cases of possible infringements of IFPMA Code of Pharmaceutical Marketing Practices (1981) for review, and offered to report to the Health Assembly on progress in applying the Code.

1984 **International Conference at Harvard School of Public Health:**
Cosponsored by WHO Action Programme with UNICEF, International Federation of Pharmaceutical Manufacturers Associations, US Agency for International Development, and Swedish International Development Agency, to develop teaching materials and case studies for use in training on essential drugs in schools of public health.

1984 **37th World Health Assembly:**
Resolution WHA37.33 called on the Director-General to develop activities to ensure the rational use of drugs, through improved knowledge and flow of information, and to examine the role of marketing practices in these processes.

1985 **WHO:**
Third revision of 'The Use of Essential Drugs', Technical Report Series No. 722, including a summary of information services provided by the WHO Pharmaceuticals Unit.

1985 **Action Programme:**
The Programme began publication of *Essential Drugs Monitor,* a newsletter with worldwide circulation, on Programme activities, publications, teaching and research, and field experiences.

1985 **WHO and Action Programme:**
Conference of Experts on the Rational Use of Drugs, 25–29 November, Nairobi, Kenya. The conference addressed a broad range of issues, including national drug policies, drug information, education and training, drug marketing, prescription patterns, distribution systems, national essential drugs programs, and WHO certification scheme.

Sources: M. Helling-Borda, 'The Essential Drugs Concept and Its Implementation', in *Health in Developing Countries,* International Colloquium organized by the Royal Academy of Medicine of Belgium, 28–29 October 1983, pp. 169–186; and other documents from the WHO Action Programme on Essential Drugs.

gramme, the scope expanded again to encompass nearly all aspects of national drug policies (as presented in the plan of action approved in 1982 by the World Health Assembly), including selection of drugs, supply of drugs, assurance of quality, manpower training, legislation and regulatory control, and financial resources. The Action Programme has also grown significantly, with a doubling in professional staff in Geneva between 1982 and 1986 and a 1.8 times increase in budgetary funds between 1982–83 and 1986–87 (Table 2). Table 1 presents the Programme's concerted efforts to spread the word about essential drugs and to include more aspects of drug policy within the Programme. In addition, the Action Programme has developed an active consulting service on drug policy for national governments. According to the Programme's own count, since 1981, 'more than 80 countries have adopted the essential drugs concept and many are operating active programs' [14].

Within the United Nations, a rough division of labor has evolved on topics related to the pharmaceutical industry. The UN Industrial Development Organization (UNIDO) has promoted local production and formulation of pharmaceuticals in developing countries [15]. The UN Council on Trade and Development (UNCTAD) has studied issues related to trade of pharmaceuticals and its implications for domestic

TABLE 2

Budget for Action Programme on Essential Drugs (US $)

	1982–83	1984–85	1986–87
Country			3,150,100
Regions (and inter-country 1985–86)	3,228,900	6,176,400	2,619,800
Global and inter-regional activities	1,056,000	1,142,000	1,843,300
Total	4,284,900	7,318,400	7,613,200
Extrabudgetary funds		approx. 3,000,000	

Staff for Action Programme on Essential Drugs

	1982	1983	1984	1985
Headquarters				
Professional	4	4	7	8
General service	3	4		
Regions				
Professional, including assigned experts	6	6	7	10

Source: WHO, Action Programme on Essential Drugs and Vaccines, November 1985.

production [16]. The UN Centre on Transnationals has examined the global pharmaceutical industry and its role in national development [17]. The Special Programme for Research and Training on Tropical Diseases supports the development of new drugs and vaccines for tropical diseases [18]. UNICEF has become actively involved in procurement efforts through international competitive tenders and in packaging essential drugs, at the UNICEF Packing and Assembly Centre (UNIPAC) in Copenhagen [19]. But the WHO can probably claim the greatest success on the conceptual level, through its promotion of the idea of essential drugs—with important potential consequences for pharmaceutical policy and management.

SOCIAL AND POLITICAL CONTEXT FOR ESSENTIAL DRUGS

The concept of essential drugs emerged from the WHO, but also reflected larger social and political processes worldwide related to poor countries, multinational enterprises, and consumer organizations. WHO staff can be credited in large part for the surge in acceptance and in controversy over the idea of essential drugs. The global environment in the late 1970s and early 1980s, however, also created favorable conditions for the concept.

Drugs are a key component of any health system. Drugs serve multiple social, psychological, and political functions; they are not simply used to treat disease. One study identified 27 'latent functions' of pharmaceutical preparations, shown in Table 3, and readers can no doubt think of others. These multiple material and symbolic functions make drugs a potentially powerful and volatile issue in public debate. These traits contributed to the intensity of the controversy over essential drugs.

The notion of a limited formulary of drugs existed long before the WHO officially adopted the concept of essential drugs. Hospital formularies have been widely used in the United States [20]. Recent studies show that hospital formularies can be effective and acceptable to hospital staff and can improve the quality of prescribing while reducing drug costs [21]. Cuba, in the 1960s, adopted a national formulary that reduced the number of registered medicinal products from about 20,000 to just over 600 [22]. In addition, UNICEF and PAHO used limited lists of drugs in supplying countries and assistance programs prior to the 1970s. The WHO's innovation was to use these ideas to promote national policy for essential drugs in poor countries.

The 1970s witnessed increasing recognition by established institutions that appropriate drugs are a necessary element of a health system, especially in poor countries [23]. It is impossible to provide good quality care without appropriate drugs. For some diseases, drugs are also a highly cost-effective technology in terms of benefits, in the prevention of diseases through vaccines, and in treatment and further illness avoided, for example, through antibiotics [24]. Shortages of drugs adversely affect the credibility of a health care system and the morale of health workers. On the other hand, a supply of appropriate drugs is not sufficient for assuring the effective operation of a health system. Attention must also be directed to the processes of distribution, prescription, pricing, and use of pharmaceuticals [7].

A second element that contributed to the acceptance of the concept of essential drugs was the growth of an international consumers movement in the 1970s. Established consumer groups in the United

TABLE 3

Latent Functions of Pharmaceutical Preparations

1.	Visible sign of the physician's power to heal (drug)
2.	Symbol of the power of modern technology (drug)
3.	Sign that the patient is 'really' ill (drug)
4.	Legitimizes the long-term illness without cure
5.	Concrete expression that physician has fulfilled his contract
6.	Reasonable excuse for human contact with physician
7.	Satisfactorily terminates the visit
8.	Fits the concept of modern man that he can control his own destiny
9.	Expression of physician's control
10.	Indication of physician's concern
11.	Medium of communication between physician and patient
12.	Forestalls lengthy discussions
13.	Source of satisfaction to the physician
14.	Identifies the clinical situation as legitimately medical
15.	Legitimizes sick role status
16.	Symbol of patient control
17.	Means of patient goal attainment
18.	Excuse for failure
19.	Symbol of patient stability
20.	Evidence of physician as an activist
21.	Evidence of pharmacist activity
22.	Research source of utilization and treatment
23.	Political tool
24.	Medium of exchange
25.	Sampling medium
26.	Method of clinical trial
27.	Method of differentiating legal drug status

Source: Mickey C. Smith, *Principles of Pharmaceutical Marketing*, Lea and Febiger, Philadelphia, 1983, p. 112.

States, Britain, Germany, and Japan turned to the environmental and health problems of poor countries. And developing countries began to establish their own consumer and public interest organizations. The selection of a Malaysian president for the International Organization of Consumers' Unions — the first Third World president — reflected those two processes.

Consumer groups in the late 1970s viewed pharmaceuticals as a major target in efforts to create an international consumer watchdog network, to serve as a countervailing force to multinational corporations [25]. Among the most active organizations were the International Organization of Consumers' Unions, Social Audit of the U.K., Oxfam, and BUKO, a West German coalition of development action groups. These groups and others collaborated in the formation of Health Action International (HAI) in 1981, an organization of some 50 consumer and other public interest groups, in both rich and poor countries. As its goals, HAI seeks 'to further the safe, rational and economic use of pharmaceuticals worldwide, to promote the full implementation of the World Health Organization's Action Programme on Essential Drugs, and to look for non-drug solutions to the problems created by impure water and poor sanitation and nutrition'. In working toward these goals, HAI has actively lobbied the annual World Health Assembly since 1982 and engaged in other campaign actions [25].

Another factor that affected the debate over essential drugs was the controversy over infant formula in the 1970s. That controversy focused public attention on multinational firms and health problems in poor countries, and compelled the WHO to address the role of the private sector and the issue of regulation. Various public health experts and consumer groups identified a decline in breast feeding in poor countries and attributed that trend to marketing practices of infant formula producers. High infant mortality rates were said to be linked to the use of infant formula, often in unsanitary conditions or improper ways (such as the use of contaminated water to prepare the formula), and to the overpromotion of this product. In 1978, the WHO passed a recommendation that member governments take measures to promote breast feeding and to regulate 'inappropriate sales promotion of infant foods that can be used to replace breast milk'. In 1981, the WHO, under heavy lobbying from consumer organizations, passed as a recommendation an 'International Code of Marketing Breast-Milk Substitutes' [26].

The controversy over infant formula held different lessons for the various participants. The Reagan Administration — the only government to vote against the infant formula Code — regarded the Code's passage as an undesirable event, an overpoliticization of the World Health Assembly, and a pattern to be avoided again. The Reagan Administration argued that the WHO should not be involved in such regulatory recommendations. Consumer groups, on the other hand, regarded the Code as a success, representing a new-found legitimacy at the international level, raising real problems of marketing practices to public scrutiny, and changing corporate and WHO consciousness about these issues. Individual corporations responded to the infant formula controversy with different strategies. Nestles, the main target of the consumer campaign, underwent a dramatic transformation in its approach from outright rejection to conciliatory bargaining, ultimately agreeing to abide by the WHO Code in all countries that passed a version of the Code [27]. The pharmaceutical industry viewed the events around infant formula, and especially the code, with nothing less than 'panic', sensing that drugs were next on the agenda [28]. The formation of the WHO Action Programme, and Health Action International, shortly after the 1981 World Health Assembly, seemed to confirm industry fears.

The concern with essential drugs also reflected increasing awareness in poor countries about the need to manage the process of economic growth with appropriate government intervention, to avoid possible negative consequences. The spread of environmental regulations during the 1970s illustrates this trend [29]. Environmental protection was no longer seen as a luxury of rich countries, but a necessary element to assure quality along with growth in poor countries. The broader acceptance of national regulation helped to promote reforms of pharmaceutical policy, in efforts to control the safety and efficacy of drugs available in the market.

The economic crisis of the 1980s provided a final element to promote the concept of essential drugs. In poor countries, government expenditure on drugs represents a significant portion of the health budget, often ranging between 20% and 40%, and in some cases reaching 60% (although data are scarce and of variable quality) [30]. Moreover, teaching hospitals tend to promote the prescription of relatively high-cost brand-name drugs, while rural dispensaries lack essential drugs such as penicillin, chloroquine, and iron tablets, indicating serious problems of equity and the lack of training in cost-effective prescribing [31]. In addition, as Brian Abel-Smith noted, 'In many developing countries even relatively poor spend more on the health services they buy than the government spends on providing them with services' [32]. One study of drug expenditures in poor countries without production facilities calculated the per capita average in 1975 at $1.32 (both government and personal costs). The author wrote that the rate of growth of such expenditures has been 'extremely high. In most less developed countries, medicines expenditure has been a rising proportion of total health expenditure. . . . Most striking of all, in most less developed countries expenditure on medicines has been rising very much faster than the rate of growth of the economy' [33].

These trends have encouraged health ministries to search for ways to reduce their drug costs. The debt crisis in the 1980s, which is squeezing the foreign exchange reserves and earning capacity of many poor countries, puts additional pressure on governments around the world to reduce import expenditures, including energy, food and drugs. Even rich countries, including Britain and Japan, have imposed cost control measures on drug expenditures, reflecting budgetary constraints, the high costs of drugs, and the relative administrative ease of cutting drug costs [34, 35]. Poor countries have felt even greater pressure to decrease total drug costs—particularly when the International Monetary Fund has required adjustment measures, such as currency devaluations and import reductions, to guarantee additional loans—making the cost-effective promises of an essential drugs policy especially attractive.

ACCOMPLISHMENTS AND REMAINING ISSUES

The major accomplishment of the WHO's Action Programme has been to transform the concept of essential drugs into a major issue on the international health agenda of multiple organizations around the globe, to transform the nature of discourse on pharmaceutical policy and poor countries. Topics related to essential drugs have been debated at international conferences and at national workshops by policy makers in national governments, international agencies, private corporations, industry federations, consumer groups, donor organizations, and educational institutions. The scope of the issue has expanded from a concept to a list to a policy, now seeming to include all aspects of a national pharmaceutical system. This expansion represents a successful form of conceptual marketing by the WHO, getting other organizations to accept the WHO's evolving definition of essential drugs as legitimate. The WHO in effect outmarketed the industry.

But the WHO's actions on essential drugs have rarely occurred without controversy. The measures have been criticized by the pharmaceutical industry, by conservative critics [28], and by the Reagan Administration, all seeking to protect the private market from the restrictions of national formularies, constrain the WHO program to the public health system in poor countries, and keep the WHO from becoming an international regulatory agency. Criticisms have also emerged from consumer groups such as Health Action International, which seeks to push the WHO to accept HAI's principles of real medical need, significant therapeutic value, acceptably safe, and satisfactory value for money, as applicable to private as well as public health systems and to rich as well as poor countries. Moreover, while industry staunchly has opposed a WHO marketing code [36], HAI and others steadfastly demanded one (at least until 1984).

The WHO, in response, has sought to maintain some intentional ambiguity in its recommendations on essential drugs, perhaps to solicit the continued support from industry groups as well as consumer groups and to meet the diverse ideological demands of different governments within the WHO. The intentional ambiguity involves the definition of essential drugs, and related policies, especially whether they are designed to promote essential drugs or to exclude certain 'nonessential' drugs and whether they apply only to the public health system or also to the private sector. These ambiguities allow for vastly different ethical, political, and economic interpretations concerning the role of national governments in regulating and controlling private firms and individual decisions. The ambiguities may be necessary, however, to contain the level of controversy and provide a measure of consensus within the WHO and within the World Health Assembly, the annual gathering of country representatives (usually the minister of health) who vote on WHO reports and resolutions.

This point reflects a common problem in international agencies: developing a global recommendation for policies that require national implementation. The more directly a recommendation relates to diverse national values and potentially controversial issues, the more ambiguity may be necessary to gain acceptance by different parties. While the ambiguity may be functional for the international organization, it does not help national policy makers who must make difficult choices.

The WHO's first major controversy in this area focused on the list of essential drugs published in 1977 [10]. The Organization's leaders may have been unprepared for the complexity of problems and intensity of controversy raised by the list. The list took the WHO into areas in which the organization had limited expertise, including international trade, economic development strategy, and industrial policy. The primary source of opposition was the pharmaceutical industry, especially the research-oriented multinational firms. Medical associations also expressed concern that the list would restrict the physician's choice of drugs and thereby compromise good care.

In April 1978, the Council of the International Federation of Pharmaceutical Manufacturers Associations (IFPMA) adopted an official statement on the WHO's report on essential drugs, noting 'serious reservations' about the policies recommended and deep concern about 'the manner in which these policies are being represented and promoted'. The IFPMA reported that 'the pharmaceutical industry is entirely sympathetic to the desirability of improving health care and the access to drugs in developing countries'. But the Federation concluded that 'adoption of the misguided measures recommended by the WHO Report could severely retard medical care and would discourage investment by the pharmaceutical industry in research'. In 1979, the U.S. Pharmaceutical Manufacturers Association issued a point-by-point rebuttal to the reports from various UN agencies, including the WHO [37]. An evolving dialogue between the industry and the WHO, however, has helped reduce the sharpness of rhetoric on both sides, although some tensions have persisted. Indeed, the IFPMA changed its position and now supports the concept of essential drugs for the public health sector of poor countries [38].

The WHO's initial publication on 'The Selection of Essential Drugs' seemed to suggest that national policy makers simply needed to produce a list in order to achieve the objectives of availability, low cost, proper dosage, and total coverage [10]. Some countries adopted lists, but exerted little effort on distribution or logistics, and achieved no significant progress toward the stated goals. In countries where attention focused first on excluding unlisted products from import or private sale, without measures to improve distribution, the availability of drugs may even have worsened. In that sense, the industry's comments about the importance of distributional problems were on target. The first revision of the list in 1979 made only minor changes. But the establishment of the Action Programme in 1981 marked a recognition that a list alone would have little positive impact, that countries needed to deal with the broader issues of management and policy— a point reflected in the new title for the 1983 list, 'The Use of Essential Drugs' [13], as noted earlier.

In recent years, the Action Programme has developed increasing expertise in assisting countries with national policy and management issues. Most of the Program's staff and budget are now devoted to technical support to countries. Compared to its initial assistance measures, the Programme now uses 'a more flexible pragmatic approach to problems taken if possible in order of priority' [39].

One innovative measure is the use of drug ration kits in Kenya, in which medicines for 3000 patients are packed centrally and then distributed directly to local health units. This approach was designed with the assistance of consultants from the WHO and the Danish International Development Agency, primarily to improve the distribution of a limited number of essential drugs to rural health facilities. But the measure also sought to improve the quality of drugs supplied, reduce losses in transit, and provide training for health personnel [40]. Kenya's use of sealed ration kits (provided according to attendance rates at health facilities) has reduced losses from breakage, pilferage and wastage and increased the supply reaching health centers and dispensaries in the periphery [41]. Problems remain, however, in the lack of flexibility for drugs in the ration kits (especially in responding to different incidences of diseases in different areas) and in the difficulties of paying recurrent costs in a health system with free drugs [42]. The ration kits nonetheless seem to provide a more cost-effective distribution, allowing Kenya to achieve 'more bang for the buck' it spends on drugs.

The WHO's efforts to improve the efficiency of the public health management system for drugs, through such measures as Kenya's ration kits, now meet with little criticism from the private pharmaceutical industry. Indeed, a number of pharmaceutical companies are working with national governments to help improve the management of the public health drug system, including logistics, information, and distribution [43]. But conflict between the industry and the WHO is likely to persist on three points that involve both public and private sectors in policies for essential drugs: the extent of regulation, the role of the market, and local production. These points are briefly discussed below.

The Extent of Regulation

Governmental regulation of the pharmaceutical sector covers a broad range of issues. The multinational firms seem to oppose regulation in principle, despite the fact that some kinds of regulation can benefit the research-based multinational firms. Regulation can thus affect different segments of the industry in different ways, benefitting one while costing another. Quality control for safety and efficacy, for example, can remove low-cost producers of poor quality drugs from a market as well as the producers of spurious drugs, and thereby benefit the competitive position of high-quality drugs. The application of quality control to traditional medicines could also benefit international firms. Other examples of governmental regulation that benefit these firms are patent and trademark protection, which represent important elements of research-based firms to protect their products and recoup the costs of research. Of course, the potential benefits of these forms of regulation depend on effective implementation. But these examples suggest that a position opposing regulation in principle and supporting the 'free' market does not fully represent the interests of some multinational firms.

The WHO, on the other hand, seems to stress only certain forms of regulation. Quality control is an area that the Action Programme recognizes as important for achieving the goals of essential drugs, and as a key component in a national drugs policy, applicable to the private as well as the public sector. But the Programme does not explicitly recognize the different problems in assuring quality from small domestic producers in poor countries (which tend to have inadequate quality standards), compared to the major multinational firms of rich countries (which tend to have highly developed quality control systems). The WHO also seems critical at times of the ideas of patent and trademark protection [1]; those elements are certainly not supported in the documents of the Action Programme.

The issue of regulation provides an arena for direct conflict between governments and the private sector, and represents an expression of national values regarding politics, economics and society. Neither the WHO nor the industry can decide what forms of regulation are most appropriate for a particular country. Those decisions are the prerogative of national sovereignty. But there is some ground for convergent interests between the industry, the WHO, and national governments, which could be pursued through joint programs. One example is the training program in quality control for government employees in poor countries—funded by several pharmaceutical manufacturers [44]. That program reflects an implicit recognition that regulation is not in principle bad but can benefit certain segments of the pharmaceutical industry, as the regulation affects the structure of competition in the market.

The Role of the Market

The role of the market in the pharmaceutical sector represents another key area for conflict between the WHO and the industry as well as an important expression of national identity. The market for drugs usually reflects a nation's larger political and economic strategies for development. This point tends to produce positions just the opposite from regulation. The WHO seems hesitant to recognize the market as a potentially efficient or effective mechanism for allocating resources, while the industry seems to suggest that the market can and should do everything. Yet here again some complexities in the positions exist.

While the WHO is ambiguous about the role of the market in the domestic pharmaceutical sector, the Organization has supported the use of the international market for procurement. The WHO collaborative program with UNICEF promotes the use of international competitive bidding to obtain the best price for good quality generic drugs. This use of the international market, of course, requires a certain level of sophisticated strategy and bargaining ability on the part of national governments, which UNICEF and the WHO seek to upgrade through technical support. The approach represents a form of selective national linkage with the international market, perhaps with broader implications for development strategy. Industry generally encourages this effort to increase the efficiency of national procurement for the public sector through essentially market mechanisms, so long as a private market is allowed to operate as well. Indeed, some tenders have been filled by generic products manufactured by research-based multinationals or their subsidiaries. And some firms have actively pursued this emerging market for essential drugs, reflecting different corporate strategies to meet the changing global market [45].

The role of the market in the domestic economy, however, is more controversial. The WHO is ambiguous about whether its list or its concept should apply to the market while the industry is adamant that it should not. Efforts to apply a list to the market and thereby exclude drugs from commerce and import, rather than to apply a list to the public health sector and thereby promote the use of certain drugs, have apparently met with mixed success in achieving the objectives. The Bangladesh Drug (Control) Ordinance of 1982, for example, has generated substantial controversy by banning about 1700 drugs from production or sale and by taking measures to promote local manufacture and restrict sales by foreign firms [46]. A PMA-supported study of the Bangladesh policy reported vast problems of implementation, scarcity and smuggling [47]. On the other hand, a government perspective presented significant progress in reducing imports and prices while increasing national self-reliance [48].

On a more limited scope, the WHO seems reluctant to consider uses of the market that could promote the distribution of essential drugs to peripheral geographic areas. For example, social marketing techniques (the use of marketing to influence the acceptability of social ideas) might be effective in promoting a small number of essential drugs through the private distribution system [49]. Or using economic incentives, a government might provide subsidies to certain private pharmacies, to assure that essential drugs are available in the periphery. The drug policy of Norway (one that the Action Programme likes to cite as a successful case of a restricted national formulary in a rich country) uses such subsidies to assure availability of drugs at restricted cost in remote areas [50, 51]. This approach might be an area of convergence of interests for the WHO, the industry and national governments.

Local Production

The issue of local production provides a third area for conflict between the WHO and the industry in pharmaceutical policy. The question of 'make or buy?' represents a fundamental decision in any business organization, to meet the objectives of procurement: 'to obtain the right materials, at the right time, in proper quantities, and at as little cost as possible' [52]. This statement is remarkably similar to the objectives of the WHO's essential drugs concept, reflecting broad similarities between private and public decisions over whether to make or buy. Yet conflict has commonly arisen among the WHO, the industry, and national governments on make-or-buy questions for pharmaceuticals, indicating different interests and perspectives on the issues involved.

Statements in the 1970s on the new international economic order called for local production of all goods possible in the Third World. UNIDO and UNCTAD, for example, argued that poor countries should develop a local pharmaceutical industry to reduce drug costs, cut foreign exchange expenditures, and provide employment opportunities at home, as part of a broader strategy of import substitution and economic development [53]. But the objectives of local production can conflict with the objectives of essential drugs, especially if local production costs more than imported goods (due to economies of scale, high capital start-up costs, inadequate trained staff, poor quality controls, etc.). In this way, domestic economic policy can conflict with domestic health policy. Moreover, if a government seeks to promote local production through subsidies and restrict imports through taxes and duties, conflicts can arise between domestic and foreign producers.

Potentials for cooperation in this area also exist. A government might aim to promote different levels of production—from packaging and formulation, to production of simple products, to complex manufacturing—depending on local resources and manpower available. Foreign corporations might cooperate in local production, depending on market access for other products, the size of the market (with potential economies of scale), as well as other factors that affect profitability. The industry recognizes the 'enormous potential for market increase' in the Third World, a majority of the world population which consumes about 15% of the global drug market [54]. The industry is also aware, therefore, of the need to promote economic development, as a means of long-term market development.

On the make-or-buy question, the WHO now takes a reasonably conservative and explicit position. As one recent document put it: 'It is generally accepted today that the establishment of formulation plants to produce essential drugs at competitive prices requires careful study of technical and economic feasibility' [55]. Broad recognition exists today that the pharmaceutical industry needs economies of scale to reduce costs per unit produced, and that international competitive bidding is generally cheaper than local production (which often requires importing raw materials). A review of how the WHO reached its current position, with an analysis of successful and problematic case studies, could be quite useful.

NAIROBI AND BEYOND

In late November 1985, the WHO convened a Conference of Experts on the Rational Use of Drugs, known as CONRAD, in Nairobi, to bring together specialists from widely different perspectives, including industry, consumer groups, academics and national policy makers. In the words of the WHO's Director-General, the meeting sought to stress the 'importance of cooperation rather than confrontation' [56].

Overall, however, CONRAD was marked by disagreements, postures, and consensus.

Conflicts of opinion among the participants occurred on various topics, reflecting the divergent views and interest represented at the meeting. The topics of disagreement included the role of a medical needs clause, the idea of a WHO marketing code, and the relation of an essential drugs list to the market. As anticipated, disagreement arose mainly between the industry group and the consumer group, each of which maintained a support organization outside the closed conference. The points of disagreement are not covered here, since they have been briefly described in earlier sections of this paper.

The WHO organized the conference so that most interventions took the form of statements to the chair rather than discussion among experts, resulting in a good deal of posturing among the limited number of participants. This format, not unusual for such international meetings, may not have been the most productive approach for substantive discussion of the issues. But the statements did produce a record of the diverging viewpoints on numerous topics related to the rational use of drugs, as reported by the WHO [57].

Remarkably, the meeting also produced consensus on a number of topics. Dr. Mahler's summary remarks offered something positive for each of the major groups at the meeting, as he covered issues of drug information, national drug regulatory programs, ethical advertising for drugs, the need to assure access to drugs for all individuals, rational prescribing, better training, and a proposal to study ways to contain costs and recover costs. He stressed that the WHO was not an implementing or enforcing agency, not a supranational regulatory agency, but would serve a coordinating and catalytic role. Dr. Mahler reviewed the responsibilities of six groups involved in making drug use more rational, and stated that no contradiction should exist between working for social equity and for an expanding market.

The WHO Action Programme on Essential Drugs has now operated for over five years since its establishment in February 1981, and it is a critical time to evaluate its accomplishments, limitations, and future directions. While it is still too early to assess the consequences of essential drugs policies for health status, the WHO has accomplished major changes at the level of ideas, expressed in policy and management of drugs. This paper raised issues important to the WHO and the pharmaceutical industry, and suggested trends in the actions of both parties. As illustrated by the Nairobi meeting, the potential for increasing cooperation exists, while the likelihood of continued conflict persists. An unavoidable tension may reside in the fundamental objectives of the two sides: the WHO's mandate to improve health conditions, especially in poor countries, and to stress equity and health; and the industry's mandate to use health resources as a means to achieve organizational growth and profit. The concept of essential drugs provides an area for overlap between these objectives, especially when the concept is used to stress principles of managerial efficiency in the public sector, which can directly and indirectly benefit the private sector.

Ultimately, pharmaceutical policy is predominantly domestic policy, and therefore the prerogative and responsibility of the government to decide and implement. As described in this paper, however, national policy takes shape in an international environment of unequal distribution of economic and political power, and in a national context of competing demands for scarce resources. The industry, the WHO, and governments must deal with the complex relationships between the public and private sectors in pharmaceutical policy, if they are to work effectively toward the objectives of the essential drugs concept.

The experiences with essential drugs illustrate two broader themes. First, a new pattern has emerged for setting the agenda of international health issues, with open participation in international organizations by industry associations and by consumer groups. The pattern is still evolving, but it represents a significant change and poses a complex challenge to the leadership of international agencies. The more open participation also raises questions about whose interests are being represented and whose interests should be represented at agencies such as the WHO.

Second, changes in the international agenda-setting process may influence national policy but will still leave difficult problems of implementation at the country level. The evaluation of the new agenda's impact on policy, services, and health conditions poses complex and controversial problems. Who decides whether the new policies are helping? According to which criteria? How can an evaluation obtain legitimacy from the various parties involved, so that the objectives of improving the health of poor people in poor countries can in fact be achieved?

ACKNOWLEDGMENTS

An earlier draft of this paper was presented at the Conference on Third World Health Problems and the Role of Pharmaceuticals, at the University of Notre Dame Program on Multinational Corporations and Third World Development, 11–13 December 1985. In preparing the final draft, the author appreciates the thoughtful comments of C. Peter Timmer, Klaus M. Leisinger, Thomas McLaughlin, Ann Gardner, and an anonymous reviewer, as well as those of participants in a research seminar of the Takemi Program in International Health at the Harvard School of Public Health.

EPILOGUE

Global activities on essential drugs have demonstrated both continuities and discontinuities with the described themes since the original essay was published in 1987. This note identifies important trends along these two dimensions to bring the reader briefly up to date on several issues.

Continuities exist in the accomplishments and the problems related to essential drugs. The concept of essential drugs has received increasing acceptance at the national level throughout the world, with innovative policies introduced in various countries. Increasing acceptance has occurred within international agencies, as reflected by programs in the World Bank, the EEC, and the UNICEF/WHO Bamako Initiative, and within bilateral aid agencies, including SIDA (Sweden), DANIDA, and others. WHO's Action Programme on Essential Drugs has continued to expand its activities, mainly through extrabudgetary funds (over $22 million in 1990–91). The Programme published a report on the world drug situation in 1988, and continues to publish its biannual newsletter, *Essential Drug Monitor,* with articles of recent policies, research, and other activities. These accomplishments were substantiated by an evaluation completed in 1989 by a team from the Royal Tropical Institute of Amsterdam and the London School of Hygiene and Tropical Medicine. The evaluation supported many of the points in the chapter and concluded that the Programme had contributed to a greater availability of essential drugs in many poor countries.

Continuities in problems have occurred for the three points of conflict that I discussed (the extent of regulation, the role of the market, and local production). These problems have remained difficult for the Programme to address and resolve. At the national level, essential drugs programs have confronted many complex problems of implementation, yielding mixed results (although in many countries NGOs have succeeded in implementing essential drugs policies at the local level). Finally, the health impacts of the essential drugs strategy have remained elusive and difficult to measure.

Discontinuities also have emerged in the political economy of essential drugs policies since 1987. Within WHO, various organizational changes followed the election of Hiroshi Nakajima as Director-General in 1988 and his replacement of Halfdan Mahler. The Programme on Essential Drugs was removed from the Director-General's office, where it had received high priority and relative freedom from bureaucratic constraints, and was placed within a new Division of Drug Management and Policies, reflecting a lower priority within the organization. The dynamic leader of the Programme, Ernst Lauridsen, subsequently resigned. The Programme reduced its emphasis on advocacy and implementation of policy and adopted a more traditional WHO role of coordination and technical advice. In 1990, WHO and the International Federation of Pharmaceutical Manufacturers' Associations adopted a Memorandum of Intent on cooperative projects to improve health care in the Third World, suggesting that WHO became more influenced by industry's positions and less by consumers' positions, a change from the situation in the 1980s. The more active role of UNICEF in pharmaceutical policy for poor countries also represented an important change from its previous role mainly in providing drugs through UNIPAC.

Even in the midst of these discontinuities, many national governments and international agencies have placed the issue of essential drugs higher on the agenda. Without a doubt, WHO's Action Programme on Essential Drugs contributed to increased attention to pharmaceutical policy in poor countries around the globe. Given the complexity of the problems involved, it should come as no surprise that all was not solved and that many people in poor countries still lack access to essential drugs. Much remains to be done, for WHO and for other organizations concerned with this matter.

REFERENCES

1. Mahler, H., Report to the 28th World Health Assembly, Official Records of the WHO, 1975, No. 226, Annex 13, pp. 96–110. For an article based on this report, see: National drugs policies, WHO Chronicle, 29 (1975) 337–349.
2. Resolutions of the World Health Assembly from 1948 to 1975 related to various aspects of drug policy appear in: The Role of WHO in the Transfer and Dissemi-

nation of Information on Drug Quality, Safety and Efficacy, Prepared for the Conference of Experts on the Rational Use of Drugs, Nairobi, Kenya, 25–29 November 1985. (WHO/CONRAD/WP/1.2).

3. Antezana, F.S., Essential drugs—whose responsibility? Journal of the Royal Society of Medicine, 74 (1981) 175–177.

4. Greenhalgh, T., Drug marketing in the Third World: beneath the cosmetic reforms, The Lancet, i (1986) 1318–1320.

5. Silverman, M., Lee, P.R. and Lydecker, M., Prescription for Death: The Drugging of the Third World, University of California Press, Berkeley, 1982.

6. Jayasena, K., Drugs—registration and marketing practices in the Third World, Development Dialogue, 2 (1985) 38–47.

7. Fraser, H.S., Rational use of essential drugs, World Health Forum, 6 (1985) 63–66.

8. Lall, S., Problems of distribution, availability and utilization of agents in developing countries: An Asian perspective. In Institute of Medicine, Pharmaceuticals for Developing Countries, National Academy of Sciences, Washington, DC, 1979, pp. 236–249.

9. Resolution WHA 28.66, Official Records of the WHO, 1975, No. 226, pp. 35–36.

10. WHO Technical Report Series No. 615, The Selection of Essential Drugs, 1977.

11. Lauridsen, E., But some are more essential than others! World Health, (July 1984) 3–5.

12. World Health Organization (WHO), Declaration of Alma Ata: Report on the International Conference on Primary Health Care, Alma Ata, U.S.S.R., 1978, WHO, Geneva, 1978.

13. WHO Technical Report Series No. 641, The Selection of Essential Drugs, 1979; and WHO Technical Report Series No. 685, The Use of Essential Drugs, 1983.

14. Essential Drugs Monitor, 1 (1985) 2.

15. United Nations Industrial Development Organization (UNIDO), Global Study of the Pharmaceutical Industry, UNIDO, Vienna, 1980.

16. United Nations Commission on Trade and Development (UNCTAD), Guidelines on Technology Issues in the Pharmaceutical Sector in the Developing Countries, UNCTAD, New York, 1982.

17. United Nations Centre on Transnational Corporations (UNCTC), Transnational Corporations in the Pharmaceutical Industry of Developing Countries, UNCTC, New York, 1983.

18. Vane, J. and Gutteridge, W., TDR and the drug industry, World Health, (May 1985) 21–23.

19. United Nations Children's Fund (UNICEF), The Supply of Essential Drugs and Vaccines Utilizing UNICEF Reimbursable Procurement Facilities, Memorandum from Arne Jensen, Director, Supply Division, UNICEF, 10 May 1984.

20. Collier, J. and Foster, J., Management of a restricted drugs policy in hospital: the first five years' experience, Lancet, i (1985) 331–333.

21. Rucker, T.D., Superior hospital formularies: a critical analysis, Hospital Formulary, 17 (September 1982) 9.

22. Capo, L.R., International drug procurement and market intelligence: Cuba, World Development, 11 (1981) 217–222.

23. Institute of Medicine, Pharmaceutical Innovation and the Needs of Developing Countries, National Academy of Sciences, Washington, DC, June 1979.

24. Feldstein, P.J., Health Care Economics, 2nd edn., Wiley, New York, 1983, pp. 444–446.
25. Fazal, A., The right pharmaceuticals at the right prices: consumer perspectives, World Development, 11 (1983) 265–269.
26. WHO, International Code of Marketing Breast-Milk Substitutes, WHO, Geneva, 1981.
27. Sethi, S.P. and others, New sociopolitical forces: the globalization of conflict, Journal of Business Strategy, 6 (Spring 1986) 24–31.
28. Starrels, J.M., The World Health Organization, Resisting Third World Ideological Pressures, The Heritage Foundation, Washington, DC, 1985.
29. Leonard, H.J. and Morell, D., Emergence of environmental concern in developing countries: a political perspective, Stanford Journal of International Law, 17 (1981) 281–313.
30. Lohse, A.W. and Vaughan, J.P., Editorial: a review of essential drugs and primary health care. What are the important next steps? Journal of Tropical Medicine and Hygiene, 86 (1983) 131–137.
31. Speight, A.N.P., Cost-effectiveness and drug therapy, Tropical Doctor, 5 (1975) 89–92.
32. Abel-Smith, B., Value for Money in Health Services, Heinemann, London, 1976.
33. Piachaud, D., Medicines and the Third World, Social Science and Medicine, 14C (1980) 183–189.
34. Deitch, R., Commentary from Westminster: more pressure on the profits of the pharmaceutical industry, The Lancet, i (1984) 521.
35. MacKnight, S., U.S.–Japan competition in pharmaceuticals, Japan Economic Institute Report, No. 45A (22 November 1985) 1–8.
36. International Federation of Pharmaceutical Manufacturers Associations (IFPMA), Medicines and the Developing World, IFPMA, Geneva, May 1984.
37. Pharmaceutical Manufacturers Association (PMA), The Pharmaceutical Industry: International Issues and Answers, PMA, Washington, DC, April 1979.
38. Peretz, S.M., An industry view of restricted drug formularies, Journal of Social and Administrative Pharmacy, 1 (1983) 130–133.
39. WHO, The Role of the WHO Action Programme on Essential Drugs and Vaccines, Prepared for the Conference of Experts on the Rational Use of Drugs, 25–29 November 1985, Nairobi, Kenya (WHO/CONRAD/WP/2.5).
40. Moore, G.D., Essential drugs for Kenya's rural population, World Health Forum, 3 (1982) 196–199.
41. New Drugs Supplies Management System for Rural Health Facilities in Kenya, Prepared for the Conference of Experts on the Rational Use of Drugs, 25–29 November 1985, Nairobi, Kenya (WHO/CONRAD/WP/2.4.3).
42. Ministry of Health, Kenya, DANIDA, SIDA, and WHO, Evaluation: Management of Drug Supplies to Rural Health Facilities in Kenya, November 1984.
43. Prominent examples include the US industry's efforts in the Gambia, the Swiss industry's work in Burundi, the German industry in Malawi, the French in Senegal, and Warner-Lambert's Tropicare program in several African countries.
44. Peretz, S.M., Pharmaceuticals in the Third World: the problem from the suppliers' point of view, World Development, 11 (1983) 259–264.
45. Ciba-Geigy and the Third World: Policy, Facts and Examples, Ciba-Geigy, Basel, n.d.

46. Bangladesh: Government's drug policy assailed again, The Lancet, i (1984) 97.

47. Jayasuriya, D.C., The Public Health and Economic Dimensions of the New Drug Policy of Bangladesh, Pharmaceutical Manufacturers Association, Washington, DC, September 1985.

48. Ghulam Mostafa, A.B.M., Bangladesh: the nettle grasped, World Health, (July 1984) 6–9.

49. Manoff, R.K., Social Marketing: New Imperative for Public Health, Praeger, 1985.

50. WHO, Drug Control and Distribution in Norway, A Case Study, Prepared for the Conference of Experts on the Rational Use of Drugs, 25–29 November 1985, Nairobi, Kenya (WHO/CONRAD/WP/2.4.5).

51. Bakke, O.M., Drug selection in a regulated society: the Norwegian experience, Hospital Formulary, 19 (1984) 411–421.

52. Culliton, J.W., Make or Buy, A Consideration of the Problems Fundamental to a Decision Whether to Manufacture or Buy Materials, Accessory Equipment, Fabricating Parts, and Supplies, Business Research Studies No. 27, Harvard Graduate School of Business Administration, December 1942.

53. UNCTAD, Technology Policy in the Pharmaceutical Sector in Developing Countries, UNCTAD, Geneva, 1976.

54. Griffin, R.J., Pharmaceuticals in Third World markets, special opportunities, special problems, American Pharmacy, NS22 (1982) 130–133.

55. WHO, The Role of the WHO Action Programme on Essential Drugs and Vaccines, Prepared for the Conference of Experts on the Rational Use of Drugs, Nairobi, Kenya, 25–29 November 1985 (WHO/CONRAD/WP/2.5).

56. Rational use of drugs, cooperation prevails at WHO Conference, WHO Chronicle, 40 (1986) 3–5.

57. WHO, Conference of Experts on the Rational Use of Drugs, Report by the Director-General, Summary of the Debate, Thirty-Ninth World Health Assembly, Provisional agenda item 25, 19 March 1986 (A39/12).

The World Health Organization Action Programme on Essential Drugs

FERNANDO S. ANTEZANA

Only twenty years ago the concept of essential drugs was an isolated issue, although strong in a small number of countries. In WHO, it was in the process of development. Since then, the establishment of national drug policies linking health needs with drug consumption together with a series of important events, both within and outside the health sector, have influenced the rapid development of the concept.

In the last twenty years, we have observed remarkable progress in basic sciences, pharmacology, biotechnology, drug regulations, health care delivery (including primary health care strategies), health financing, the pharmaceutical industry, and various other health-related societal issues. At the same time, a clear awareness of the role of pharmaceutical products and vaccines in health care has evolved considerably, not only among policy makers and health planners, but also particularly among patients, consumer groups, and the community at large.

The financial resources needed to satisfy the demand for pharmaceutical products, including vaccines, in developing countries have escalated over the past twenty years: often consuming more than 25 percent of the annual health budget. This situation is often aggravated due to shortages of foreign exchange. In spite of the allocation of additional expenditure on drugs, most rural populations and other under-

Fernando S. Antezana is the programme manager of the Action Programme on Essential Drugs of the World Health Organization (WHO) where he also served as the senior scientist of its Drug Policies and Management Unit. Prior to his association with the WHO, Antezana worked with the Peruvian Ministry of Health and was senior health advisor to the Andean Pact countries.

served groups have no regular access to the most essential drugs and vaccines.

Could we have identified these changes twenty years ago? Could we have anticipated the present scenario at that time? Would the policies have been different? Could we have forecast and assessed the consequences of the economic crisis that developing countries are facing today? The rapid and dynamic development in the field of pharmaceuticals, the many influencing forces, and the world economic situation make prediction of future activities particularly difficult. Nevertheless, the importance of a wider, more forward-looking view cannot be denied, particularly in the pharmaceutical sector, due to constant scientific and technological innovations and their scientific and social relevance.

The expansion of primary health care in the developing world, the increasing tendency towards decentralization, the deficit in financial resources, and the social demands for equity will require new thinking, reforms, planning, and efficient execution for programs in the health sector, particularly related to essential drugs. In addition, continuous progress in biotechnology (including recombinant DNA technology), drug delivery systems, bioelectromagnetic variations, computer-assisted drug design, increased generic product usage, prospective epidemiology, ecological issues, and others will also affect the present situation with regard to the availability and use of essential drugs. It is also important to note the relation between risk-placer and risk-taker in therapy and, finally, the relationship between body, mind and spirit.

However, in the 1980s progress was recorded in many countries. A policy on essential drugs, improved procurement under generic names, and improvements in storage and distribution as well as in training of health staff have enabled a number of countries to significantly improve both accessibility and rational use of a carefully selected number of drugs which meet people's common health needs. The selected drugs and vaccines are called "essential drugs," indicating that they are of the utmost importance and are basic, indispensable, and necessary for the health needs of the population. The WHO model list of essential drugs should be regarded as a contribution to solving the problems of those Member States whose health needs far exceed their resources and who may find it difficult to initiate such an endeavor on their own. The WHO Expert Committee updated the model list in 1979, 1982, 1985, 1987, and again in 1989.

There has been an outstanding level of scientific and technological advance in the past fifty years, and in particular over the past three decades, in developing potent drugs for a wide variety of health problems. In addition to the achievements of individual scientists in research institutions, major credit for these advances must go to the pharmaceutical industry, especially to multinational corporations. However, industry has not paid the same attention to ensuring the availability of the products of its research and know-how to the underprivileged of the world. Although in the past it may have claimed that this was not part of its responsibilities, there are signs that the industry is becoming increasingly aware of the tragedy whereby the populations of developing countries—who make up the vast majority of the world's population—are often unable to enjoy the fruits of pharmacological and pharmaceutical research. Following such widespread acclaim of the goal and strategy for attaining health for all by the year 2000, no individual or group conscience can remain untouched by this situation.

ACCESS TO DRUGS IN DEVELOPING COUNTRIES

In the context of WHO's Revised Drug Strategy a group of experts met in 1987 to draft "Guidelines for Developing National Drug Policies." The guidelines were reviewed by the Executive Board's Ad Hoc Committee on Drug Policies and published in 1988; they are addressed to policymakers and administrators for adaptation in the light of local circumstances.

The formulation of national drug policies linked to health needs is particularly important for developing countries. The main objective of a national drug policy should be accessibility for all people to the most effective and safe medicinal products of established quality at the lowest possible cost. Clearly formulated national drug policies should aim to improve the efficiency of the pharmaceutical supply system through better cooperation and coordination of the different components and sectors involved.

National drug policies and practices (including quality control, distribution systems, and proper utilization of drugs) have, by themselves, been deficient in assuring the availability of even a limited number of safe and efficacious drugs for curative, preventive, and diagnostic purposes to large segments of the world population. In spite of the general recognition that medicinal products should be viewed as essential tools for health care and the improvement of the quality of life, it is not uncommon to find that drug policies are also directed towards industrial and trade development. These policies are sometimes contradictory and can be implemented in different sectors of the administration. Problems of cooperation and coordination vary accordingly, not only between the pharmaceutical supply system and the health care system, but also among the different components of the pharmaceutical supply system itself.

In addition to complex technical considerations, political, social, and commercial factors influence drug policies and their implementation. Thus, the health sector has a low priority in many countries where health expenditures represent a small fraction of the gross domestic product. In spite of attempts by WHO Member States to encourage governments to devote more resources to the health sector, growing economic problems and competing domestic demands often result in governments being unable to do so. In such situations, the ability to satisfy drug requirements is correspondingly inadequate.

Although progress in formulating and implementing national drug policies has been impressive, it must be recognized that a vast number of people — perhaps as many as two billion — still lack regular access to the most-needed essential drugs, either because these are not available or because their cost is beyond the reach of most of the rural and urban poor. From a global perspective, access to essential drugs remains critical for reasons which include lack of resources, poor infrastructures, and shortage of trained technical and managerial staff at the national level.

The economic crises of the 1970s and 1980s had a dramatic effect on the health sector in developing countries. The reduction in health budgets, together with the limited availability of convertible currency, led to drug shortages for most developing countries. In general, owing to the disproportionate allocation of resources for urban hospitals, the shortages were most acute for primary services in rural areas. The supply of drugs to the primary services therefore became a major priority for the countries concerned. Success in the years to come will depend on the capacity of health systems in a period of economic crisis to create efficient, flexible sources of finance to ensure the sustainability of essential drugs programs and to nationalize those projects supported by foreign aid.

Drug programs have too often been implemented in a vertical fashion, establishing parallel supply, training, and supervision systems that are inadequately integrated into the existing health services. While considerable attention has been placed on developing and strengthening national pharmaceutical supply systems, even the best managed and most efficient supply system cannot deliver its products in a vacuum. Supply systems must be a completely integrated part of the health care system.

In countries where national programs do not exist, separate programs may be implemented in various parts of the country, often by different donors. Coordination between agencies, donors, and lending agencies is often difficult, so that services are fragmented and there is an unnecessary duplication of efforts. In the absence of coordinated programs, systems to deliver essential drugs to the end users will be very difficult to sustain on a national level. This effort needs all the combined experience and expertise in both the pharmaceutical and health care systems to find workable solutions to the problems of how to measure health care coverage and to expand accessibility to essential drugs.

Government decisions on whether to rationalize drug supply are often conditioned by factors outside the control of the ministry of health. WHO has demonstrated that rationalization based upon the essential drugs concept can make substantial foreign currency savings for the country and contribute to the objective of supplying the most necessary drugs to the majority of the population.

Experiences in some developing countries demonstrate that WHO can be wholly effective only when governments have the political will to develop and implement national policies. At the same time governments attempting to rationalize their drug systems face enormous political and economic pressure from various national and international interests. WHO — as the United Nations specialized agency for health — can provide crucial leadership as well as moral, political, technical, and, to some extent, financial support to countries in mobilizing political will to overcome these political and economic pressures.

Evidence from some countries suggests that since the early 1980s general availability of essential drugs at the primary care level has been increased through the rationalization of drug supply. Where availability of essential drugs has increased, there appears to have been a corresponding increase in the credibility of health services and the morale of health workers. This, in turn, has facilitated preventive and promotional health activities.

External funding has sometimes been conditional on the purchase of "drug kits" from European donor agencies or from UNICEF's Supply Division. The kit system was developed during the early 1980s for use in vertical operations as an emergency answer to acute shortage and should not become a long-term strategy.

Unfortunately, there are many indications that problems still exist in the prescribing of drugs at all levels of the health system. As suggested at the 1985 Conference of Experts on the Rational Use of Drugs, WHO prepared a report on the world drug situation. This provides a systematic description of the drug situation in both the public and private sectors.

Many drug utilization studies or analyses of national morbidity and drug consumption patterns reveal discrepancies between disease incidence and the availability of drugs that actually cure illness or provide reasonable, long-term symptomatic relief. Many physicians and other prescribers, rather than ensuring a correct diagnosis, often prescribe several drugs where one might have been enough. The many combination products on the market contribute to irrational prescribing practices. In turn, the existence of effective drugs for many diseases has raised expectations, and medication is frequently demanded for self-limiting diseases, or other conditions for which there is no effective drug treatment.

Efforts are being made in many countries to stem grossly excessive use of drugs. Paradoxically, the ever-increasing demand for drugs is frequently associated with poor compliance in their use: often because patients are dissatisfied with the drug, do not understand how to take it, or are unable to pay for the full dose. In urban areas of many developing countries, unrestricted over-the-counter sales of prescription drugs remain the rule rather than the exception. This is in sharp contrast to the situation in slums and rural areas where residents lack access to even a few necessary drugs.

THE WHO DRUG ACTION PROGRAMME

At the country, regional and global levels, the WHO Drug Action Programme (DAP) addresses the need for a change in resource allocation to ensure the regular supply of essential drugs to underserved populations; it is a comprehensive reponse by WHO to an economic and technological imbalance that has hitherto denied large segments of the world's population access to the most essential drugs and vaccines. Vigorous advocacy and promotion of the essential drugs concept—

as a technically sound and realistic approach both to rationalizing drug supply systems and to making drugs accessible to the whole population—have been, and will continue to be, a very important component of the Programme.

The approach most commonly used by DAP in assisting Member States improve their country conditions begins with a situation analysis that is performed jointly by nationals and WHO staff or consultants. Following this, a national seminar is held for all interested parties, in which priorities are selected and constraints identified. Subsequently a country action plan is prepared with the help of WHO, including cost estimates, time schedules, and assignment of specific responsibilities. The action plan constitutes the project document that is submitted for funding.

WHO support to country programs is now provided through the regional offices. Most essential drugs programs are being implemented with external financial support. WHO's involvement in the funding of programs may take one of the following forms: (1) direct support to country programs; (2) responsibility for the management and execution of the country programs for which donors' funds are channelled through WHO; or (3) program planning and financing the preliminary activities while finding donors for specific country programs (situation analyses and development of project proposals). This latter form—using "seed money"—is normally effective in generating additional funds from other sources.

When funding for a national program is assured, implementation of the plan starts. The government usually creates an essential drugs management unit with a program coordinator and support staff. Staff from WHO regional offices and headquarters identify consultants for specific technical areas, give technical and administrative support, monitor progress, report to donors, and initiate evaluation of the program. Because trained personnel are scarce in many countries (particularly in smaller ones) the essential drugs program is often accommodated within the country's pharmaceutical and regulatory control services. In others, the essential drugs management unit is a separate operational unit which coordinates procurement, storage, and distribution of the drugs in the public sector and undertakes training of health personnel in their management and use.

Many countries receive technical support to streamline procedures for procurement, storage, and distribution of essential drugs. In a few cases, technical support is provided to a Member State under a special tripartite agreement between the Member State, a development agency, and WHO. Some external aid agencies request that management or steering committees be created to include all parties concerned in the implementation of the essential drugs program at country level.

The availability of essential drugs in many developing countries is hampered by the lack of foreign exchange, the absence of a rational system of procurement directed to appropriate selection and quantification of needed drugs, and the difficulty in obtaining information on suppliers and on the prices and quality of finished goods and raw materials. However, a large number of countries have achieved some progress by taking advantage of the international market of generic drugs at low cost. Quality assurance is an important consideration for generic products as well as brand products, and demand for generic products has increased because of their wider use in some industrialized countries.

Few countries have centralized procurement systems. In those that do, international tendering by generic name is usually limited to the public sector. Countries with a national essential drugs list may apply it to both the private and public sector, in which case the process of procurement can be centralized, but in most countries procurement systems for the public and the private sector are distinct.

Too often purchasers pay far more than necessary for their drugs. Many developing countries issue regular tenders for their quarterly or annual drug purchases through national tender boards, but it is not unusual for higher prices to be paid than those prevailing in international competitive markets. Few developing countries have access to continuous market intelligence. UNICEF's indicative price list on essential drugs helps address this problem: it provides information to bargain for better prices. Another opportunity to ensure lower prices is to coordinate procurement by the ministries of health, social security, the hospital sector, the military, and other departments. Unfortunately, many developing countries have no such coordination. Tendering mechanisms have other drawbacks: the purpose is defeated if the best suppliers do not bid, and procedures can take several months to complete.

Pool procurement by groups of countries has not been easy to implement because of difficulties in establishing the necessary international legal and commercial agreements, and creating compatible administrative and financial mechanisms. However, a new collaborative effort in this regard is the WHO / African Preferential Trade Area (PTA) joint project in essential drugs. The Action Programme on Essential Drugs has engaged in different modes of collaboration with UNICEF, but from the beginning the focus has been on procurement of drugs and vaccines. Thus one of the main aims of joint action was to establish a group bulk-purchasing scheme to lower costs to governments.

Distribution in most countries tends to follow standard patterns for central, provincial, and district stores (if they exist), and finally for health units. It is often affected by factors such as seasonal destruction of roads, inadequate transport, fuel shortages, and the inaccessibility of large areas for supply. The Bamako Initiative in the African region can also be an important instrument for improving more equitable distribution of essential drugs at district level as well as financial mechanisms.

One of the aims of essential drugs schemes is to encourage self-reliance in local production, but this raises many economic, infrastructural, and technical problems. Political problems can arise as well, when local production conflicts with the interests of the multinational companies.

Pharmaceutical technology transfer has met with mixed results. While some developing countries have become almost completely dependent on external assistance for their drug needs, some of the larger developing countries have the capacity to produce the necessary raw materials for the production of some pharmaceuticals and to meet most of their own requirements for essential drugs. Some countries see production as part of overall industrial development and have established a profitable pharmaceutical industry. Regretably, some of these countries have done so without paying much regard to the actual health needs of their populations. Multinational drug companies have subsidiaries in many developing countries, but this does not necessarily secure self-reliance or cost reduction, since the parent company often owns the technology and the expertise.

Drug formulation plants in numerous small and medium-sized developing countries do not always operate at efficient levels of production. Experiments in producing drugs on a regional or subregional scale have shown it not to be a viable alternative to importation or domestic production. In such situations, governments often subsidize the operations of their national operations and/or import drugs at lower cost, therefore further complicating the economics of local production.

Countries that import most of their pharmaceutical products are largely dependent upon the competent authority in the country of origin for assurance of the quality of their purchases. The WHO Certification Scheme on the Quality of Pharmaceutical Products Moving in International Commerce provides the administrative basis for attestation. Efficient control of the quality of pharmaceutical products is based upon: statutory licensing of all drug products as a condition of marketing; regular inspection of indigenous manufacturing facilities to ensure that they operate in compliance with specified "good manufacturing practices"; testing of products within the distribution chain in a quality control laboratory to exclude substandard and degraded products; and enforcement of standards through penal sanctions. Several countries now use regional or subregional quality control laboratories for their drug testing.

Much still needs to be done to assist small regulatory authorities to undertake their complex tasks in a way that is efficient, comprehensive, and feasible within the limitations of their budgetary allocations. The tasks have been made more demanding in recent years by the sharp increase in the number of companies worldwide engaged in pharmaceutical manufacture and the many intermediaries involved in the formulation — or simply the supply — of finished products.

Training in all aspects of drug supply management and rational use is one of the most important components of a national program on essential drugs. The development of training materials for various groups and the training of these groups in national or regional seminars and workshops are important components of the strategy. Also, fellowships and individualized sessions should be used to facilitate the training of nationals. In rational use, the training of health workers is often unsystematic. Crash training programs have generally not been followed up by refresher courses and supervision. New approaches are being developed to improve the situation, including the development of standard drug treatment schedules.

The Programme is always searching for new methods for improving the effectiveness of country interventions. Current operational research includes: socioeconomic studies on the level of household expenditure on drugs and its variation in rural, urban, and peri-urban settings; the effects of the price of drugs on their utilization as well as on the use of health services; whether the drugs paid for are in fact essential; and socio-cultural research. The projects aim to collect information on people's perception and use of drugs, to evaluate the impact of educational intervention on the use of drugs, and to develop methodologies for assessing the main cultural and contextual factors influencing drug use.

Financing of drug supplies remains a crucial issue, and reliance on donors continues to be great in many countries. But the situation in the past in which many countries were reluctant to impose a charge for drugs appears to be gradually changing under the pressure of economic constraints. WHO has been assisting countries to find ways of generating additional resources for the purchase of drugs, as well as in identifying alternative mechanisms for financing essential drugs programs.

A conference on cost recovery held in early 1988, at which representatives of countries compared experiences with different types of cost recovery and drug financing schemes, concluded that the major problems jeopardizing cost-recovery schemes were, once again, lack of convertible currency, inequities for users, and insufficient staff with the managerial skills required to make financing mechanisms work effectively. Moreover, participants concluded that it was crucial that such schemes should avoid making financing be dependent upon charges on the sick and disadvantaged. Rather, the community as a whole should bear the burden of financing. Further studies in the field of financing drug supply have been undertaken by DAP and alternative financing mechanisms are being tested.

THE POTENTIAL FOR MULTINATIONAL PHARMACEUTICALS

It is against this background that I present my perception of the possible roles for the multinational pharmaceutical industry's cooperation in the essential drugs effort. In my view there are two main modalities for possible cooperation: (1) institutional cooperation at the global level (between WHO or other international health organizations and the International Federation of Pharmaceutical Manufacturers Associations as the international representative of the pharmaceutical industry) or regional level (between WHO Regional Offices and the regional associations of pharmaceutical manufacturers); and (2) direct cooperation between companies and/or associations with WHO Member States or national projects. A third possibility could be where the WHO Secretariat acts as honest broker to facilitate cooperation between Member States and the pharmaceutical industry.

I consider it important to recall here today's prevalent economic, social, and technical circumstances such as the developing world's external debt, the major events in Europe and the European profile in

1992, the revolution in communications, the Gulf Crisis and the rocketing of oil prices. Such developments in a rapidly changing world cannot be neglected when cooperation in health is discussed. We can no longer consider pharmaceuticals and vaccines in isolation. In the same way, we cannot consider cooperation with developing countries as a charitable issue or mere good will. In the health sector we are heading towards a future of broad participation of the entire world community in a contribution to global equity, well-being, and peace. It is here where I see the real challenge for the multinational pharmaceutical industry.

As you know, there are several programs in WHO with which the industry has been collaborating such as the Special Programme for Research and Training in Tropical Diseases; the Special Programme of Research, Development, and Research Training in Human Reproduction; the Divison of Mental Health; the Pharmaceuticals Unit; and the Action Programme on Essential Drugs. This cooperation can be seen as a step towards the common objective of assisting Member States in increasing the accessibility of essential drugs of quality to all those in need at a price they can afford. This, obviously, is the ultimate goal for cooperation, but it has many components for collaboration. To help reach this goal, the pharmaceutical industry can contribute effectively due to its unique position—in which capital, technology, research, scientific knowledge, and managerial know-how are closely interwoven.

Some of the areas in which I see potential for cooperation are the following:

1. *Development of infrastructures.* This includes not only the infrastructures for drug procurement, distribution, delivery, and quality control, but also—as an important issue to promote more rational use of drugs—the development of capacities for clinical management of drugs and vaccines.

2. *Transfer of technology.* This includes transfer of both software (know-how, planning, and management expertise) and hardware (machinery and supplies for pharmaceutical management and production). In this regard, joint venture arrangements should be considered.

3. *Research and development.* This concerns the search for new medicines or new therapeutic uses of already known substances and for new drug delivery systems (both sustained and controlled release systems). Such research and development is important for the future of disease control and management, particularly for tropical diseases.

4. *Training.* Relating to all components of programs on essential

drugs, the multinational pharmaceutical industry is uniquely qualified to produce material and expertise for this purpose.

In collaborative activities in health, flexibility and imagination must be emphasized, provided that knowledge, understanding, and goodwill are already in place. I am certain that multiple opportunities will arise for international cooperation in health, particularly for the multinational pharmaceutical corporations, in a real spirit of partnership in those areas where there is mutual interest and understanding. Considering that change is constant, the question is: should one influence their direction or merely await their occurrence, i.e., adopt a prospective versus a reactive stance. Finally, I would like to suggest that cooperation in the field of health between developing countries and the pharmaceutical industry should not be seen as a defensive mechanism but as a positive building of respect, understanding, and partnership.

Health Services Delivery: UNICEF's Bamako Initiative

AGOSTINO PAGANINI AND STEPHEN JARRETT

The delivery of basic health services suffered considerably during the 1980s due to the severe economic crisis experienced by many countries in Africa. The sight of run-down health centers and hospitals, with demotivated health personnel, has become common. Health budgets have shrunk, with greater proportions of what is left being spent on staff salaries, leaving practically nothing for the vital operational costs of such essentials as drugs and medical supplies, training, and supervision. This has been exacerbated in many instances by international donors heavily supporting capital investment costs without due concern for the ensuing recurrent cost needs.

In many countries, people have lost confidence in government-run facilities due to the lack of drugs and the often negative attitude of health workers, whose salaries have lost up to 80 percent of their purchasing power and who have become increasingly abandoned by the absence of supervision and opportunities for professional development. Patients prefer to seek alternative forms of care for their ailments, often at a high cost to the household budget, or simply to deny themselves proper care. The public health delivery system itself has entered a period of crisis, deepened by the AIDS epidemic. This has a detrimental impact on primary care for mothers and children.

This paper was presented in the seminar by Agostino Paganini, M.D., the manager of the Bamako Initiative Management unit of UNICEF. Paganini's work on tropical medicine includes service with the Nutrition Support Programme of the WHO, the Ugandan Ministry of Health, and the Italian government in Tanzania and Rome.

Stephen Jarrett, the paper's co-author, is a member of the staff of the Bamako Initiative Management Unit.

Faced with almost insurmountable odds, a call to action was nevertheless made by the ministers of health of sub-Saharan Africa in 1987 to return again to the principles of primary health care in order to revitalize those services most urgently needed by the vulnerable groups, namely children and mothers. The key was seen to be to rationalize community spending on health, to direct local resources into revitalized services, but, at the same time, to make sure that no one was left out because of inability to pay. The generation of local resources, under increasing community control, would ensure the availability of resources for drug supplies and other local operating costs. This call to action became the "Bamako Initiative," given that the ministers were at the time meeting in that city for the World Health Organization Regional Committee Meeting.

The Final Resolution, approved at the end of the Bamako meeting, stated that the aims of the Bamako Initiative were to accelerate primary health care; to give priority to women and children; to define and implement primary health care self-financing mechanisms at district level; to encourage social mobilization for community participation in maternal and child health and primary health care; to enable communities to be principal partners in health care development; and to ensure the regular supply of essential drugs (UNICEF, 1988).

Financing was seen primarily in the context of district systems, appropriate to local circumstances, and would take into account all available resources, including essential drug supplies.

The Initiative has continued to receive political support in Africa through the Organization of African Unity, showing that the will to tackle the deteriorating health situation in Africa is strong. The Initiative's link to structural adjustment has begun to place it as a central action among countries' economic decision makers, given that cost-sharing in the provision of government services is rapidly becoming the norm in sub-Saharan Africa. The initiative, since its inception, has evolved to play a critical role in focusing attention on maternal and child health care, promoting quality service at an affordable price, rather than simply relying on market forces.

The Bamako Initiative Resolution called upon both UNICEF and WHO to support the Initiative, with particular emphasis on mobilizing the necessary technical and financial resources that would be needed.

The Bamako Initiative's Broad Policy Agenda, as set by the ministers of health themselves (WHO, 1988), is:

- National commitment to universal primary health care, with emphasis on priority maternal and child health problems;
- Incorporation of universal primary health care policies within long-term national plans and budgets;
- Government commitment to continued and increasing financial support to these services, maintaining budget integrity;
- Decentralization of Ministry of Health management of primary health care to district and community levels;
- National commitment to ensure equity of access to these services for the poorest sectors of the population, through measures such as fee exemptions, subsidies, additional budgetary provisions, and links to income-generating activities;
- Policy provision for community participation in the management and financing of these services;
- Commitment to the local management of community resources with a proportion of funds generated at the local level remaining in the community;
- Policies promoting essential drugs and the rational use of drugs.

KEY COMPONENTS—FOCUS ON COMMUNITY ACTION

The Bamako Initiative, in reviving and extending basic health services, highlights four key components.

1. The *basic health services* themselves represent the central element of concern, as the premise put forward is that health status improvement and goals attainment can only take place if appropriate and timely health care provision is easily accessible to the majority of the population. The aim is, therefore, to have well-functioning, peripheral health centers and health posts at sub-district and village levels, supported by community health workers to reach those still not within easy reach of a specific health facility. Mothers' and children's health clinics within district and national hospitals and urban health facilities are also important elements of back-up to rural health facilities and as primary providers of care to the urban poor. Building up capacity refers not only to an adequate physical infrastructure for the provision of services, but also to properly trained and motivated staff, as provider attitude is clearly one of the main variables in the determination of the patients' use of the services.

2. Another main variable in the credibility of services to patients is the availability of *essential drugs and supplies*. There are two basic sides to essential drugs: first, the overall logistics of making appropriate drugs available on a timely basis, and second, the assurance of their rational use, which is largely an educational effort of changing both provider and consumer habits. Consideration is also to be given to other supply needs, such as vaccines, medical items, and stationery, which are no less important than essential drugs.

3. The economic crisis of the 1980s has pushed to the fore the issue of the *financing of health services*. Much of the deterioration of health facilities and the decline in their utilization has been due to the inability to mobilize sufficient resources for their upkeep, both in terms of physical infrastructure as well as staffing.

4. Experience indicates that *community involvement* is one of the most challenging aspects of primary health care. Community action in health already exists in many places. The long-term effect of community involvement is to increase the effectiveness of health services and the respect in which health staff and services are held. Community control, through local organization, is seen in the context of the community being a full partner in health care development and expecting to pay part of the costs. Community financing, managed by the communities themselves, can contribute effectively to the local costs of providing health services, covering some recurrent costs, including essential drugs and supplies, operating expenses of local facilities and incentives for health workers.

THE ROLE OF DRUGS

Drugs comprise a strategic element of primary health care and of the overall health system at every level. Their presence in health facilities improves the quality of service provided and helps motivate health workers. In addition, their constant availability in the system inspires confidence in the public who put considerable emphasis, misguided or not, on the curative powers of drugs, particularly injections.

This is seen in the pervasive nature of self-medication. Recent research in Sierra Leone (Fabricant and Kamara, 1990) shows from a survey of four chiefdoms that between one-half and two-thirds of patients choose market drugs or native remedies as a first course of health action. Those nearer to a primary health care unit were more likely to go to the unit first (27.3%) as opposed to those living further away (9.6%). Similar data have been cited for Ethiopia (Kloos, 1987). For malaria treatment in Sierra Leone, drugs obtained from peddlers generally cost less than those in health facilities but this was often due to the purchase of only a partial course of treatment of chloroquine or perhaps some other preparation. The partial purchase may have been due to the limited availability of cash in the household in the context of the purchase price of drugs, with only around 50 percent of households in Sierra Leone having cash available for such use. In a similar survey in Uganda, a much lower percentage of households (8%) had cash available for health care costs (Waddington, 1989). Selling assets is at the heart of financing health care and clearly household contributions to health care need to always be kept to the lowest level possible, in accordance with both cost and necessity (Litrack, 1989). Comparatively speaking, however, the data from Sierra Leone tend to show that a primary health care unit can provide the most cost-effective treatment, taking into account full recovery of the cost of generic drugs.

The lack of any controls in drug availability and use clearly represents a dangerous situation. The way out of this points to having accessible primary health care facilities with a constant supply of a limited range of appropriate cheap drugs administered by trained personnel. Restrictions in the range of drugs available have been seen to influence improved drug use more than health worker training alone (Hogerzeil, 1989). No less important is public education in the use of drugs. Effective health services, combined with education, are at the heart of the Bamako Initiative which sees community management and control as a means to providing local initiatives to manage and use essential drug supplies appropriately.

UNICEF has always endorsed the essential drugs concepts as defined by WHO. Essential drugs are those that satisfy the health care needs of the majority of the population; they should be selected to assure: (1) adequate quality (including stability and bioavailability), (2) efficacy, (3) safety, (4) reasonable prices, and (5) constant availability. UNICEF follows the related policies of the WHO, which remains the specialized U.N. agency which defines technical recommendations, although UNICEF provides input whenever necessary.

For many years UNICEF has provided support and services to developing countries in the area of essential drugs. Historically, UNICEF assistance has been mainly linked to the direct supply of essential drugs and medical equipment. The 1989 value of drugs and vaccines supplied was approximately US $90 million (the UNICEF catalogue contains about 200 items from the WHO model list; these drugs are supplied under generic names). Data from recent years show constant increase (600 percent increase compared to 1984). Procurement Services provided by UNICEF are extended as well to those governments or international organizations who request them (50 percent of total supplies in 1989).

With the Bamako Initiative, considerable UNICEF support has been channeled to training activities in drug management and in prescribing and dispensing practices. Benin, Guinea, and Nigeria, for example, joined together to produce health worker training manuals to improve local management, including the development and use of standard treatment flow charts allowing for improved diagnosis and prescribing by peripheral health workers.

Considerable amounts are already being spent by households on drugs so the rationalization of this expenditure on more cost-effective treatments and with funds staying under community control is one of the fundamental strategies of the Bamako Initiative. The key is to avoid drugs assuming a greater importance than preventive action (Bennett, 1989). Experience in Benin, however, has begun to show that revitalized services with better quality care not only produce an increase in curative care but also in preventive care (ICC, 1990). Interestingly, in a recent evaluation of the Initiative in Benin, mothers who perceived funds generated in the health center to be community property were more willing to pay for services, including drugs, than those who perceived them to be government or health worker controlled (Benin MOH, 1990).

This same evaluation also shows a relatively high degree of public dissatisfaction with essential drugs as opposed to injections, which has given rise to sustained debate on the possible use of placebos (such as vitamins) as an interim measure until a more widespread change in public behavior on drugs is achieved. Action in public education in drug use, less prominent so far than other features of the Bamako Initiative, is clearly a priority area of action, but one that is dependent on having put into place a network of strengthened health services. It will also have to contend with the potential opposition of the many who benefit from drug selling, including the private sector and, in some cases, health workers themselves.

ISSUES IN FINANCING

The complexity of the Initiative cannot be underestimated, especially as it relates to the revitalization of existing government-run health services, as well as to closing the large gaps in access that currently persist and that require a doubling or tripling of capacity in order to provide a minimum of preventive and curative care for the majority of the population. Action in planning, while reviewing the implications of the four key components, will have to take account of a number of issues in financing that have been seen to be generic to the implementation of the Initiative.

How *government commitment* is expressed in implementing the Initiative takes several forms. The policy agenda is clear in those aspects on which specific statements are necessary and these often exist in some form or another. Financial commitment, however, is fundamental in enabling policy to be translated into action. Universal primary health care will require significant budget modifications as well as a long-term perspective in order to reorient budgets in line with strategies for strengthening these programs. Coupled to this is the need to secure *foreign exchange* commitments for eventual drug and supply imports, particularly in those countries with non-convertible currencies. Initial measures are being used in several countries such as Sierra Leone by utilizing local U.N. offices' requirements for local currency to provide equivalent amounts of foreign exchange for international procurement. Realistically, however, continued adverse economic conditions in Africa severely limit the financial capacity of the government, in terms of both local currency and foreign exchange, the implication being that implementation will have to proceed at a carefully measured pace.

Linked to financial commitment is the overall *status of health workers*. One aspect is to have a minimally acceptable level of staffing for the services that are to be provided, taking into account that community involvement will substantially increase the demand put on health workers. Investment in human resources will ultimately determine the success of the Initiative and a significant improvement is required from the present situation in which health workers in many countries often do not even receive their salaries or receive them very late and, therefore depend on other jobs, including private health practice. Low salary levels are an added problem, but are common to the whole civil service structure, so any move to address this issue would have much wider implications. The underlying point is that worker motivation has to be reasonably assured in order for the demands being created to be satisfied. In this regard, Uganda is seriously considering that community resources be used principally to pay health workers salaries with government funds used for supply and drug inputs, training, and logistics.

In planning and implementing the Initiative, a clear measurement of *access and utilization* will be needed. Access to primary health care is presently very low and many countries will have to expand their infrastructure, particularly at the peripheral levels, or introduce outreach activities as a transitional measure. Of importance is the fact that delivery costs in many parts of sub-Saharan Africa are much more expensive than elsewhere due to low population density (Foster, 1987), thus exacerbating the situation. Limiting the Initiative to existing health facilities, often only to the health center at sub-district level, may not substantially increase geographical access to health services. The introduction of payment for treatment (user fees) has been associated with decline in utilization of services when this has been enacted arbitrarily. On the other hand, utilization increases when services are perceived to be of high quality, as witnessed in Benin and Guinea, both for curative and preventive case. *Equity* and the possible exclusion of a considerable proportion of poor inhabitants in urban and rural areas due to inability to pay represents a continuing major concern in implementing the Initiative. The policy agenda makes explicit provision for determining measures to protect those who cannot pay. While it is true that traditional structures exist as safety nets, some evidence, such as from Sierra Leone, tends to suggest that household assets are sold or money is borrowed to pay for health services. In many situations, however, the health workers and community are aware of those families who cannot pay and provide free treatment for them. This issue of equity, nevertheless, cannot be lightly dismissed as part of the community's responsibility; rather managers at all levels should be provided with ongoing information that will immediately detect exclusions due to inability to pay. Likewise, equity throughout the health system should be maintained, particularly with regard to the introduction of user fees in urban areas. Both fees and exemptions (including those for some chronic illnesses) should be reasonably uniform to avoid mass movements of patients to those facilities known to give preferential treatment financially or in terms of quality of service.

No hard and fast rules can be established for *community financing*. Even if the expectation is that communities will eventually contribute the costs of essential drugs and local operating expenditures, full recovery of these may not be immediate and may be reached only after a number of years, depending on the economic status of the community. Additionally, different communities will have different goals and levels of performance in community financing, thus requiring flexible approaches and support at the local level. In this regard, there are no preconceived ideas that any particular type of community financing is more advantageous than any other. User fees, charging for drugs, prepayment, and payment in kind all have advantages and disadvantages that need to be assessed in every locality in the light of local customs and past/prevailing experience.

Another point requiring considerable attention is the *management of community funds.* It has been seen in Benin, Guinea, and Sierra Leone that community funds tend to accumulate in local bank accounts, especially as cost recovery is only achieved on a partial basis initially. There is often considerable reluctance to use funds being generated and this may be due, in part, to unclear guidelines on this particular aspect of operations, as well as the relative lack of experience of communities to take on such management. The risk exists that funds left in bank accounts will devaluate (particularly non-convertible currencies) and possibly even revert to the National Treasury, thus defeating the purpose of the communities' financial involvement. Each country will need a clear policy for the funds' management during the planning stages, as well as a clear plan for preparing communities for these financial resources.

Many of the above issues and concerns have implications for *information management.* For efficient management at the local level, registration cards, charts, monitoring forms, stock reports, and accounting sheets will be some of the information tools used, although with care not to unduly overload health workers with mountains of paperwork. Conscious efforts to streamline paperwork, to produce in the most efficient way the minimum acceptable amount of information within the confines of good bookkeeping and transparency of financial management, will be key in successful management and monitoring.

Finally, there is every indication that the AIDS epidemic continues to spread rapidly through Africa, with adult infection rates in some countries over 20 percent. The impact affects both mothers and children, with increasing numbers of AIDS orphans. This strains both national and community means to cope, overburdening health services with long-term patients and reducing resource availability for local development.

Communities in high HIV-infection areas will be less able to be partners in the management and financing of health services but more in
need of health care support. This creates a different environment for
the reviving and extending of health services, inevitably leading to a
long-term dependency on external support.

WOMEN AND HEALTH

The woman's situation is at the center of Bamako Initiative action, inasmuch as increased access to and quality of maternal and child
health services are its central aims. The fact that 30 percent of rural
households in sub-Saharan Africa are headed by women, that women
produce 60 percent of the household food consumed and generate a
third or more of all household income is significant to community development. Within the many areas of poverty that afflict women, poverty
of health is associated with reduced productivity, hence the need for
services and facilities that support women's management of pregnancy
and child care (Jiggins, 1989).

Of concern in financing is the fact that "ability to pay" is addressed to the family unit whereas in reality it is often the woman-
head of household who is required to pay maternal and child health
costs from her own funds. In community organization, family and social
structures still often deny women decision-making roles in a process
to which they often have to contribute financially.

Action in maternal and child health care is, nevertheless, seen
as a way to break through the barriers confronting women, enabling
a real change in their situation. The maternal and child aspects of
primary health care which commonly represent the major components
of the services' utilization, particularly of out-patient care, include:

- education of families on mother and child health,
- prevention of pre-pregnancy risks,
- essential obstetric care, including ante-natal, labor and post-partum
  care and the identification and referral of high-risk pregnancies and
  complications,
- birthspacing and family planning,
- child care, including perinatal care, especially for low birth-weight
  babies, growth monitoring and promotion, immunization, nutrition, and the management of sick children.

INITIAL POSITIVE RESULTS

The Initiative builds on many long-standing forms of community initiative. Indeed, since it has been launched, more and more such experience has been discovered, with something in virtually every country in Africa. Non-governmental organizations, especially, have a wide-ranging experience in the provision of basic health services based on user financing.

Three years after the Initiative was launched, twelve countries constitute the core group of the Bamako Initiative (Benin, Burundi, Cameroon, Equatorial Guinea, Guinea, Kenya, Mali, Mauritania, Nigeria, Rwanda, Sierra Leone, and Togo), with several more involved in preparatory action. The approach has begun to prove viable and timely in response to health needs in African countries, where access to health care services are estimated at around 50 percent of the population on average. For several years, primary health care projects in different parts of the country, financed by the governments of the Federal Republic of Germany, the Netherlands, and Switzerland, have been recovering a percentage of drug and local operations costs through user fees.

Benin's experience in community financing is probably the most advanced to date, with a pricing system and the necessary mechanisms for the local management of drugs and finances securely in place. The Bamako Initiative was already being implemented in 100 commune health centers and 50 district health centers. Data from 44 health centers, which have benefitted from a process of revitalization, show two and threefold increases in utilization between 1987 and 1989, for preventive and curative care respectively. Similar increases in utilization are seen in Guinea, where work has already begun in 101 health centers. In both countries, communities have achieved the ability to cover local operating costs, in partnership with the government, which contributes staffing and supervision, and donors, which provide supplies and equipment and training costs.

From these initial experiences in Benin and Guinea, user charges per consultation, which includes full treatment with essential drugs, have averaged from between US$1.10 and US$1.37, representing community-level support of around 45 percent of the overall costs of providing local health services. Such a level is well below the expenditures otherwise incurred through a mix of traditional healing plus the purchasing of drugs in private pharmacies. As seen by the rising utilization of services, it has been considered affordable by the majority of the population. Community health committees are taking a lead role in organizing and managing these initial efforts at revitalizing the basic health service.

Guinea is probably the country most advanced in implementing the Bamako Initiative, although the initial phase concentrates on establishing fully functioning health centers at sub-prefecture level. Village-level outreach is planned for the future, but full coverage, including the eventual establishment of village health posts, will only be possible after several years. The incorporation of Conakry, the capital, into the program has posed problems for which solutions are being sought.

In Burundi, a pre-payment system will be continued, with families paying in advance for health cards, although careful monitoring of this will take place to ensure its effectiveness. Health care will remain free for children under five years of age, thus creating an incentive for families to follow appropriate child health practices.

The government of Cameroon is taking advantage of a relatively extensive health infrastructure, health committees at each level including village health committees, and a specialized semi-autonomous national pharmaceutical company. Some experience in cost recovery exists, with support from German, American, and Belgian bi-lateral assistance and from NGOs. A national commission has been formed with UNICEF and WHO support, and initial implementation will begin in twenty-two health centers located in four regions of the country.

A gradual expansion of the primary health care network is planned in Equatorial Guinea as of 1991 under the guidance of a national technical committee, in which both WHO and UNICEF participate actively. Intensive staff training has taken place at central and district levels in anticipation of start-up action and supply systems are being strengthened, consolidating EPI (Expanded Program on Immunization) action in this area.

The Bamako Initiative in Kenya centers on community action to increase effective access to basic primary health care, initially in twelve districts over the next four years. Alliance between the village health committees and community health workers will be strengthened through the opening of community pharmacies, with these workers trained to handle a small number of drugs for the most pressing health problems in the community. The pharmacies will provide sustained supplies of essential drugs at affordable prices, as well as allowing for small incentives to be paid to the community health workers. Linkage to the formal health system will be cemented by the continued strengthening of the rural health infrastructure, which will provide comprehensive maternal and child health care, complement simple action carried out by the community health workers, and closely supervise health work in the community.

Since the signing of the Bamako Initiative Resolution in 1987, Mali has taken great interest in moving ahead with preparatory action. A number of studies on topics such as drug supply and health financing mechanisms have been conducted, and these have contributed to policy development for the Bamako Initiative.

The World Bank has recently entered into loan negotiations for consolidating pharmaceutical management and strengthening primary health care in four regions. This will follow the lines of the Bamako Initiative and will be mutually supportive of action envisaged by UNICEF, in collaboration with WHO. There are issues still to be overcome, such as health worker remuneration and mechanisms for supporting primary health care in very low-income areas.

Strong political commitment to implement the Bamako Initiative exists in Mauritania and a national coordinating team has been established, with active participation from many sectors of government, UNICEF, and WHO. Initial planning has designated a demonstration area for implementation, initially covering two regions in the country (Oued Naga and Kankossa). A process of national extension during the period 1991–1994 will follow. This will be linked to the World Bank and the African Development Bank who are collaborating to develop a plan for comprehensive support to the health sector, with emphasis on an adequate drug supply and on strengthening the National Public Health Training Centre, management structures within the Ministry of Health, and the infrastructure in four regions. A range of charts for prevention, hygiene, pregnancy supervision, treatment, and management have been designed, including models for illiterate workers, and these are being used in the villages by the community health workers, after thirty days of training, and by the village health management committee, which assists the community health workers and manages essential drug stocks.

The Nigerian government saw the Bamako Initiative's relevance to their own effort of rebuilding their primary health care system and initiated action in four pilot local government areas. In addition, it initiated negotiations with the World Bank for a major loan to strengthen the purchasing, logistics, quality control and regulatory aspects of essential drugs management and specific assistance in drugs to four states.

The key financial objective of the Initiative in Nigeria is to ensure financing of essential drug supplies at the local level, and to provide a basis for strengthening primary health care management. A major constraint concerning any cost-recovery system based on essential drugs in Nigeria is the long-term availability of foreign exchange required to purchase these drugs at internationally competitive prices. The issue of equity and protection of the poorest has been discussed at the village level. At higher levels of the health system, Nigeria already has a policy for the exemption of indigents from payment at public hospitals and clinics for specified conditions such as leprosy, tuberculosis, and sexually transmitted diseases. Most communities consulted have felt that the exemption of the poorest could be left to them to decide, as villages have traditions for aiding the indigent.

Considerable preparatory work on the Bamako Initiative in Rwanda has already been undertaken. Various existing prepayment schemes for health financing have been examined for possible adaptation on a wider scale. A major review of the pharmaceutical sector is underway to establish a complete system for the selection, procurement, distribution, and use of essential drugs. A National Commission for the implementation of the Initiative, including UNICEF and WHO participation, is guiding the work. Eventual collaboration with other donors, such as French, German, and Belgian bi-lateral assistance, is planned in order to broaden the scope of Initiative in Rwanda.

The government's efforts in Sierra Leone are firmly reoriented towards the principles of the Bamako Initiative, leading to an updated National Primary Health Care Action Plan. Nationwide primary health care coverage is being phased in, district by district. By the end of 1990, seven of the country's twelve districts and the Western Area (containing Freetown) will have begun implementing the program according to the Bamako Initiative strategy, with cost-sharing as the financial basis for action. Full country coverage is planned for 1995.

After strengthening existing primary health units in the country through the provision of basic equipment and an initial supply of essential drugs, other maternal and child health components will be introduced gradually, beginning with growth monitoring and promotion and maternal care, followed by control of diarrheal diseases, improved nutrition, and child spacing. The three primary health care components (EPI, essential drugs, and water and environmental sanitation) that are already national in scale as well as the strong logistics system established by the EPI and essential drugs program, provide a solid base for the introduction of other interventions. Eventually, 700 primary health units will be fully functional, providing access to basic health services for 90 percent of the population.

Togo approached the Bamako Initiative with an in-depth assessment of the primary health care situation, with an emphasis on the district level. The country has a relatively accessible health infrastructure, with coverage around 60 percent, and a well-established organization for health development through the district health committees. Only around 35 percent of women, however, receive regular maternal care and 45 percent attend clinics for childbirth. The Initiative, therefore, aims to strengthen peripheral health services through greater community involvement in management and financing, leading to greater sustainability. Training has taken place both at national and district levels in preparation for implementation in an initial twenty-nine subdistricts. Eventually, 380 peripheral health units will be strengthened to provide essential maternal and child health care, in line with local epidemiological patterns. Essential drug lists have already been established accordingly, with seven preparations to be managed at village level, and twenty-seven at the subdistrict level.

REACHING HEALTH GOALS
THROUGH STRENGTHENED SERVICES DELIVERY

The continued political support of all African countries for the Bamako Initiative is of great significance and underscores the need to concentrate efforts and mobilize additional resources. In looking at the Health for All goals for the 1990's, their attainment will be largely dependent on the degree to which accessible, affordable, and appropriate health care is made available to the population. Not only does the existing health infrastructure need to be fully functioning, but it must be expanded to cover the 50 percent of the population in sub-Saharan Africa currently without access to health services. This is at the center of the Bamako Initiative challenge, moving forward from the positive results already being achieved in the core group of countries.

The Freetown conference on Community Financing in Primary Health Care, sponsored by UNICEF, Health Action International, and OXFAM and held in September 1989, strongly recommended increased

attention to operations research (HAI 1989). This was mainly addressed with key topics concerning the Initiative:

1. Role of VHW'/TBA's,
2. (Cost) Effectiveness of service delivery strategies,
3. Appropriateness of different methods for drug supply,
4. Financing and managerial feasibility of drug management systems,
5. Rational use of drugs,
6. Effectiveness of health education in rationalizing drug use,
7. Feasibility of drug management at community level,
8. Influence of Bamako Initiative on maternal and child health coverage and service utilization,
9. Appropriate methods to link the community and the program,
10. Affordability and equity of access to services,
11. Pricing levels and systems maximizing community involvement
    while not deterring people from service use,
12. Most effective financing mechanisms.

Several countries, such as Benin, Mauritania, and Sierra Leone,
have begun action in operations research. A more comprehensive and
sustained approach to operations research, however, will be one of the
priorities for the next several years, analyzing both successes and failures in order to establish sustained action into the next century.

Financing and other issues will continue to provide constraints
to action. Most critical among these will relate to human resources development, particularly the recruitment and motivation of field-level
health workers. New models for paying salaries and ensuring in-service
training and supervision will have to be found, within a greater move
towards decentralization and community control. Essential drugs will
remain a focal point of the Initiative in order to attract and sustain
local investment by communities. Educational efforts to promote the
rational prescribing and use of drugs will, however, have to be given
more attention in order to reduce potential hazards as well as to increase the cost-effectiveness of local investment.

The Bamako Initiative can only work with the decided efforts of
governments, communities, and donors, in active partnership. It is felt
that, as the new decade begins, it is opportune for every country to
gather together all the local, national, and international participants
in health care development and analyze how universal accessibility to
primary health care can be a reality by the turn of the century. To date,

UNICEF has already contributed over US$24 million to on-going action. The composition of this partnership will vary according to national circumstances; for example, in better-off countries, it is expected that governments and communities will take the major share in financing, with donors concentrating on the poorest segments of society, particularly the unreached. For countries hard-hit by economic recession and the AIDS epidemic, however, a major financial burden will have to be assumed by donors to respond to needs beyond the normal levels of support, both in type (including recurrent costs) and quantity.

The role of international solidarity, in support of both the increasing local empowerment in health and renewed government commitment to providing basic health services to the majority of the population, will be a critical factor in the next decade if significant progress is to be made. Short-term support to vertical interventions will have to give way to long-term international commitments to a broad-based delivery of health services, aided by improved information management to provide solutions to key issues and monitor progress towards "Health for All by the Year 2000." Encouraging news in this regard has recently come from the second U.N. Conference on the Least Developed Countries, with potential increases in development aid for the poorest nations, including twenty-eight in Africa.

REFERENCES

Benin Ministry of Health. 1990. Review of the Extended Programme on Immunization Integrated to Primary Health Care, 19 February–23 March.

Bennett, F.J., 1989. The Dilemma of Essential Drugs in Primary Health Care, Soc. Sci. Med. Vol. 28, no. 10, 1085–1090.

Fabricant, S.J. and C. W. Kamara. 1990. Community Health Financing in Sierra Leone (draft), July 1990.

Foster, S.D., 1987. Logistics and Supply Aspects, Bellagio Conference on Case Histories in Development, Italy, October.

HAI, OXFAM, and UNICEF 1989. Report on the International Study Conference on Community Financing in Primary Health Care, Freetown, 23–30 September.

Hogerzeil, H.V., et al. 1989. Impact of an Essential Drugs Programme on Availability and Rational Use of Drugs, The Lancet, 21 January.

International Children's Centre. 1990. The Bamako Initiative: Primary Health Care Experience, Children in the Tropics, no. 184/185, Paris.

Jiggins, J. 1989. How Poor Women Earn Income in sub-Saharan Africa and What Works Against Them, World Development, Vol. 17, no. 7, 953–963.

Kloos, H., et al. 1987. Illness and Health Behaviour in Addis Ababa and Rural Central Ethiopia, Soc. Sci. Med. Vol. 25, no. 9, 1003–1019.

Litrack, J.I., et al. 1989. Setting the Price of Essential Drugs: Necessity and Afford-
ability, The Lancet, 12 August.
UNICEF. 1988. The Bamako Initiative, Recommendation to the Executive Board for
Programme Cooperation, 1989–1993, E/ICEF/1988/P/L.40, New York, 15 March.
Waddington, C. 1989. Drug Sales—A Solution to the "Sustainability" of PHC? Mimeo.,
September.
WHO, Regional Committee for Africa. 1988. Guidelines for the Implementation of
the Bamako Initiative, AFR/RC38/18 Rev.1, Brazzaville, 7 September.

Response

ROBERT T. McDONOUGH

There seems to be little disagreement on the basic challenge facing this group—to get the products our companies manufacture to the people who need them. Within that challenge are a whole range of problems from pricing to corruption to counterfeiting to protection of intellectual property rights. The core problem on which we need to focus as corporations, as organizations, as people working for governments, or supergovernmental organizations is, "How do we work together to overcome the problems?"

The problem is not that people do not care enough about Third World health. Governments around the world care about the health of their people. Pharmaceutical companies care about the health of their consumers. This is not an evil, corrupt society focusing on this problem. None of us would attend a seminar on this subject if we did not care. The problem is that we do not care enough. We do not care enough to force our organizations, whether the Upjohn Company or the World Health Organization or the United States government, to break the barriers that keep us from finding ways to help the people who need pharmaceuticals.

The challenge is clear. However, even for those who do care, there are few guidepoints. Sister Regina Rowan spoke about a lack of trust for the pharmaceutical industry. That is legitimate. There are some good reasons why outside observers might view the pharmaceutical industry as being untrustworthy. Corporate executives also lack trust for a number of groups which try to get them to move in one direction or another. Why do people who have the same goal or share similar

Robert T. McDonough has served as the manager for public planning at the Upjohn Company since 1987. An attorney and an accountant, he previously worked with international mergers and acquisitions.

goals have an inability to agree and work together? Perhaps there is a devil, or a source of evil.

Karl Marx said, "One of the great problems of the world is that there are too many Christians but too few followers of Jesus." Remember, when push came to shove, Jesus put his life on the line and set the ultimate example for pushing for change in society. It would serve us all well to reflect upon the message that Jesus meant to leave for us. We need to resolve the distrust we have for one another. We need to believe that we can work together. We need to accept the fact that we are going to have to work for small victories whether in Indonesia or Kenya or elsewhere. We need to work with the people and help them make their own decisions, whether it is in providing essential drugs or facing another problem.

Beyond that, what we all have to do, either through our own corporations or the World Health Organization or the United Nations International Children's Emergency Fund, is to not let the politicians of the world convince others that health care can be something less than the highest priority. We must communicate to the decision makers, the people who set the priorities, even in places where there are few resources. We must convince them to move from the status quo, not to accept things as they are, and to get the services and the medicines to the people who need them. We must force our governments, force our corporations, and force the World Health Organization to eliminate the bureaucracy that is taking eighty percent of their budgets. Instead, they must discover what the needs are and how to get products to those in need.

Most of what I have said is obvious. But it is imperative to keep moving forward, to get beyond the confrontations, and start moving together in the same direction.

One of my favorite stories is about a man who was caught in a flood, sitting atop his house as the waters rose. The Red Cross rescue boat came and he was invited to get aboard. The man on the house said, "No, God will save me." The rescuer in the boat said, "I don't have time to argue, have it your way." So the waters kept rising. Later the Red Cross worker decided to return to again invite the man to get in the boat. "I may not be able to return. This is your last chance, the waters are rising." The man on the roof repeated, "No, God will save me." The Red Cross rescuer said, "I have other people I can save who aren't crazy," and so he went off and saved a few others. Then he decided he must return. It was the same story the third time. The man in danger said, "God will save me." The would-be rescuer said, "I am sorry. I cannot force you to get in the boat." The waters kept rising and the person drowned. He arrived at Heaven and looked at God and said, "I had such faith in you that you would save me!" The good Lord said, "I sent the boat three times." The point is that the Lord, however he or she is defined, works through us. We can make a difference. We are needed to get in the boat and go to help others still on the roof.

Within my own company, I am not the lone voice. People do care and they do want to work together. We must move beyond periodic confrontations that only result in going our separate ways. We have to identify specific opportunities such as the Bamako Initiative or other projects we can support, work toward building some cooperation, and then move to the next challenge.

Seminars such as this one are critical for accomplishing objectives. We will find ways. There are ways we can get drugs to the poorest people in the world without bankrupting the industry or causing the cessation of research. It requires moving beyond the rhetoric to the solving of problems.

Response

PAUL A. BELFORD

In 1806, Napoleon had a senior officer executed. One general asked another general what he thought about it. The other general said: "Worse than a crime, it was a blunder." It its Third World activities, the industry has been the target of a long list of accusations including mislabeling and bad marketing. These are more on the order of blunders than crimes and should be avoided. It is clearly in the interest of the multinational pharmaceutical not to blunder.

When a responsible executive becomes aware of a problem in Third World marketing, he or she fixes it. Over the last ten years, an informal, woefully underpaid infrastructure has developed throughout the world that brings corporate blunders to the attention of industry. And, we have tried to fix them. I think we can say honestly that in the last ten years, industry has done a much better job. But, in committing these errors industry has taken it on the "free," in the sense that it hasn't paid for having these things brought to them.

I could not agree more with Fernando Antezana. He presented a collage that gave us a sense of where WHO wants to go and where WHO wants industry to go. I would especially endorse Antezana's focus on training and on the notion that most of the problems of pharmaceutical availability in the developing countries can be fixed without outside dollars. What is needed is outside manpower and understanding of local situations.

This is also the case for the Bamako Initiative. As Agostino Paga-

Paul A. Belford has followed the U.N.-related North-South issues at the Pharmaceutical Manufacturers Association over the past decade in his position of assistant vice president international. Prior to this, he served the government as an international economist with the Treasury Department and then as director of the International Economics Impact Analysis at the Overseas Private Investment Corporation. He is now the president of the Association Executive Resources Group.

nini said, the Bamako Initiative must fit into the existing structure. But the Bamako Initiative is being placed on top of a nonexistent fabric. The people who are supposed to operate within the Initiative have never had any experience of health care. The Initiative would work against the background of the United States or in Europe where health care was provided prior to national socialism. This lack of experience and infrastructure in the Third World is a great challenge.

Research-based pharmaceutical companies do not know how to go about infrastructure development. When we did The Gambia Project, we blithely expected that three pharmaceutical experts in primary health care logistics were going to appear from our companies, fly over to The Gambia, and organize the project. Well, there were not three experts. We had thousands of people who could run a 15,000 square feet wholesaling or holding facility, but we didn't have anyone in our companies who knew how to select twenty-five or thirty basic drugs and how to organize and train people to be sure that these drugs were available at all the primary health care systems throughout the country. That is expertise we do not have. When Africare got involved, Gabriel Daniel knew how to do it and hired three people through the Indian Health Service.

Extensive industry participation is not very practical in many places. In most of the countries whose names I have heard mentioned in this seminar, there is no corporate presence. Most of the products that are available in these countries are brought in by wholesalers operating out of the United Kingdom, France, or Germany who distribute regionally across Africa. That is how the pharmaceuticals are getting down there. We must agree that this kind of distribution does not relieve the company of responsibility. We cannot say that it is not the company's problem. I am saying, however, that wholesaler distribution means the pharmaceutical companies have limited assets and resources in place to bring to the task. In large countries such as Nigeria, where a company may have marketing and production activities, the problem is not that no one within the country knows how to get the drugs to the people who need them.

The Pharmaceutical Manufacturers Association has spent over a million dollars on three projects in The Gambia, Sierra Leone, and Ghana. One million dollars is a lot of money even if it is spread over eight years. Philip Ellsworth, Malcolm Barlow, Alberta Edwards, and Mike O'Neill were the ones who got the million dollars out of their chief executives. We had to prove that a relatively small amount of money could significantly increase the availability of pharmaceuticals (25 or 30 basic drugs).

That million dollars should not have had to come from the pharmaceutical industry. It came from the pharmaceutical industry because we were desperate to show we were good people. We are also desperate to make the point that the nonavailability of pharmaceuticals in Malaysia or wherever has absolutely nothing to do with the fact that we have patents on our research products in the First World. They are totally distinct, separate phenomena. In the early 1980s we were being attacked in the United States for our patents and for our trademarks, as the killers of children in the Third World. We showed through our Gambia-type projects that this was not true.

In addition to our projects in The Gambia, Sierra Leone, and Ghana, we are initiating a project in Togo. There, we hope to initiate a pilot project on quality assurance. We are trying to make the point to developing country professionals and officials that quality control stops at the dock. You can make the best product in the world, with the absolute best quality control, but once it gets to the dock, quality assurance is the responsibility of the people who have purchased it.

We expect that the industry is going to help support this project. We also need some money from WHO and, perhaps, from the World Bank. The PMA should not be in the funding business. They should be providing organizational and managerial resources.

Beyond these projects the industry should press multinational institutions to initiate and fund their own projects. The WHO should go beyond its current mode of activity to become an actual transfer of resource agency. The Action Programme should initiate projects in the Third World that are similar to the ones we did in The Gambia, Sierra Leone, and Ghana.

On other issues, I personally believe that a pharmaceutical marketing code is a bad idea. If it were to be adopted by the World Health Organization and become a cause célèbre on which companies were called to task, the chairmen of companies would say to their people, "This just isn't worth it. Don't sell to anyone who sells in Africa. We can't control it. No one can control it."

I do think international consumerism is a good idea. This industry is better because of the pressures that have been brought by the consumers. We all drive better cars because of Ralph Nader (although I doubt I would enjoy his company over an extended period of time). We have a process going, a process that I think has been highly successful and should be continued, but we have to be realistic on what results we can expect. Do not ask from the companies what they cannot provide. The pressures have to keep up, and if they keep up, more will happen.

Response

LINDA PFEIFFER

This group agrees on three principles: (1) National and international efforts and resources relating to health care which focuses on the poor in underserved parts of the world should target the basic essential drugs that the majority of the population needs for the majority of its ills. (2) The ultimate success of any of these programs lies with the community. (3) Cost recovery is necessary.

Agostino Paganini deals with the enormous problems that must be addressed on the national level of the Bamako Initiative—how the funding is going to be handled, how to overcome graft, and how to ensure proper training for people. These problems involve all the dimensions of the Bamako Initiative. While Klaus Leisinger holds that drugs are not really the major problem in health care delivery to the poor of the Third World, Paganini insists it is still one of the most costly problems. Thus the overall cost recovery issue associated with health care quickly focuses on drugs. Nongovernmental organizations have been practicing cost recovery or partial cost recovery relative to drugs for a long time. These organizations, of course, have the luxury of dealing with a contained area, an individual community. Thus, NGOs have faced the cost recovery problem but on a much smaller scale than a program such as the Bamako Initiative.

NGOs have substantial experience and a desire for partnership to bring to the problem of health care in the Third World. The whole premise of International Medical Services for Health (INMED) is partnership, a private-sector partnership with nonprofit, nongovernmental

Linda Pfeiffer is the president and chief executive officer of International Medical Services for Health (INMED). She has been instrumental in establishing a lasting partnership between multinational corporations and nonprofit agencies around the world to work toward common goals for health and sustained development.

149

agencies and industry, particularly pharmaceuticals. INMED, formed in 1985, is a young organization.

From the beginning, INMED contacted industry representatives seeking and finding cooperation. The second step was to meet with the manager of the Action Programme on Essential Drugs of the World Health Organization to discuss this partnership. He also was supportive. I remember not understanding at the time his knowing grin and his shaking head while discussing this partnership between NGOs and industry. He was wise. However, in some cases it is an advantage to be naive because then one does not discourage easily. Some things that seem impossible can be worked out. The INMED relationship with industry is comparable to the tunnel under the English Channel. Comic strips during the early days of the building of the tunnel depicted a Brit on one end and a Frenchman on the other, each with a shovel. Someone fires a gun to begin the race, and they shovel as fast as possible. The comic strip then shows them passing each other on the way. INMED has built a number of tunnels. Where these tunnels are now joined there is partnership among NGOs, INMED, and industry. There also remains much to accomplish.

To continue the analogy, the tunnel is complete but there are Brits who say, "There is no way they are getting me down into that hole." It brings that dreaded continent closer. This is a good analogy for NGOs and the industry because they have common goals but different points of view. On the other hand, a lot of our British friends are saying, "It is dangerous down there, you know; we could get blown up." This parallels the view of many corporate managers when dealing with NGOs. Companies can envision people shooting at them if they do something too "up front."

INMED was established to focus on both medical supply and health education. On the medical supply side, we do a good deal of planning and fulfilling of supply needs through low-cost purchasing arrangements with companies. When we talk about purchasing arrangements and good prices for nonprofit groups, companies are naturally concerned about the international pricing structure. But there are creative ways to deal with this. Sometimes it can be straightforward, other times it can be addressed in the context of overall project costs.

NGOs usually do not purchase drugs from major companies. The relationship has been mainly one of donations. At this point, most companies and most agencies believe that donations are something we need to move beyond. This means a more creative, reliable partnership. When NGOs purchased drugs in the past, they used discount brokers for convenience and for cost reduction. It has been easier than working with the pharmaceutical industry, even though there have been problems with quality. INMED has tried to make it easier for NGOs and large producers to work together directly.

If this creative partnership is to be successful, it must move beyond this seminar's participants. Most corporate delegates to this seminar are with the public affairs departments of their companies. It is better for INMED to interact with the company as a whole. If we go strictly through the public affairs department, the marketing people are uncooperative. In a couple of instances INMED has initiated a relationship with people in a marketing department and public affairs personnel were uncooperative. However, cooperation *can* be realized if there is overall understanding.

Marketing departments often support collaboration with INMED because they can see its potential within host countries. Good public relations is good for business. INMED's program is good for NGOs and good for companies.

An illustrative example is INMED's work with a group of Tibetan refugees in India and Nepal. They were a contained group with a major tuberculosis problem. They also had an effective plan for monitoring it: they knew the multiple-drug therapy; they knew they had to actually be present in remote communities on a daily basis to ensure patients' dosages daily for six months. They had the structure. They needed the drugs. A number of different drug firms had given drug donations. The people knew there was a cost. Donations always cost something in importation or distribution. INMED helped the people formulate a proposal. We also submitted our own proposals and raised money to purchase drugs. This process introduced the natives to a number of international agencies, and they then raised the remainder of the money. There can be many positive results with a well-planned, long-term planning project.

Another advantage of the small, contained projects of INMED is that both companies and NGOs are able to see results more quickly. WHO and UNICEF normally deal with macro issues. INMED is often opportunistic. For example, INMED moved rapidly on a project in Southern Guatemala, which focused on eighty villages where the local NGOs and the Ministry of Health wanted a certain deworming drug. We went to a company and got a low price for the drug to start the program. Rotary International became involved because the local Rotary had put together some of the funding sources. Another multinational company provided health education materials. Because of the NGO and corporate initiative, funding was obtained from the Pew Foundation. With this model, which includes deworming and the education to make sure the problem does not keep recurring, the Ministry of Health is now setting aside a day a week in the schools for health education. What started as a small opportunity turned into a major government policy. It was the corporate response that enabled INMED to obtain the other international funding. Companies and NGOs can both move quickly, encourage other outside funding, and enable local agencies to take the initiative for their programs.

Discussion Summary

Hans Wolf, the chairman of the session, opened the floor for discussion with a distinction between communal and corporate responsibility.

I have heard agreement among not just the speakers, but all those in the room, that health for all is a valid and essential goal. There should be a focus on priorities which in the case of pharmaceuticals means a limited number of the most commonly needed drugs; there should be community participation by the people who are to be helped; there should be systems for partial cost recovery. The multinational pharmaceutical companies have both a self-interest in promoting these programs and some responsibility beyond self-interest by virtue of their power, their wealth, their strength, and their expertise.

There is also an implicit statement on a communal responsibility. All of us as citizens of wealthy nations have a responsibility both through voluntary donations and through government aid programs. An area for discussion, then, is the appropriate borderline between corporate responsibility and communal responsibility.

A look at the "health for all" goal reveals an enormous gap. Unless there is expeditious progress, that enormous gap will only be slightly smaller by the year 2000. The problem is growing almost as fast as the solution. In what ways can the pharmaceutical industry move to close that gap? How can both nongovernmental organizations and governments move to close the gap? Each side is looking to the other for the principal effort.

Rosemary Sabino raised the question of cooperation among pharmaceutical companies.

Institutions in the health care field have trouble cooperating with each other as hospitals strive to contain costs for local communities. Do pharmaceutical companies have trouble working together? If we

153

cannot work together among our own disciplines, then working with other, dissimilar institutions is an impossible task.

Hans Wolf explained that cooperation with dissimilar groups might be easier than cooperation with competitors.

The members of the Pharmaceutical Manufacturers Association have varied interests which make it difficult to work together. The pharmaceutical firms comprise an industry of competitors. Therefore, there are limits to the kinds of cooperation that are appropriate. Obviously there are appropriate forms of cooperation in areas such as Third World health care. Still, pharmaceutical firms are competitors with an array of viewpoints. In many cases, it is easier to come to a cooperative arrangement with someone with whom one is not directly competing. It is usually easier to cooperate elsewhere in the chain that links multinational corporation and patient.

Second, what pharmaceutical firms need from nongovernmental organizations is to have areas delineated where they should take action. NGOs tell corporations, "Do more." Firms ask, "But, what?" Multinational corporations have massive responsibilities; they need the expertise and research of NGOs translated into specific suggestions. While meeting their responsibilities to their owners, shareholders, and employees, managers need suggestions as to where they can go further in practical ways.

Michael Privitera reported progress in this area.

I see some evidence of specific suggestions and an increasing promise of collaboration in the last six months. Pfizer has had a number of people who are members of medical-related kinds of NGOs—the president of the Diabetes Association, the president of the World Psychiatric Association—approach the firm to discuss cooperative ventures in the field of education, specifically for identification of diabetes and for working on the diagnosis of certain psychiatric illnesses on a more global basis. Also, there seems to be a perceptible shift at the World Health Organization—a willingness and openness to start cooperative processes with the industry. This is encouraging.

Paul Belford pointed out the cooperation in the Togo project.

The work of the Pharmaceutical Manufacturers Association in Togo overcame problems of cooperation within the industry as well as developing the possibility of working with the World Health Organization. In discussing a project in Southeast Asia, a few member firms did not agree with the concept, but all were concerned and resolved to try to work on a joint project with the WHO. The chosen area of cooperation was quality control. Questions were free-flowing: "What is quality control? Will this be another discussion about getting a $200,000 quality control lab somewhere? At the end, what will we have done? Will we have achieved anything at all?" After the questioning stage, there was a focus on the next step of quality control which is quality assurance. Here manufacturers have an educational edge. In Togo, the plan is to use corporate expertise to teach quality control and quality assurance.

We will look to organizations such as the WHO, the World Bank, or the Regional Development Bank to fund the pilot project in conjunction with industry. The quality assurance project could then be extended, and further areas of collaboration explored. On some other issues, however, it is inappropriate for the PMA and the WHO to cooperate.

Ved Kumar pointed out the need for a more active role for industry.

I welcome this message from Paul Belford about the multinationals' involvement. It is very good that the companies are willing to join in cooperative ventures. However, what I hear is, "You have to do business on our terms. We are only willing to play a passive role. You come to us, we will discuss with you if it is workable. Then we will join you and make a pilot project out of it."

We want the companies now to move from the passive role to an active role, and come to institutions like the World Bank with programs and ask us to join in.

Paul Belford responded:

The industry has been proactive. The PMA has mounted projects in The Gambia, Sierra Leone, and Ghana to design systems for the distribution of pharmaceuticals. We reached out to the World Bank without much success. The PMA was responsible for a project in The Gambia because there was nothing coming out of the Action Programme in the early 1980s. Please note, this is in no way a criticism of the acting president or Fernando Antezana.

We are now sufficiently convinced of WHO's capabilities, resources, and intention that we can say that we want the WHO to stop being an advisory group on drugs and focus on the supply of drugs, backing that action with funds. I am not talking about buying drugs and throwing them off the back of a truck somewhere. I am talking about establishing quality assurance seminars to enhance capabilities in developing countries — the training to which Antezana referred.

The PMA is proactive and reaching out. In the particular case of Togo, the PMA is funding an opportunity to join together staffs from the WHO, IFPMA, corporate, and national associations to collaborate on a program to improve the quality of the products available in the countries at the level of the people who are responsible for it in the countries themselves. The people in the seminar are people from seventeen West African countries. The purpose is to make clear to them that quality assurance is their responsibility, and that the PMA can help.

Paul Maxey suggested another point for collaboration:

I represent an NGO perspective, which has received in the last three years three major donations of approximately 50 million corporate products from companies represented at this seminar. Some in this room are models of corporate product donations. One of those companies provides the major distribution organizations in America with a cash equivalent grant to purchase products from their warehouses for distribution in the Third World. Several corporations represented here plan the manufacture of certain products for donation. Some deliberately produce needed basis essential drugs. Others donate products that are right in the heart of the essential drugs list and allow us to distribute them. Yet there are still some who need to look at their corporate policies of donated materials in light of these other models.

Earlier, it was suggested that the industry might approach the United States Agency for International Development (USAID). For many years the mission boards of both Catholic and Protestant health care efforts have been subsidized in shipping American products through a program of AID called Ocean Freight Reimbursement.

The Ocean Freight Reimbursement program is a treaty exchange between countries in which duty and other kinds of blockages at the dock are eliminated. Now in our own instance and in the instances of the other two organizations of which I am intimately aware, we are delivering to responsible mission hospitals in the Third World and they have expatriate assistance or backup with this program. We have not experienced the kind of dock delay and pilferage that so often occurs in many instances.

Recently, we have encountered some objections from the USAID people over problems associated with corporate donations. USAID needs to be more aware of the responsible corporate donations when they are measuring the effectiveness of Ocean Freight Reimbursement. We need the collaboration of industry in convincing USAID that Ocean Freight Reimbursement is an effective part of our national development efforts.

Hans Wolf summarized:

In reaching the goal of health for all, there is a systems problem and there is a money problem. The lead responsibility for the systems problems rests with governments and international organizations, but the pharmaceutical industry can and should play an important role in helping to solve those systems problems through its technical know-how. The financial problem is one we all share. I don't think there is any question that the wealthy pharmaceutical industry can do more than we are already doing. But so can governments, so can voluntary charitable organizations. We can all do more and we all need to do more if this conversation is not going to be repeated in the year 2000.

Counterfeit Drugs

Drawing on his extensive grassroots health care experience in India and Africa, Ved Kumar sets the stage for analysis of the counterfeit drug problem. He frames the overall issue of illicit pharmaceuticals in terms of fake, spurious, mishandled, or substandard drugs. Other practices include the substitution of drugs or repackaging of samples and other expired products. Although a problem in every country, Kumar outlines why these practices are so widely spread in the Third World. Policies for governments, pharmaceutical professionals, and manufacturers are suggested.

Gabriel Daniel, a pharmaceutical health specialist for Africare, reports on a recent trip to West Africa where he encountered this "worst and ugliest form of medical corruption." He presents reasons fake drugs are so widespread, the damage they do, and possible approaches for their control.

Alberta Edwards and Michael Privitera bring the managerial view to the issue. Edwards represents Schering-Plough to international organizations and governments on the issue of counterfeit drugs. She shows why counterfeiting can only be controlled through close interaction among manufacturers, governments, and companies involved in local channels of distribution — a cooperation that does not now exist. With his extensive experience in the United States government and his current work for Pfizer, Privitera views the issue from both the public and private sectors. He lays the responsibility for lack of effective action against counterfeiting squarely at the feet of host government bureaucrats.

Following the presentations and responses, the participants heatedly debate the impact of pharmaceutical demand/supply imbalance as a root cause of the problem.

Global Syndicates and the Threat to Third World Health

VED P. KUMAR

Counterfeiting is as old as modern civilization and all through this period there have been and there are unscrupulous elements in society who tend to exploit the marketplace and the unsuspecting consumers by palming off lookalikes, adulterated substitutes, substandard, or misbranded items as genuine to reap quick profits.

The exploitation of the marketplace by these antisocial elements is directly linked to the issue of demand and supply. If there is a strong consumer demand for certain items and the supply is restricted due to economic, ethical, moral, or statutory limitations, the resultant gap is filled by smuggling, counterfeiting, and all other allied illegal activities. This is evident in large-scale illegal supplies of narcotic and psychedelic drugs in the Western world and of pharmaceutical drugs in the developing world, especially in sub-Saharan Africa. In the past, however, the problem of counterfeiting was generally localized with limited impact due to the absence of vast industrial infrastructure, poor communications, and the absence of intellectual property rights. It was confined to adulteration, substitution, and substandard manufacture; detection was comparatively easy.

However, with the expansion of the manufacturing sector and the explosion in the variety and numbers of new research products, coupled with the communication expansion making the whole world more of a global village, counterfeiting and allied clandestine activi-

Ved P. Kumar is a senior pharmaceutical specialist with the World Bank. With extensive managerial experience in the Indian pharmaceutical industry, the government of India, the Asia Development Bank, and the World Health Organization, Kumar has concentrated on Africa during his decade with the World Bank.

ties have graduated to a fine art. The individual operators have been replaced by syndicates with vast resources and a global network with a capacity to strike simultaneously at various vulnerable spots. The operations of these syndicates are always underground, not in the knowledge of the licensing and enforcement authorities, and are often located in countries with weak legislation or lax controls.

These syndicates have the necessary resources to buy the most sophisticated manufacturing, packaging, and printing equipment, resulting in an array of items which escape detection even by the most experienced handlers. In addition these syndicates have a vast sensor network to monitor the enforcement environment. At the slightest hint of a possible crackdown, they have the capacity to fold up and shift operations with lightning speed from a hostile theater to a more benign theater. These syndicates also run a parallel distribution network which is as efficient as the distribution network operated by any big industrial corporation.

Counterfeiting has now assumed such an alarming size that it and associated activities (misbranding, substitution, adulteration, and spurious manufacture) are becoming a major threat to the industry, to future research and development, to employment, individual and community safety, and public health. For people involved in drug supply and management, counterfeiting is a constant headache requiring constant vigilance. The health care professionals, the pharmaceutical industry, and the academic and research community see the problem from different perspectives. For health care professionals, fake drugs frustrate all attempts to improve health care delivery. Industry is concerned about their image, reputation, and profits. Researchers and academics are concerned about the economic and social cost.

Counterfeiting spans the entire industry spectrum from entertainment, auto industry spares, food and beverages, spirits and wines, and worst of all, in pharmaceutical drugs, which pose a major threat to public health and safety, prolonging human misery and endangering lives.

It has been estimated that globally the counterfeit trade may account for 3 to 9 percent of the total world trade, i.e., almost $60 billion a year. The percentages for the pharmaceutical drugs conterfeit trade may be higher than other sectors because of the acute shortage of drugs in many developing countries. Substandard manufacture under poor conditions, sale of physician samples, substitution, etc., in those countries further adds to the problem. Rising costs of product development, screening, approval, and market introduction, and the consequent higher consumer prices to cover such costs has made this industry a major target of counterfeiters.

Though the developed world is not free from the problem of counterfeiting, the incidence is fairly low as compared to developing countries. Counterfeiting in Europe and America is mainly directed at the skillful duplication of trademarks or fast moving new products. (For example, in the Naghdi case, a person reportedly offered to FBI undercover agents seven million bottles of Tagamet for $27 million. The same person earlier unsuccessfully tried to sell in the U.S. market about eight million pharmacy packs of Tagamet, Anspor, and Naprosyn for $700 million). In spite of strict surveillance and monitoring, counterfeits find their way into these countries by the use of legal parallel importing and distributing channels in Europe and America or the re-import of goods to the country of origin on different pretexts. They may also go through the diversion market which is often used by hospitals and institutions to sell drugs bought on special discounts for extra profits. The ease and speed with which over two million packets of fake ovulin contraceptive pills entered the U.S. market is a case in point.

A congressional subcommittee study concluded that the current distribution system in the U.S. is not foolproof. The study also identified as weak points the sale of drugs at deep discounts to non-profit institutions and hospitals (and bogus charity groups) far in excess of their normal needs and their subsequent resale through parallel distribution channels for profit, goods exported to foreign buyers, stolen merchandise, and the sale of physician samples — all serving as the main conduits for entry of counterfeit drugs.

The main factors responsible for the lower incident of counterfeiting in developed countries are:

- Effective legislation with stringent penalties and quick dispensation of justice. In addition, laws are updated to meet newer challenges.
- Strong enforcement and surveillance machinery.
- Limited self-medication and a clear-cut demarcation between over the counter and prescription drugs.
- Qualified and conscientious professionals prescribing and dispensing drugs and an organized and duly licensed wholesale and retail drug trade.
- Large manufacturing sector ever watchful of protecting their good will and profits.

- Strict enforcement of manufacturing norms and storage requirements for drugs and regular inspection of manufacturing and retail pharmacies to ensure compliance.
- A healthy cooperation between health care professionals and the enforcement authorities in reporting adverse drug reactions or suspect products, a good record in monitoring stock movement in trade, a well-organized drug recall system, and the machinery to inspect and seize suspected drugs.
- Active national quality assurance programs supported by statutory quality control laboratories. This is further supported by very efficient in-house quality control at the manufacturer's level.
- A responsible and alert media, an educated and aware public, and organized consumer groups.
- Recent proactive role of manufacturers to track and prosecute counterfeiters which has been fuelled by the spate of person injury suits. Until recently manufacturers maintained a low profile to avoid adverse publicity.
- Responsible legislators who quickly respond to public outcry and introduce appropriate legislation to plug any loopholes in current laws, procedures, and policies. (The enactment of the prescription and drug marketing act by the U.S. Congress in 1987 is an example of how the proactive role by legislators can further strengthen the hands of the enforcement machinery to control and monitor counterfeit trade.)

On the contrary in most developing countries and especially in Africa counterfeiting, misbranding, substitution, adulteration, and spurious manufacture are rampant across the board, covering all types of drugs. Counterfeit drugs account for more turnover than genuine drugs entering these countries through legitimate channels. Almost 60 percent of all drugs are reported to be counterfeit, substandard, or spurious in the Nigerian market. There are similar reports of mass circulation of counterfeit drugs in other countries. The recent report of the death of 250 children in Nigeria due to ingestion of a common drug mixed with a poisonous base is distressing but not unique. Such catastrophes have been reported in other countries too. Unfortunately, in spite of frequent mishaps in the developing world, in most cases the government response is ad hoc, aimed at crisis management and pacification of public anger rather than addressing the real problem.

This sometimes makes one wonder how serious the government efforts are in tackling the problem.

The Nigerian case is a clear example of a panic reaction. The case involved wrongful manufacture of paracetamol syrup using the wrong solvent, ethylene glycol, instead of propylene glycol. Instead of finding the cause of the manufacturing mishap, the government banned sale of paracetamol syrup, denying even legimate products to sick children. All manufacturers were asked to certify that they use propylene glycol and that their product is duly tested. All these actions would certainly be useful if the real culprit was relentlessly pursued. There were no real signs of that until November 1990. This all happened in spite of a massive investment in quality control laboratories and manpower.

One would certainly wonder, if counterfeiting is so widespread in Africa, why the impact on public health is not so visibly high. There are three probable reasons. First, the counterfeiters are generally merciful. Barring exceptions, they either use inert materials or subclinical doses of active ingredients. Such drugs may not do any good, but also do very little harm and may act as placebos. In addition most common ailments are self-limiting in nature; patients generally recover after the disease has run its course. Second, in most critical conditions, the response failure is attributed to the severity of the disease and the fatal outcome is considered an act of God. Third, other consequences of consumption of counterfeit or substandard drugs, like the development of resistance, appear too late on the scene and due to the absence of any tracking or surveillance system, the outcome can seldom be attributed to any specific drug.

The proliferation of counterfeits in developing countries is the cumulative result of various factors including policy and planning failure and the relegation of health, especially the provision of drugs, to secondary importance. Most countries, on gaining independence, had a limited health infrastructure and consequently limited drug needs. These countries embarked upon expansion of modern health care services to cover the majority of the population — an emphasis which got further impetus after Alma Ala and the adoption of primary health care. However, while expanding infrastructure, drugs were not viewed as an essential ingredient for the provision of health services, both from resourcing and technical standpoints. This planning failure in allocating adequate resources for drug supplies resulted in a widening availability gap, leading to the current situation of widespread shortages.

In the light of more pressing problems of national development demanding attention, the problem of drug supplies and the regulation of the pharmaceutical sector was considered somewhat of secondary importance and did not receive broad policy or financial support. No efforts were made to develop cohesive national policies to encourage local production to meet the rising need for drugs. In the absence of a congenial environment and a policy framework, very few foreign companies and hardly any local entrepreneurs ventured into local production, resulting in near total dependence on imports. Though the genuine demand for drugs has increased during the past two decades, the available resources have decreased. In Africa, since the oil crises of the 1970s, deteriorating economies and increasing debt burdens have made it impossible for many countries to provide adequate resources, especially in foreign exchange, to provide drugs for major segments of the population. Against competing demands for scarce foreign exchange, drugs seldom get an adequate share. For instance, in Tanzania, against a projected estimate of $55 million per annum for import of essential drugs for hospitals and dispensaries, only 10 percent of the required foreign exchange was made availabe. Even the limited available resources are unevenly used in favor of urban facilities and often for buying expensive drugs and even unessential exotic drugs for VIPs who exercise tremendous authority and clout. The result is a virtual drug famine in rural areas. Some marginal relief is provided by donors, which is often offset by pilferage, misuse, and poor logistic management.

A weak and often non-existent drug legislation cannot regulate and monitor the drugs moving in the commerce and manufactured in the country. Most countries inherited some legislation from colonial days that is totally inadequate and unsuitable for the local environment and has not been updated to respond to current concerns like counterfeiting. Some existing legislation tends to address relatively unimportant problems like drug advertising, drug sampling, etc., rather than the more pressing problems of quality assurance, drug enforcement, sale and manufacture. Absence of appropriate legislation allows anybody with money to start manufacturing and trading in drugs, and drugs from any source can freely circulate in the country. Even in those countries with reasonable legislation, the enforcement machinery is too weak—limited by shortages of trained manpower. (For instance, Ghana until recently had only one full-time and eight part-time drug enforcement officers for the entire country.) The laws are easily circumvented by influential people with political connections and by those who are able to pay bribes to corrupt machinery. This is further complicated by frustrating bureaucratic procedures, too many agencies involved with little coordination, and a slow justice process which often makes it impossible to punish culprits.

There is no nationwide network of retail and wholesale pharmacies due to the shortage of qualified personnel. Pharmacies are generally located in urban areas and operate on a western-style system with very high retail mark ups. They serve an elite population. The common people find the place too daunting to enter and too expensive. (In Ghana, out of a total of 36 wholesale and 194 retail pharmacies, 35 wholesale and 133 retail are located in two principal towns, Accra and Kumasi. For the rest of the country there are only 26 outlets, with two regions having no pharmacy at all.) The shortage of licensed pharmacies has resulted in the emergence of a parallel market of unlicensed dealers who run their own wholesale and retail network. They operate from any place, fixed or mobile—in the trains and buses, boutiques and restaurants, and Duka shops—under the most unhygienic and unhealthy conditions. A recent study in Senegal revealed that the parallel market for illicit drugs is very well structured inside the social and economic system. The turnover of the illicit market is about ten times the national health budget for the study area and is as large as the authorized drugs sold through the pharmacies. These small shops adjust their selling practices to popular money management practices, offer an alternative for symptomatic treatment at low cost, and often are willing to sell drugs in fragmented form on a single or daily dose to the poor who don't have enough money to buy standard packs.

Due to the absence of any effective control on the therapeutic use of drugs, the line between over the counter and prescription drugs is blurred. Most shops dispense any drug without prescription and often prescribe exotic drugs. In some countries very potent drugs are specially promoted and displayed at pharmacies. Even where legal restrictions exist, the shortage of qualified persons and the high cost of obtaining a physician's prescription make it difficult to enforce the regulations.

A well-intentioned effort by some countries to relax the drug rules to license general retailers in rural areas to stock and sell a few common over the counter drugs to service the poor rural population has come back to haunt the authorities. These outlets, variously described as "patent-shops," "chemical sellers," etc., operate in many West African countries. These shops, which now outnumber registered pharmacies in a ratio of 10:1, stock and sell all sorts of drugs and operate more in urban areas than in the rural countryside. Recent raids in Nigeria revealed that a large number operate without license and sell all kinds of suspect drugs. These drug shops, which are not supervised by any qualified person, are more prone to buy drugs on the basis of price and price alone, irrespective of the source of supply.

In addition, drug and pharmacy legislation does not stipulate maintaining prescription records by the pharmacies. This makes it difficult to track down a patient or a doctor, even in the case of an accidental dispensing of a wrong or unsafe drug.

Drug registration and drug regulation to control the movement of approved drugs are generally not existent. Where they do exist the backlog of drugs awaiting registration—a process which can take years—renders them meaningless. Nor does legislation stipulate any record keeping for prescriptions dispensed under different schedules. In addition there is hardly any system to report and monitor adverse drug reactions or drug recall procedures in the event of any untoward reactions. Thus not only can any drug enter and circulate in the country, once in, it is totally lost in the system and can continue being sold to unsuspecting consumers long after any negative reports appear abroad.

The absence of a quality assurance program and lack of supporting quality control laboratories further complicate the problem. Most countries have no system to periodically test drugs moving in the market for a quality check. A few countries have laboratories which are inadequately staffed, lacking the necessary testing skills, equipment, reagents and chemicals, and reference standards for testing. Often the test response time is as much as six months or more. During this period any suspect drug continues to be sold. Total absence of a regulatory mechanism, enforcement capacity, and a quality assurance program in most countries provides a safe haven for counterfeiters.

COUNTERFEITING: MODUS OPERANDI

Various terms like fake, misbranded, and spurious are used interchangeably to describe counterfeit activity. In a broader sense they all convey the impression of a clandestine activity designed to defraud the consumer for easy gains. However, there are subtle differences in the application of these terms, their focus, and how they are employed to the manufacture and supply of illicit drugs. A clear appreciation of modus operandi will probably help in developing strategies to curb such illicit operations.

Counterfeiting: "an attempt to copy with an intent to deceive." This is directed to skillful duplication of well-known established trademark products which have an international reputation of efficacy and quality. These state of the art lookalikes even fool the most experienced handlers and are the handiwork of skillful operators. Generally manufacturers of such lookalikes do not tamper with active ingredients, which are the same as stated on the label. As these duplicates represent very popular fast-moving items, the speed of distribution and consumption is the essence. Counterfeiters move swiftly, distribute drugs to a wide customer base to ensure quick consumption before such drugs undergo any physico-chemical degradation and become suspect. This type of counterfeiting with the infringement of trademarks is of greatest concern to international companies as it not only affects their market image, but their profits as well.

Fake drugs: "worthless imitation passed on as a genuine item." These are crude copies of the most popular drugs and are generally the work of fly-by-night operators, for sale in less sophisticated markets with poor consumer conscientiousness. In these fakes, the operators often replace the active ingredients with inert or sometimes harmful substances. They are generally sold in developing countries to unlicensed outlets.

Spurious drugs: "superficially like and morphologically unlike." In such cases the labels and carton are only suggestive of the genuine article and the active ingredients are often cheap inert materials like chalk or talc. Spurious manufacturers rarely go after highly sophisticated trademark items. Their preference is for mass consumption items commonly used in public sector institutions, like chloroquine, tetracycline, Ampicillin, etc. Such spurious drugs are often introduced into public sector purchasing systems through a local agent bribing willing officials. Some bogus companies still exploit the commonly held belief in ex-colonial countries that any goods manufactured in Europe are of standard quality by selling spurious drugs labelled as made in England or Germany.

Misbranding: "to brand falsely or in a misleading way; to label in contravention of statutory requirements." This is another form of crude copy. Often a small manufacturer designs the packages, labels, and lettering in such a manner that on a cursory look the product looks similar to a reputable brand and can easily be sold to unsuspecting consumers. These are sometimes referred to as "Made As USA" products.

Substandard drugs: "of a quality lower than prescribed by law." Unfortunately a lot of substandard drugs circulating in the developing countries are the products of licensed or overground manufacturers. Though unintentional, the substandard quality is due to a lack of knowledge and expertise for formulation development, of stability parameters, and of good manufacturing practices. Immediately upon manufacture these drugs may pass required quality tests, but they seldom maintain the quality during the stipulated shelf-life. Of course some manufacturers take advantage of lax enforcement and weak quality assurance programs to intentionally produce substandard drugs which contain much less than the stated contents.

Substitution. This is another commonly practiced activity in developing countries which requires only simple skills. In this case either the labels or the contents are substituted to make a quick profit. In the first category, the label of a cheaper drug is replaced by that of an expensive drug. Most common is the replacement of aspirin labels with that of chloroquine or other costly drugs, though this interchange is not restricted to generics only. In the second category, the contents are switched to sell restricted or controlled items such as narcotics and steroids. The labels have a special code which is easily deciphered by the regular distributors of such contrabands. The most common is labelling ampoules containing morphine as distilled water and bottles containing mandarin, amphetamines, and steroids as antacids.

Repackaging of samples and expired products. Repackaging of sample and expired goods is a thriving business around the world. In the Western world, trade is limited to repacking the pharmacy pack samples. In many Western countries legal and procedural measures are being put into place to prevent this misuse of samples. However, in developing countries there is a set of entrepreneurs solely engaged in the business of repackaging samples and expired goods who have developed an excellent network for collection, repackaging, and distribution. The problem is further complicated by the promotion of modern drugs by detailmen to quacks and traditional practitioners, often trading samples for an on-the-spot business transaction. These samples then find their way to the illicit market for repackaging into larger pharmacy packs. Similarly expired drugs are collected from various sources, especially public sector facilities where such losses are generally high due to tardy procurement practices and poor inventory management. Staff at these institutions sell such stock to the unscrupulous entrepreneurs but account for it as a write-off in the books. The work of these con-artists is further facilitated by a thriving trade in empty bottles and containers with intact labels. The bottles of expensive drugs command a premium. Often the contents are switched from an expired lot into a container with adequate shelf-life and are generally sold through itinerant vendors who sell on the basis of a single or daily dose.

There is no quick-fire solution for curbing the counterfeiting and other illicit operations. It has to be tackled both as an issue of criminality and illegal production and sale of drugs. A multipronged cooperative effort by all concerned, including governments, professionals, manufacturers and the public, will be required to get the desired results. The process is bound to be painstakingly slow.

TOWARD A SOLUTION

Role of Governments

Governments need to enact appropriate legislation which addresses the problem of counterfeit drugs and the importation, distribution, storage, movement, and sale of drugs. The legislation should provide enforcement authorities with adequate search and seizure powers. A mechanism should be established between different government entities including the Department of Justice for quick disposal of cases and for awarding exemplary punishment. The penalties should be very severe for repeat offenders including the confiscation of all equipment, stocks, and other assets of the person or organization on the second conviction, as is the case in India.

In situations where there is a shortage of trained doctors to diagnose and prescribe drugs, it may not be possible to strictly enforce drug prescription requirements. However, interim steps should be taken to regulate the prescription practices of the paramedical staff according to their skills and qualifications and the type of work performed. The range of over the counter drugs should be enlarged as in the West and chemical sellers and patent-shop type outlets could stock and sell such drugs.

Governments also should mandate strict procedures for importing, manufacturing, and selling drugs in the country. The enforcement machinery should be strengthened to monitor all imports and to inspect manufacturing and retail premises to ensure compliance. Where relaxation of the rules is required to supply common over the counter drugs, violations should be severely dealt with.

The government should establish a quality assurance scheme and a supporting quality control infrastructure. Periodic sample collection and testing of drugs moving in commerce should be done to rebuild public confidence, and the results should be disseminated to physicians and pharmacists.

In cooperation with the physicians in the public and private sectors, the government should establish an adverse effect reporting system with a recall procedure to ensure that suspect products are intercepted in the distribution chain immediately.

Since most African countries depend on imports, the governments should seek help from the regulatory agencies of exporting countries, reputable manufacturers, and international organizations to ensure quality of supply. Using the WHO certification scheme for bulk procurement will be of great help in ensuring quality. However, there is no substitute for in-house facilities in the long run.

Moreover, the government should mount education campaigns about the hazards of self-medication and of purchasing drugs from unlicensed vendors. The campaign should encourage the public to report any suspect activities or products to regulatory authorities for necessary investigation. The electronic and print media should be actively involved in these campaigns.

Professionals

Medical and pharmaceutical professionals should play a very active role in educating their colleagues and in supporting the government efforts to track down counterfeiters. The professionals should not only educate the public about drug usage, but also desist from buying drugs from unknown or uncertain sources. When there is any doubt about a drug source, they should report the matter to the regulatory authorities. Professional associations should be actively involved in promoting government efforts to enforce the laws and monitor movement and usage of drugs in the public and private sectors. They should also cooperate with regulatory authorities in reporting on response failures or adverse reactions to drugs.

Manufacturers

Since local manufacture is limited, this role will be filled by international companies who are the principal exporters or suppliers of drugs. Considering the present state of drug enforcement and quality assurance programs and the scarcity of resources to start up a series of activities simultaneously, the international manufacturers could certainly accelerate the process if they would:

1. take a proactive role to track down counterfeits and help governments prosecute the offenders;
2. transfer technology and information on how to address the problem of counterfeits based on global experience;
3. train developing country professionals in quality control in their own laboratories and support a training program for enforcement staff with the federal regulating authorities in the West;
4. provide reference standards, test protocols, reference books, and even used equipment for setting up quality control laboratories; and
5. provide quality control back-up in the early stages, along with reference samples and the know-how in the subsequent stages for the physico-chemical detection of counterfeits.

Public

Because of the problem of illiteracy, the public can play only a marginal role in the entire process. However, it is hoped that the public would support these efforts by being more vigilant and by cooperating with authorities, while avoiding the purchase of drugs from street vendors, boutiques, and unlicensed drug shops.

The Ugliest Form
of Medical Corruption

GABRIEL DANIEL

Irrespective of the why, the who, the where, or the when of counterfeiting, the faking of pharmaceutical products is surely the worst and ugliest form of medical corruption. It is a crime against humanity and science. Aware of the potential adverse effects of even the so-called safe drugs, I am especially concerned about the consequences of other forms of fake practices: the use of expired and out-of-date drugs, the irrational use of drugs, incorrect prescriptions, and poor patient records. It is necessary to discuss the practice of faking drugs and examine all its manifestations so effective preventive and control measures can be planned.

WHY ARE DRUGS FAKED?

Because of their life-saving and pain-reducing properties, and the relative ease with which they can be copied, drugs have become the most vulnerable targets of counterfeiters. Fake drugs come from sources with various levels of sophistication ranging from the highly technical and capital-intensive international cartels and the intermediate comprehensive laboratories to the desk-top or kitchen concoctions of the lay culprit. Although the reasons for faking drugs vary, the bottom line for most is economic.

Gabriel Daniel is a pharmaceutical health specialist for Africare, an organization devoted to improving the quality of life in rural Africa through the development of water resources, increased food production, and the delivery of health services. A pharmacist, Daniel has worked at the grassroots on health care problems across Africa, particularly as an administrator for a number of programs in Nigeria.

When a government does not have the hard currency to undertake international procurement from reputable and dependable sources and does not have a controlled local industry of its own, it is forced to make local purchases of drugs of questionable quality and origin. The inability of countries to control drugs and/or provide hard currency creates fertile ground for the proliferation of both international and local counterfeit drugs.

There can be two categories of people who directly or indirectly deal with counterfeit drugs. The first group are those in the health sector who are economically strained because of low and/or delayed salaries. This condition encourages them to use products of questionable quality, including expired drugs. The same syndrome can lead officials to relax control of the importation and distribution of such fake products. The second group are nonhealth-related persons whose primary objective is to make as much money as they can in the shortest possible time, irrespective of the means and the consequences.

The following are representative prescriptions obtained during a visit to a developing country:

Rx #1

Diagnosis: lower abdominal pain, vomiting, . . .
Treatment: erythromycin, Metronidazole, ampicillin, Vermox, Novalgin

Rx #2

Diagnosis: general pain, cough, PID
Treatment: paracetamol, chloroquine, iron, tetracycline, Metronidazole

Examples of irrational prescriptions such as these are widespread across Africa and the developing world. Hence, even medical officers contribute to the problem in the course of their practice by wrong diagnoses and treatments, by over-prescribing, or by the use of incompatible combinations.

WHEN IS FAKING AT ITS HIGHEST?

Shortage of commodities, whether real or artificial, is one of the important conditions that favors proliferation of counterfeit products. Such shortage creates a crisis situation where spurious drugs easily find

their way into the void market. This is also common where the supply
of a popular brand product becomes short for some reason, and the
shortage is countered by a counterfeit product.

Governments and other agencies receive wholesale gifts without
questioning the source of the donation. Such donations could have
been purchased cheaply because they were repackaged to conceal ex-
pirations or substandard qualities or because they were products that
failed quality-control scrutiny. I have seen a whole room of pharmaceuticals donated by physicians and corporations that were either expired
or inadequate samples of new products. These donations do not serve
the purpose of the recipient's relief program. Although the donations
might have been made with the best of intentions, the recipient had
to spend money to store and dispose of these inappropriate donations.

A donation of a disinfectant was made to Africare. I requested
from the donor verification of the quality, safety, and effectiveness of
the donation. The following statement was sent to Africare:

> Warranty: This information is, to the best of our knowledge, accurate,
> but may not be complete. *XXXX* Company furnishes this information
> in good faith, but without warranty, representation, or guarantee of its
> accuracy, completeness, or reliability.

It was discovered that the disinfectant could not be sold in the United
States because it did not meet quality standards. It is easy to speculate
how unquestioning agencies receive such spurious donations for their
work in developing countries.

Many health workers give expired drugs to their patients because
they do not have active drugs. Many try to rationalize their actions by
the notion that something is better than nothing — the patient could
die without the drug. Expiry dates for most of these pharmaceuticals
can range from a few months to a few years. This is another form of
usage of fake drugs. Shortage of drugs should not be an excuse to give
the unsuspecting patient a drug whose safety and effectiveness after
expiry cannot be guaranteed. This type of professional irresponsibility
encourages other, less reputable, health workers and lay persons to freely
use expired pharmaceuticals and present them for sale under various
disguises.

Strict control of the conduct of the drug business through legislation and strong quality control makes the availability of prescription
drugs difficult, especially for general merchants who are accustomed

to distributing drugs without permission — peddlers, quacks, and antibiotics abusers. It takes time and effort to exclude these groups from
the scene. They continue to get drugs through illegal sources, and in
many cases, the illegal sources are counterfeit drugs dealers.

WHO ARE THE VICTIMS?

The first line of victims are the unsuspecting patients who face
the consequences of loss of life, continued suffering, or the acquisition
of a new disease. The most recent, painful example is the death of
over one hundred Nigerian children in September 1990 who were victims of paracetamol syrup prepared with poisonous diethylene glycol
instead of propylene glycol. The supplier of this chemical labeled the
container "propylene glycol" when, in fact, it contained the toxic
substance. It then was obtained by a chemist who prepared the syrup
in a hospital. Physicians and other health workers, as a consequence
of unintentional use of counterfeit drugs, could face legal action for
failed treatment, lose clients as a result of providing ineffective drugs,
or find themselves unable to treat conditions they correctly diagnosed.

The pharmaceutical industry suffers from a blemish on its name
when its products are faked. A failed treatment with a counterfeit brand
name results in loss of confidence for the genuine product. Rebuilding
of trust is a lengthy process. In Nigeria the government prints the names
of faked drugs and their manufacturers in the national papers. That
may be the reason why some manufacturers have hired their own agents
to pursue counterfeiters in Nigeria.

The national health system loses credibility if patients become
more ill, or even die, after treatment. In Plateau State, Nigeria, residents have blamed oral rehydration therapy for the death of children.
As a result of these accusations, program attendance has decreased.
The following is an excerpt from an article published in *Vanguard,* a
national paper with the headline "Plateau Parents Blame ORT Syrup
for Kids' Deaths."

> The turnout for mass immunization campaigns in some local govern-
> ments in Plateau State may be low as some parents who lost their chil-
> dren to the killer paracetamol syrup are blaming the EPI vaccines and
> ORT for the death of their children.

TARGETED PRODUCTS

The technologically advanced international pirates of counterfeit drugs are not limited by the form and type of products they mimic. The faking is done so professionally it is difficult to tell the difference between the genuine product and the copy without effective quality-control laboratory tests performed by experienced chemists.

In the developing countries, faking is directed toward popular products. Targeted products include syrups, capsules, and injectables. Common examples include filling empty capsules with milk powder or flour to fake tetracycline and ampicillin, filling an empty container with inexpensive drugs like aspirin then labeling the container with an expensive drug name like chloroquine.

The following list from the Nigerian Food and Drug Administration shows that most of the reportedly fake drugs are syrups. Note that almost all are preparations used in the treating of children.

In 1988 the Food and Drug Administration/Control Laboratory (FDAC) of the Nigeria Federal Ministry of Health released a list of ninety-two drugs found to be fake, substandard, contaminated, poorly labeled, or having no active ingredient.

Breakdown: Fake, substandard, no active ingredient   49
             Heavily contaminated   17
             Poorly labeled   26

Affected Products: chloroquine syrup, paracetamol syrup, baby cough mixture, vitamin B complex syrup, cough linctus, worm elixir, multivitamin syrup, Benylin with codeine syrup, promethazine elixir, ampicillin capsule

CONSEQUENCES OF FAKING

Treatment failure is the foremost disastrous effect of counterfeiting of drugs and medical practices. The use of inert substances or a reduced quantity in counterfeit preparation results in the nontreatment of disease followed by the patient's worsening condition. If the faking is performed with toxic chemicals the effect could be lethal or result in acute or chronic toxicity.

Loss of confidence is another damaging result of counterfeiting. Unsuspecting health workers who have prescribed counterfeit drugs are the immediate targets of their communities. The patent product which had been counterfeited and its parent company can become the target of attack by consumers, health workers, and the government. Some countries have reacted by halting importation of pharmaceuticals from countries with reputations tainted by counterfeiting.

MEASURES TO PREVENT AND CONTROL COUNTERFEITING

1. An effective and comprehensive drug policy supported by legislation, authority to enforce, and adequate finances will assist the responsible governments to register products, premises, and professionals; issue certificates for import, export, manufacture, and distribution of drugs and related products; undertake regular inspections; and establish and operate quality control facilities.

2. Ensuring foreign exchange facilities to all officially registered bodies and ensuring adequate supplies at all times and all levels is one effective way of controlling counterfeiting.

3. Improved pharmaceutical management and distribution systems assist in uniform operation of all aspects of the supply system from initial selection to final use by the patient. It addresses the proper storage, inventory control, record keeping, and rational use aspects of the system. Africare is involved in introducing such systems in countries like The Gambia, Sierra Leone, Ghana, and Nigeria.

4. Public education and increased awareness of all concerned is an approach that will especially assist rural communities which do not have the benefit of modern control facilities or trained professionals.

5. Professional ethics and moral values are nontechnical but effective methods that instill a sense of responsibility in both health professionals and business managers.

6. International and regional collaboration plays an important role in exchanging information, controlling drug traffic, and regulating the overall conduct of pharmaceutical products.

The ultimate and lasting solution to the problem of the counterfeiting of drugs is to be found in the improved economic situation in developing countries. To improve economics is to free people to do the right thing.

Response

ALBERTA R. EDWARDS

I brought along an example of a counterfeit drug because I think it would be interesting for those who haven't examined counterfeit products before to see just how skillfully they are made, particularly in printing. If they spent half the time formulating products that are correct as they do in trying to get packages that look exactly like the original, maybe the drugs would be a little better. Because the counterfeiters not only use the same layout, they use our logos, they use our colors, they really do a terrific *printing* job. But pity the poor patient who buys and takes one of their products and gets no relief from his illness.

This sample illustrates that these counterfeiters, indeed, are multinational corporations. We have found counterfeit products in some of the African countries, but then when we looked where they are made, we found that they put an Indian address on it, in Bombay. So the products not only go from country to country within a continent, they also go between continents. In trying to track them down, we found that the Indian company sent us to the U.K. to an address that did not exist at all. This is the kind of problem that you run into.

I think from a company point of view, I will have to talk primarily for Schering-Plough because it is not a problem that many of us discuss with each other. I think this is one message that all of us here would agree on: with greater cooperation, not only among companies but with governments, with other institutions, with non-governmental organizations, etc., we could probably help a lot to alleviate this problem. It is not just a problem in the Third World or in developing countries: we know that counterfeit Zantac reached the U.K. from Greece;

Alberta R. Edwards is the vice president for public affairs of Schering-Plough International. She has worldwide responsibility for representing the company with international organizations and governments.

we know about Lasix, which was counterfeited in this country some years ago. It is a worldwide problem, and from an industry point of view, I would say each company looks primarily after their own products. Whenever we find one — and it is difficult sometimes to even know that counterfeits exist — we certainly do everything possible to track them down. As you can see, we track them not only in the country where we found it, we tracked it to India, we tracked it to the U.K. Why?

We are very concerned that people may be using drugs that don't work. We have a reputation that our drugs are highly effective; we have spent years developing them; we certainly don't want anyone to take something that contains no active ingredient. I might here just answer a question that was raised earlier. "Where do the actives come from?" It is unfortunately true that many of our products can be copied by competent chemists. In the past, quite a few of the actives were made in the Eastern Bloc and were bought by generic companies. Many of them are good quality, but counterfeiters have used them in smaller than stated quantities, or some don't even bother with an active at all. So, we have pride in our products and we take great care that whatever product you buy in any country in the world, if it has our company's name on it, it will be the same quality, no matter where. Therefore we have good reason to be very concerned about counterfeit drugs and want to cooperate with others to eliminate them.

What do companies do about it? One thing is to make their products ever more difficult to copy. The outstanding example is the Valium pill of Roche which has a hole in the middle shaped like a small heart and apparently it is a very difficult one to copy. Schering-Plough had a case in one of the Latin American countries where someone counterfeited one of our injectables and put nothing but water in the vial. We re-packaged our product into a blister pack with a printed foil. Printed foil on a blister pack is an expensive process and therefore, it is much more difficult to copy; it is therefore something a pharmacist can more readily recognize as being a counterfeit drug. These are some of the things companies have tried.

The industry group has also helped to fight counterfeit drugs by helping to train quality control people from many countries through the WHO/IFPMA Program. More than eighty quality control executives or technicians have been trained by individual companies for periods of six months. This is an on-going cooperative program in which companies are given the names of individuals who need training and then arrangements are made for the six-month training period.

Another industry effort is a workshop which will be held in December 1990 in Togo. It is also a joint effort of the WHO and the IFPMA and the title of it is "Quality Assurance of Pharmaceuticals in International Trade." There will be sessions on quality assurance but also on counterfeit drugs. The PMA's Paul Belford has been very actively working on it, so if you are interested in learning more about that conference, I think Paul would be a good person to talk to.

Another thing that we could do to help this process of cooperation is to work with a British bureau called "The Counterfeit Intelligence Board." This board is specifically set up to work on this problem. There are experts in this field: one mentioned to me is a former executive with The Wellcome Foundation Ltd., Mr. Geoffrey Foote. Through them, people who have worked in this field could be enlisted in a cooperative effort. Our experience with The Counterfeit Intelligence Board was good, in that it helped us track down the address and the people in the African/Indian counterfeit problem. Unfortunately, in the end not much happened because even though they knew about it, and even though the U.K. customs knew about it, there really was no communication among the different groups involved in counterfeit drugs. So better sharing of information also with government departments would help.

The important thing is that companies per se really can only take their complaint through the legal system of a country, and if the legal system is not effective and the drug policies and the laws are not enforced, it is difficult to get action. Companies can track down the persons, but if the persons are not prosecuted, I think it is not possible for companies to take the steps the government should be taking. But that is where non-governmental organizations can be helpful in raising the will of health ministers and of legal authorities to take swift and appropriate action in these cases.

We need greater cooperation, enforcement, and prosecution with the help of legitimate drug manufacturers, the government agencies but also those in the wholesale and retail trade who buy and sell drugs. Obviously, if someone comes to you and offers you an expensive drug for one-third or one-tenth of the price, I think we would think him naive to say that he doesn't know that there is something very "fishy" with this product. Going after counterfeit manufacturers is not enough; action must also be taken in regard to those who trade in these counterfeit products and sell them to innocent buyers.

One last point not related to counterfeit drugs, which I would like to mention, since it has been raised by several participants, is the question of samples. I know that this is a controversial issue. Samples do play an important appropriate role in spreading knowledge about pharmaceutical products. When there is a new drug, a doctor will not feel comfortable in prescribing it on a regular basis until he has tried it on a few patients to judge its efficacy for himself. Therefore, to give him some samples of a new product facilitates his gaining experience as to how a product can be most effectively used. Also later on, there may be a new indication, that was not originally known, a new illness that can now be treated with the drug. Sampling for a new indication, possibly with a different dosage schedule, is valuable. Third, there may be a new dosage form that the doctor has never used before. When we talk about sampling, we must be aware that there is a very real need for *appropriate* sampling, but certainly indiscriminate dumping of big quantities is not what I am talking about.

Response

MICHAEL L. PRIVITERA

We are all in agreement about counterfeit or fake drugs. How, then, can all of our energies and knowledge be brought together in a way that encourages improvement in countries where multinational corporations operate?

Certainly the multinationals can do more, but also the feet of bureaucrats should be held to the fire. Ransome Kuti, the Nigerian Minister of Health, has been trying to be responsible, but in most developing countries there is an enormous, dormant, slow-moving bureaucracy. Also, medical doctors and others who inevitably become part of the social workings of a country are almost exempt from the same kind of legal measures for which a poor person would be held accountable. In Ved Kumar's paper, there was a wonderful use of what I call "semantic euphemisms," words like "socially unacceptable" or "antisocial behavior"— it is such a wonderful way of calling someone a "ripoff artist" or a "pirate" or a "murderer." Governments in the Third World have been allowed to set somewhat of a semantic agenda. Kumar's paper properly suggests that there is this sort of disinfecting of action by searching for a euphemistic description. This is a behavioral quality of bureaucrats, not just in the Third World, certainly, but throughout all nations. Whether the widespread counterfeiting is tied to market forces, cultural predisposition, lack of education, lack of laws, lack of enforcement, or lack of concern, the main reason it exists in such magnitude is that no one in government is taking proper responsibility for reducing it. People seem to want to absolve themselves of fault. In the 1990s,

Michael L. Privitera is the director of public affairs for Pfizer International Inc. Before joining Pfizer in 1989, he served for a decade in the United States government Environmental Protection Agency and the State Department with a speciality in Asian affairs.

with conferences like this, with the ideologies of the twentieth century having been cracked open and exposed, warts and all, communism, capitalism, and socialism, leaders can no longer skirt this kind of responsibility. The challenge for the multinationals, for the churches, for the NGOs alike, is not just to work cooperatively with governments, but to expect and to demand more from them.

In planning for this session and thinking about "What can multinationals do?" or "What have they been doing?" I contacted a person who for twenty-three years has been involved in the Pfizer production in Nigeria. I would like to share his short memo with you. This memo helped me understand that the problem is even more widespread and graver than in Gabriel Daniel's example:

> Fake drugs come from two main sources. A number of local illegal manufacturing outfits operate underground in Lagos, Initignaba, Angoo, Ipidandicango, and Ota in the open state. Here they churn out quite a large quantity of fake, adulterated, and substandard drugs, however most of the fake production is in Lagos and Onitsha. The pharmaceutical manufacturers from foreign countries have taken the greatest action against fake or imitation drugs in Nigeria, as a matter of fact Pfizer has pioneered the fight long before the government acknowledged the enormity of the problem. The legal action against one local company resulted recently in a substantial settlement of damages to Pfizer by the court.
>
> The case was a pace-setter and signaled our determination to fight any infringement on the patent in any form. Since then, we have taken several actions to check the menace of fake drugs. Our field forces are alert to the issue and when any drug product is suspected fake, samples are sent to the office and on to a laboratory for quality analysis. If confirmed fake, we would normally arrange to arrest the retailer or distributor or importer. In fact, it is possible to be very active in this sense. We have made such attempts on more than ten occasions over fake Feldene and various antibiotics.
>
> In one instance, we engaged the services of a private security agent who tried to track the fakers. Some people were arrested but could not be prosecuted because the police insist on having an independent analysis of the fake product. A recent case of arrested counterfeiters has been the most thorough to date, going through six layers of distributors to even implicate a member of our staff who had allegedly supplied some materials. The case is being handled by an attorney and we expect prosecution.
>
> We may be lucky this time but the matter has been delayed by

the police bureaucracy, they are awaiting official analysis of the fake product in the federal laboratory. Many of our previous efforts of tracking deviants have ended at this level, but we are hopeful of a breakthrough in this case.

Following an effective lobby on the issue of fake drugs pioneered by the multinationals and carried out additionally through the press, the federal government promulgated Decree 21. This decree provided for two years imprisonment or 2,000 nera fine for any infraction of the decree. Critics fear the penal sanctions are not severe enough to act as real deterrents to criminals. Others feel the decree is a good starting point. Hopefully this will be the beginning of a real fight against fake drugs. Individual company efforts by Pfizer, Parke-Davis, and Upjohn have resulted only in frightening or dislodging the drug fakers. In most cases, the criminals have regrouped to continue their nefarious activities, usually with police connivance.

The real issue is how to bring further pressure on the governments to assume their responsibility. How can the multinational step beyond its traditional role as producer, manufacturer, and distributor in these societies? To what extent can nongovernmental organizations be monitors and advisors?

Discussion Summary

Rosemary Sabino, session chairperson, repeated Michael Privitera's question to the group, "Together what influence can we have with the governments?"

Prakash Sethi pointed out that quick improvement in the governments was unlikely.

We are all barking up the wrong tree by expecting these governments to have stiffer laws or greater penalties. These governments, to a large extent, lack social controls in terms of public accountability which is the hallmark of a functioning democracy and an open information system. Added to this are the problems of insufficient enforcement of laws, inadequate procedural controls and structural safeguards that restrain bureaucracy, and poorly paid and undermotivated public officials. Under these circumstances, further dependence on government would not help the poor, but would provide additional opportunities for bribes and corruption, and more avoidance of laws. If laws were the answer, illegal drugs and narcotics would have been eliminated in the United States which has better laws, vigorous enforcement, and stiffer penalities. Yet, nothing seems to work.

The pharmaceutical companies themselves are to be blamed for the problem. They create tremendous demand for a product through their promotional and distribution policies. Then they fail to create a distribution policy to meet the demand. They create a brand awareness, a demand, with a supply system that cannot keep pace. This invites fakers to fill in the gap at a low price. The fakers could be eliminated by copying the electronics industry in its reduction of prices in those countries. Third World markets are very different from those in the developed world. The solution is to sell generic products where there is no price incentive to create such a large gap. These governments have a lot of problems in addition to counterfeiting; every one of them needs greater enforcement and more stringent penalties. It is unrealistic to think that in the next hundred years the counterfeiting problem can be solved through government control.

Michael Privitera disagreed.

Your premises are really absurd. First, the connection with the electronics industry is different. Think how quickly software and copied products are improved. In most cases it is not worthwhile to prosecute people who are pirating its products because in a relatively short time period, there will be a new patent anyway.

It takes almost ten years to commercialize a pharmaceutical; not just to invent and to develop and to package it, but to undertake all the necessary testing which sometimes has to be performed in a foreign country. In terms of the distribution network, Pfizer and other reputable firms do not try to sell products in bus stops, or on street corners, or in any of the other amazingly inventive places where drugs are sold in developing countries. Will and direction combined with available human resources are needed in these countries. Governments must be as serious and as responsible as they are expecting their people to be.

Alberta Edwards also disagreed, pointing out that manufacturers' promotions did not create the problem.

Whatever news there is goes around the world in record time. If there is a product that cures something that has never been cured before, not one piece of literature has to be distributed on that cure. If this news becomes known in any single country, the information goes around the world. Everyone wants the drug; that is understandable. Blaming promotion and the creation of demand are not realistic criticisms today. Communications and information are self-perpetuating.

The pharmaceutical industry cannot price at a level which covers only the cost of manufacturing the drug, as generics do, or there would never be a new drug. We invest and work for eight to ten years for a new product. Close to ninety-five out of one hundred of these possible products will not become marketable. It can never be predicted which will succeed. The ninety-five cannot be avoided because it is impossible to determine in the development process which compound will make it and which will fail in toxicology, clinical tests, or somewhere else in the long development process. The money must be generated that will allow pharmaceutical firms to bring the new product to marketable standards. Low-cost drugs are not the answer to getting additional products for all the illnesses that have yet to be cured.

Klaus Leisinger also supported the need for research.

I could not agree more. I have sympathy for the United Nations International Children's Emergency Fund (UNICEF) or the World Health Organization (WHO) when either proclaims, "It is better to spend a little for everyone than much for a few and nothing for the rest." Still, the generic drugs of the year 2000 are now those sold on the private markets for higher prices today. There will not be new generic drugs tomorrow if we do not sell branded products today.

Agostino Paganini questioned the price structure for older drugs.

I also agree. The generic drugs of 2000 are those we sell in private markets today. But when a drug like chloroquine or ampicillin is counterfeited, there is something wrong. That means these drugs are not available at an affordable price. Chloroquine is an old drug, ampicillin is an old drug; why are they not produced at a price affordable to people in a country like Nigeria? Why are they not priced so low that it is not profitable to counterfeit them?

Paul Belford prointed out other factors causing counterfeiting.

Sethi is arguing that high prices create the markets for counterfeits. The reality is that the greatest instances of counterfeiting are when a product has been forced off the market by a government edict as in Pakistan in 1972, Sri Lanka in 1979, and Bangladesh in 1982. Counterfeiting has been very commonplace in those countries not because the products were too highly priced but because they were outlawed from the market. There is no automatic link between price and counterfeiting.

Paganini introduces another situation. There are two types of counterfeits — those where an active ingredient is used and those where it is absent. In the first case, someone basically creates a product which does or comes close to doing what it is supposed to do, and puts it on the market; that costs money. The counterfeiters had to formulate the active ingredients — they did not go through years of experimenting and many steps of processing to get the active ingredients. Anyone who counterfeits generic products that are widely used and actually has the active ingredient is a moron. The second worst problem with counterfeiting is, for instance, when the ingredient is talcum powder, and there is no relationship between the course of that product and the generic. We must keep these two things separate.

Carol Emerling emphasized the difference in the situation in the U.S. and that in developing countries.

The counterfeit drug situation in the United States is not comparable to that of Nigeria. The United States has one of the safest, best-managed (whether or not we like what the Food and Drug Administration is doing today), best-run regulation systems in the world. It has the greatest concentration on safety, the best enforcement, the most concerned public, and the most concerned legislators. Anyone who has followed the Dingell hearings and some of the generic companies who have had substandard drugs which would never have been approved if they had not switched the tests knows what horror is. It is difficult to comprehend something of that magnitude in the United States. It goes against our standards, it goes against our beliefs. It goes against our absolute trust in safe, approved, properly labeled drugs, whether over-the-counter or prescription. Please do not compare the counterfeit drug situation in Nigeria, this absolutely criminal system, to what is known in the United States today. We just cannot put those two in the same concept.

Prakash Sethi clarified his concern.

We are talking at cross purposes. I did not mean to infer that the United States has the same kind of counterfeiting problem as Nigeria. I was talking about the prosecution and control of illegal drugs in the United States, saying that if, with all the available resources, cocaine consumption cannot be controlled or eliminated, countries in the Third World would never have enough resources to prevent counterfeiting. I am talking about the ability of governments to mobilize enough resources to control the marketplace. As Edwards iterated, information flows quickly in the international marketplace, spurred by sample drugs. When people are dying to get pharmaceuticals, they will force a supply. And as Daniel suggested, the largest part of counterfeiting is occurring in low-level common drugs where the issue is clearly one of price. It is a simple law of marketing: When enough demand occurs and pricing is too high for people to satisfy that demand, someone else will fill the gap. It happens in Gucci luggage, it happens in all known promotions. Why should drugs be an exception to this simple marketing law?

Intellectual Property Rights

The subject of intellectual property rights is perhaps the one argued for most passionately. As one industry spokesperson said: "Intellectual property rights [patents] are critical to our survival!" This section includes two presentations by persons in the pharmaceutical industry as well as highlights of the seminar discussion which focused on the activists' response to the business position.

The first presentation by Philip Ellsworth outlines why intellectual property rights are considered so crucial by the pharmaceutical industry. Since research and development are essential for discovering new medicines, it must be an ongoing task. The problem, however, is that R & D costs are staggering and only a small number of projects actually result in new products. There must be some incentive to take the risks with the vast amounts of capital needed for R & D and there must be some guarantee that a company will have an opportunity to recover its costs as well as have a return on the investment. There must be some incentive to stimulate people to use their ingenuity and creativity to discover new medicines. It is for these reasons that we have the patent system. Unfortunately, some countries do not enforce patent protection and allow "pirate" companies to steal the discoveries of others for their own gain. Ellsworth discusses the various remedies currently in place to try to curtail this widespread pirating in developed and developing countries.

The second essay by Michael O'Neill argues that patents actually do much more good than harm to developing countries. He discusses six "myths" that seem to be persuasive in arguing against patents and shows how each is fallacious. He also cites three major studies where research is clearly on the side of patent protection as being in the public interest for a developing country.

The discussion summary reveals that activists from the WHO and U.S. consumer groups largely support the notion of intellectual property rights; however, they note that every right has a corresponding responsibility. Do not pharmaceutical companies who are resourceful and poweful have some responsibility to developing countries? Should they give medicines away to the very needy? What should they do? Should not a government ensure that important medicines are available to everyone at a reasonable price? One point of common agreement was that there was a need for a better international forum where these issues might be more fruitfully adjudicated.

Intellectual Property:
The U.S. Concern

PHILIP G. ELLSWORTH

Intellectual property rights refer to our most valuable resource, human intelligence, and the rights we have to the discoveries and inventions of human intelligence. In the pharmaceutical industry there is common agreement that we must protect our newly created products through patents and other safeguards. The U.S.-based pharmaceutical industry spends 16 percent of sales—not profits but sales—on research and development.

In this industry, R & D is the most important component of the organization, for without new products we die. The R & D arms of our organizations are, by far, the most important. They are the fuel that makes our engines go. In a typical year in the 1980s, the U.S. industry spent over 8 billion dollars on R & D. It takes over two hundred million dollars on each product that we launch because we have to pay for our failures as well as our successes. It takes us a long time to get a product to market. From the time the molecule is discovered to the time a related product is launched is ten years. And it takes time to discover the product, to test it, to develop it. Once we do all that, we have to go through all the approval processes with various governments. So a lot of time and energy is spent on developing a product and for that we have a patent. From the time we launch the product, the patent's life has already half expired, so those eight or nine years that we have left to sell are extremely important to us as an industry.

Philip G. Ellsworth is the vice president of international industry and trade affairs for Marion Merrell Dow. With twenty years of experience at Marion Merrell Dow, he recently completed a term as chairman of the International Organizations and Issues Committee for the Pharmaceutical Manufacturers Association.

It is important to remember that our products are relatively easy to make; you don't have to be a rocket scientist to make an active ingredient. All you need are a couple of reactors, a few dryers, and some chemical engineers and some chemists and you can essentially make our products. This is why the patent is so important to the pharmaceutical industry. Without patents we have no way to finance new research and to pay for product development.

"Pirate" is the term used to describe those who ignore patents. "Pirate" refers to the companies who make our products in countries where there is no effective patent protection—Argentina, Brazil, Canada, Chile, Mexico, India, Thailand, and Eastern Europe. We blame the governments. In most cases it is a company that is making and selling our product, but it is the governments in those countries that allow them to do so. And the problem is that the government is sovereign and we are just a company. Since we cannot do anything about it, we go to our government and say, "You have got to help us get protection for our products."

There are three avenues to protect intellectual property: multilateral, bilateral, unilateral. Let me outline some of our successes and failures with these various responses.

The Multilateral Response. GATT, the General Agreement on Tariffs and Trade, is an organization of 100 or so countries that decided they would get together and discuss certain issues, instead of making bilateral arrangements—one country to another. It was through the influence of the pharmaceutical industry, with help from some other high-tech industries, that the question of intellectual property came into the GATT negotiations. GATT is one multilateral approach. WIPO is another, the World Intellectual Property Organization, which is a forum where many countries come together to discuss patents.

The Bilateral Response. The bilateral approach relies on two specific pieces of federal legislation to enforce patent laws, Section 301 of the 1974 Trace Law and "Special 301," a later amplification which provides strong incentives to observe patent protection. After gathering data on how a country is observing intellectual property protection, the U.S. government engages the offending country in discussion, requesting remedial action to protect legitimate patents.

The Unilateral Approach. The unilateral approach is the last resort and relies on the sanctions provided in the legislation. The key sanction is retaliation. Legislation enacted in 1984 allows the president to confer special low tariffs under the system of the General System of Preferences (GSP) on those countries, largely developing countries, that protect intellectual property rights. Legislation in 1988 (Special 301) directed the U.S. government to monitor countries' response to our intellectual property and to compile a list of offenders. The president is directed to take retaliatory action against violator countries.

It may be helpful to review some of the successes and failures in our attempts to obtain patent protection throughout the world. Korea was a success story. Some of the most sophisticated pirates in the world were in Korea, but because we brought an action against them, we essentially convinced them to give us not only patent protection but decent enforcement mechanisms and pipeline protection. "Pipeline protection" is for drugs that are still in the R & D process—between discovery and launch. Whenever we agree with the government to protect intellectual property, we want to be sure that as part of that agreement they protect those products on which we are still working.

Thailand was not such a big success story. They are on the "hit" list of those countries who do not enforce patent protection. They have hemmed and hawed on the matter. Now they are "discussing" ways to give us intellectual property protection, but I don't see them coming along all that quickly.

Brazil was threatened with retaliation under the GSP. Brazil and India were the two leaders in the Third World that everyone looked up to. We would go to Thailand and they would say, "Why are you picking on us, look at Brazil and India." So we knew we had to curtail the violations of one of those as best we could and we went after Brazil because we thought we had more leverage against them. They have come around now and they say they are going to be giving us patent protection. Who knows?

Argentina is about the same as Brazil. Chile is also the same, except that they have actually come up now with some patent laws. We do not find these laws acceptable. Chile may just be stalling for time, but we are not sure and negotiations continue.

We have had bilateral discussions with the Soviet Union, Czechoslovakia, and Poland and we have been promised product protection by the year 1992. There are going to be some problems with the Soviets on the compulsory licensing issue. Under compulsory licensing there is patent protection in the country but the government has the right to grant what they call a compulsory license. The compulsory license arrangement allows the government to decide that it is in the best public interest to provide our products to their citizens at cost or low cost. They then force us to license our products to a third-party local company, giving us in return a pittance of a royalty, 3 or 4 percent, which is irrelevant and not anywhere near the commercial value of what we are being forced to license. This is a problem with the Soviet Union as well as with Rumania, Bulgaria, and others. Hopefully this will be worked out in negotiations.

Canada has a womb to tomb mentality. Until recently Canada insisted on compulsory licenses for all of our successful products. Local Canadian firms, the generics, would watch the launching of products in Europe, to see what products were successful. By the time we got approval to launch in Canada, the generics would have already gotten their dossiers together. They would know exactly what product they were going for; they would make the application for compulsory licensing; and they were on the market just a few months after we were in Canada. After we have spent so much money developing the pharmaceutical product, to have that type of thing going on in a developed country was very unsettling and upsetting. After much negotiation, we now have a situation where they still have compulsory licensing but only if they deem our products to be excessively priced. That is still highly unacceptable and we are still working to change it. Canada has a Third World mindset. It is a problem.

In the bilateral approach, essentially we say, "Look, either you protect our products or we are going to give you some problems exporting your products into this country which is a free and open market. We would like a little parity there." Since we are a big market, we can certainly catch a country's attention. But countries like Brazil would much prefer to be in the GATT forum where they have got a whole range of countries like India who are their natural allies.

What the companies seek is both product and process patents with a minimum twenty-year term. They want reasonable working requirements. Part of having a patent is that we have to work it, we cannot just discover a patent and do nothing. Many countries will say to us, "Well, look, if you don't make it in this country, then we are not going to give you patent protection since you are not working the patent in our country." We are just not prepared to build a plant in every country in the world; it would be financial disaster. We want to be able to bring our product into those countries where we choose not to build a plant.

What do we see in the future? There is a consensus in the major developed countries, and some developing countries, that our products can be patented and ought to be patented. Why should pharmaceuticals be different from shoes, autos, belts, and mousetraps? But there is going to be some difficulty about the conditions for compulsory licensing. While these countries agree there should be restraints on compulsory licensing, they turn around and say, "Yes, but we require the rights to compulsory licensing if we want to provide medicines to our citizens free of charge."

Finally, let us briefly consider what I call "Major Thieves." That is a provocative term, but we believe by circumventing patent protection countries are stealing our products. Countries like India are not going to sign anything and we know that. While we think the multilateral discussions will be productive on paper, the "stealing" will still go on. We will continue to pursue the patent protection issue at the GATT talks, and at any other avenue that seems to hold promise, for the bottom line is this: we have no choice. The very survival of the pharmaceutical business requires that we put an end to the theft of our products and that we continue to invest new funds in research for new products.

Developing Country Concerns
from an Industry Perspective

MICHAEL A. O'NEILL

Pharmaceuticals have played a role in the medical advances of the post–World War II era and a major role in the eradication of many crippling diseases. The patent system has played an important role in the development of innovative medicines. The cost and time today to bring a drug to the market—from a laboratory bench to a pharmacist's shelf—is, by latest estimate, $231 million and about seven to ten years. After this period of testing, discovery, and government regulation, the industry ends up with six, seven, or eight years of patent protection, depending upon how good our scientific studies are. The global realities today require that more and more nations take a responsibility for subsidizing research and development. Over 75 percent of research and development over the last twenty years has been conducted in OECD countries. Research and development that was conducted in Latin America, Asia, or Africa is growing smaller and smaller. In large part, the lack of a patent system explains the diminishing R & D.

In summary, the underlying premise is that recognition of sound intellectual property rights is inextricably linked to development of new medicines and the advancement of medical technology. Before discussing some of the myths surrounding intellectual property rights, I will set the scene by describing the effect pharmaceutical patents have had on the actual experiences in a country. For instance, take the case of Turkey. Once there were twelve pharmaceutical companies operating

Michael A. O'Neill is director, industry and government affairs for Wyeth-Ayerst International, a division of American Home Products. Prior to joining Wyeth-Ayerst in 1987, he worked as a pharmaceutical detailman and as a consultant in government relations.

there. They eliminated patent legislation; now there are only seven. Canada is a classic example of how the curve has gone. In 1969 when Canada introduced compulsory licensing, the number of companies engaged in research and the level of research spending was on a rise. After the introduction of compulsory licensing from 1969 to 1989 (when they put in the new patent act), it declined. We have seen the research increase since the new legislation. Brazil and Argentina are other examples where many research-based drug companies have departed in the last decade. This is particularly so in Argentina where only a handful of R-&-D-based companies remain. By contrast, there are other examples, not in the developing world, where there has been a reverse trend. Within the last ten or fifteen years, Japan, Italy, Ireland, South Korea, and Canada are examples where patents have been introduced. This had a dramatic effect on the expenditure for research and development. The whole level of medical care has increased.

The first myth heard from people who do not think patents have substantive validity or value is this: If you give patent protection, prices will rise substantially and consumers will be prevented from affording medicines. The argument goes that if a "monopoly" is given, companies will raise prices. One of the reasons this just does not happen is that in most instances when there is a new patent law, only truly new innovation is going to be able to qualify for a patent. This might not be true if there is retroactive protection for products not yet approved. The vast majority of products that are going to be eligible for patent protection are going to go off patent by the time any of these laws go into effect. In fact, only a small proportion of products are going to be affected. For instance, less than 3 percent of the registered drugs today in Brazil, or by sales volume approximately 7 percent, would be subject to new patents. Similar figures exist in other developing countries. Also, in any given year, there are probably going to be twenty to thirty new drugs introduced on the market. While these new products are coming on patent, there are others going off patent.

The second myth says that during the patent period covered, there is going to be no competition and this will lead to higher prices. Here the basic fallacy is that patents convey market power, particularly monopoly market power. This myth ignores the fact that a doctor has many substitutes in both the same chemical class as well as the therapeutic class from which to choose in treating a given condition. To carry this further, patents allow innovators the right to capture gains from their innovations. Usually this will take the form of foothold access in a well-developed, highly populated market. It permits sellers in most instances to charge what the market will bear for that product rather than establish their own price. Unless, of course, the strategy of the company is to charge a premium for its product and to enter the market in a much smaller way. But this practice is not common in developing countries given the income levels and the nature of the drug market. Either way, consumers are going to benefit if there is patent protection as it will generate more competition in the market. If this were not the case, modern economies would be highly concentrated and overrun with monopoly power, particularly in the pharmaceutical industry. But if you look at the pharmaceutical industry, as compared with other industries, you find that the largest company in our industry has about 3 percent of global sales. In most instances individual pharmaceutical companies that depend on patents do not have a substantial part of the pharmaceutical market in any given country; the market is very competitive.

The third myth is that a strong generic industry has the effect of keeping prices low. This is not substantiated. I point to one recent example, the case of the Philippines. Two years ago the Philippines introduced a generic law that was put on the books to promote generic prescribing and generic dispensing. It required products to have the generic name in a print size equal to the brand name size and above it. The goal was to have pharmacists publish a list of all brand name products alongside their generic equivalents, with the price, so that people would be encouraged to buy generic drugs. The results, however, two years after the introduction of the law, is that generic companies have raised their prices more quickly than have their brand name counterparts. They have not taken advantage of a situation they were given, an easier access to gain market entry. Second, if you look at consumer behavior patterns, when given the choice of buying a generic at a lower price or buying the brand name product at a higher price, they are telling the pharmacist they will take fewer tablets from the familiar product. There have been a number of newspaper reports on the poor quality of some products. This is part and parcel of the new law, in that the government through this law made it easier for generic manufacturers to set up business. There have been a lot of problems associated with quality control and quality assurance. The doctors have been "up in arms" about this, totally independent from the manufacturers, in saying that this has had a chilling effect on their prescribing freedom. They have galvanized a political lobby to try to change the generics law. In my judgment, there is no compelling evidence that generics automatically result in lower prices. One can refute the argument that if patents are kept out of a country, prices are automatically going to be lower.

The fourth myth is that patent protection will put the generics industry out of business. We don't have evidence to indicate this in developing countries. However, I can point to a couple of good examples where there are viable generic industries—the United States and Germany. Thirty percent of the market in each country is controlled by the generics industry. There is a link between strong patent protection and strong generic industry. It is only logical because generic manufacturers depend upon innovative companies to give them a continual pipeline of new products which, when they go off patent, can be manufactured.

Myth five is the corollary to myth four: that the local infant industries will not be encouraged where there is a patent system. This rationale has been used in places such as India, Thailand, Turkey, Mexico, Venezuela, Brazil, Argentina, Chile, and Indonesia. Here the reality is that the policy creates an environment where fewer local companies survive. I do not deny that. I think that those that do survive generally are stronger and are more powerful. There are some exceptions to this—Argentina is an example. Argentina has had for the past twenty years a very strong generics industry. It is a peculiar case. If you look at their neighbor Brazil, however, in 1969, prior to the time when patents were eliminated, the national firms had 36 percent of the market. Twenty years after the fact, that number is down to 12 to 15 percent. That is a glaring example of the impact that elimination of patents has had. A contrasting example is Italy which is often used by our industry as a model of what patent protection can do. Italy, prior to 1978, had no patents for pharmaceuticals. If you look at the level of research and development spending alongside the level of prices, pre-1978 and post-1978, there has not been a dramatic increase in prices, accounting for inflation. But there has been a dramatic growth, 20 percent annually, for research and development expenditures. That makes a very important statement on the value of pharmaceutical patents for research and development.

The sixth and final myth is that the R-&-D-based industry merely transfers the actual goods and does not contribute to the technological base. This is the whole question of technology transfer that Dr. Antezana discussed earlier. There again, the reality is that the active ingredient, or the finished product, is really the least expensive part of the whole good. What is far more expensive and complex are the medical and scientific services that the innovator offers. The transfer of technology via the pharmaceutical firms is a fairly sophisticated process. For example, the holding of medical symposia, the medical literature that is produced by companies, and clinical research studies conducted in developing countries are all examples of transfer of technology. Transfer of manufacturing is not feasible in many cases due to the inability to generate economies of scale.

I want to turn now to the studies mentioned above. The first was done by researchers at the National Economic Research Associates (NERA). They tried to link the stage of economic development with the strength of patent protection in eighty-seven countries. They found a very strong link between the presence of intellectual property rights and economic modernization. Some examples of what criteria were used to measure modernization and economic development range from the level of energy used in the home to nutritional consumption. The point made is that robust intellectual property fosters technology transfer by facilitating licensing, disclosing innovations, and generating centers for published data. By contrast, in countries in Latin America and Africa where there are little or no intellectual property rights, research and development spending has been very poor when contrasted with the OECD countries I mentioned earlier. The other point studied was on the cost side: What effect does patent protection have on prices of pharmaceuticals in these markets? Economic elasticity studies were conducted to look at demand and how price rises will affect demand. Here the results show there is little evidence of price-level hikes arising from patent protection. Their overall conclusion is that benefits exceed costs by a wide margin. Moreover, using protectionism to develop local industry through import barriers and allowing counterfeiting are ill-fated shortcuts to innovation.

The second study, by the Latin American Economic Research Foundation, an organization in Buenos Aires, was done primarily because Argentina, like Brazil, is in the throes of introducing patent legislation next year. This study took a slightly different route in that it did not do the economic analysis of NERA. But a lot of the conclusions are the same and they address many of the myths I discussed earlier. This study summarized the major arguments for patent protection that have been espoused over the last twenty years. It examined agreements that Philip Ellsworth discussed above, such as the GATT, etc. It also looked at the U.S. Government International Trade Commission report that was done several years ago which found, after a survey of industries, that $24 billion was lost to U.S. industry as a result of inadequate intellectual property rights overseas. Pharmaceuticals accounted for one-eighth of that — $3 billion. There were four case studies in this research which provided a panoply of different experiences. They looked at Mexico, India, Korea, and Italy and assessed the costs and benefits of intellectual property protection in each instance. It was instructive because in the case of Korea there was a sweeping economic liberalization program that has been introduced recently on patent legislation for pharmaceuticals. In India, the case is closed — no patent protection, and a fairly autarkic society with respect to pharmaceuticals. Mexico is in the process of going through a transition from an import-substitution-based economy to an open economy. I have already mentioned Italy. They also looked at Argentina, the twelfth largest pharmaceutical market in the world.

The final study did not discuss pharmaceuticals, but I mention it because there are not many African development organizations that have done studies on patent protection per se and its relevance to Africa. This is a Kenyan-based organization, and the report was published in 1989. Unlike the previous examples, this does not go into pharmaceuticals but it does look at computers, biotech products, and local products from the informal economy. Its conclusions are that a culture has to be developed to place a premium on innovation as a mechanism for enhancing national sovereignty. They call for a certificate system for small-scale intermediate industrial-sector products to supplement a full-fledged intellectual property system. The value of the study is that the basic concern for innovation is similar to the rationale for wide patent protection as a valid policy for governments to adopt with respect to economic development.

Sound intellectual property rights lead to technology transfer and economic growth. These recent studies demonstrate that the benefits over the long haul exceed the cost to consumers and to industry. Patents for pharmaceuticals are not a monopoly given the wide range of choices that doctors have in both the chemical class as well as the therapeutic class. These are all more or less the theoretical bases, but more important is what is happening in today's world. What we are witnessing is heightened patent protection in places across Latin America and Asia. In part, this has been done because of U.S. trade pressures and because of the debate in the GATT. More importantly, it results from domestic political changes we have seen in many countries such as Argentina or Brazil. There is recognition by their leaders that intellectual property rights are inextricably linked with sound economic growth.

Discussion Summary

Lee Preston summarized the situation from an academic perspective.

There is a widespread feeling in this group, and I am sure in this whole area of activity in the world, about the need for the development of some international arrangements and understandings that, being an academic person, I would refer to as a "regime," not a law or a code or a committee but some kind of a way of doing things. Philip Ellsworth's observations, which I found extremely interesting, bear out the notion that the industry sees a very great need for an international regime and is trying to work with GATT on the creation of a regime that would have some features that the industry believes are needed. I am quite prepared to believe that some of those features really are needed in some form.

Others say, "Yes, we do need an international regime, but it has to have some other elements in it too; it can't just have the elements that one party wants, there are other parties with other interests." And so we need to find a forum where we can bring these different perspectives together to discuss compromises coming from this other direction. This makes me think of Paul Belford's comment: "We want the WHO to do more, we want the other organizations, the other interests here, to do more, to come in with us, to participate more." I am prepared to believe that he represents the general feeling on the part of industry. The key is to find a forum in which to establish a regime involving a number of governments and governmental organizations, private business, and users (the users are so important here) in a mode of behavior that we will find more responsive to this complex set of problems than the ad hoc, isolated kind of problem solving we have been doing in the past.

Michael Naughton raised the question of responsibilities.

In your pursuit of intellectual property rights, and I certainly don't think anyone would deny your right to those property rights, what are

211

your responsibilities? With every type of right there is a corresponding responsibility. You went through a whole presentation on rights. What are your responsibilities to your intellectual property rights? What responsibilities can you guarantee to particular governments?

Carol Emerling responded:

A company has to state what its responsibility is. Is it for Nigeria to tell us what its responsibility is, or is it in the corporate province to say that we have a great number of responsibilities and we feel we can discharge them this way? My hunch is that the answer is somewhere between the two. You err when you imply that companies do not *ever* exercise social responsibilities.

There are two companies sitting at this small table of four who have both donated patented products for the good of the Third World. Merck has donated Ivermectin freely to the developing countries. Wyeth company donated the patent on a bifurcated needle to the World Health Organization which enabled WHO to eradicate smallpox worldwide. Corporations are not ignoring their social responsibility, it is just that they want to do it in a way that draws on their expertise.

Tom Carney pointed out the relation of patents and information exchange.

I think we have to go back to why the patent system was instituted. When Abraham Lincoln introduced the patent system, he didn't do it to protect companies. He did it to stimulate genius and invention. It was not to protect people who are going to sell the product, it was to stimulate other people to invent things. The exchange for the monopoly you get is the fact that you give up all the information on your research. When you put in a patent claim, you indicate the exact structure of the chemical compound. This means that everyone in the world knows what you are doing. This has always been one of the main sources of knowing what is happening in the technical field and particularly what your competition is trying to do.

I have been in the pharmaceutical industry since before penicillin. I have seen some changes in the patent system. I have seen some changes in the perceived value of the patent system. In the early days of the pharmaceutical industry we went entirely for protection on the patent system.

Things are changing now, and not for the better. For example, the Japanese are changing their strategy. For awhile there were more Japanese patent applications in this country than there were United States patent applications. That is changing now, particularly in instruments and devices. The Japanese are now refraining from patent applications. They are "potting." They will coat the device or part of the device with plastic so that if you want to get in to see what the device is made of, you have to destroy the device by taking off the plastic. This destroys the idea of having an exchange for a monopoly, an exchange for information. The Japanese now are not giving us information in that particular field, and I am afraid they will follow the same strategy in the chemical field.

When we consider the value of patents, the actual transfer of information is one of the most important things to be accomplished. This stimulates competition.

Prakash Sethi raised the question of trademarks.

The argument was made in the Third World that while some patents may actually be protecting basic innovations, many patents protect what you call "recombinations." These simply are intended to prolong the monopoly.

The second argument is, even after patent protection has lapsed, sometimes the real effect on pricing is negligible because of brand name recognition and the trademark protection that you have. Is it possible for the industry to consider making the trademark name itself generic once the patent is lost?

The trademark is not a patent. Yet it is basically prolonging the life and exploiting the market. Shouldn't the companies let go of the trademark after the twenty or twenty-five years is granted for the patent?

John North explained the importance of trademarks.

There are a couple of things that follow here. One is the legal liability. There is a warranty, at least on a product for most of these companies, that if you prescribe it under the conditions set out in the package literature there is an implied warranty that the company will stand behind the product. Once you surrender your trademark, it becomes a liability question.

The other thing is, in reality, in 80 percent of the world there are price controls at the generic level whether you have that trademark or not; the power is in the hands of the pharmacist. You may write for the brand name but at the level of reimbursement, he probably is filling it at a very different level. So, in fact, the patent name is set aside to some extent.

Michael O'Neill agreed:

The whole purpose of a trademark is to create customer recognition, customer trust. Customers know that after buying that product, following its patent life, there is something upon which they can rely. The confidence of the physician likewise is valuable, and should remain after the patent has expired.

Alberta Edwards placed the cost of drugs in the context of overall health care.

We haven't done a very good job in explaining the economics of our industry. It is repeated over and over again that, "You've gotten your money back on that particular product." That isn't the way companies work. We are not trying, at this point, to just recoup what we have put into that one product. For one thing, most of us do research in a certain therapy area; in the early stages we don't allocate the cost to one product or another, rather we do research in the therapy area. What we are trying to do through a patent and its protection is to finance our research for future products. Therefore this argument that we always hear—you've gotten your money back on this product, or it didn't take that much money to do research—misses the point. We are trying to finance all the research of all the products that may never see the light of day, and for all the products that are going to take eight or twelve years to develop. Thus, recovering extra funds on one product isn't really the relevant point. If that is all we did, we wouldn't be doing research for the next one.

In discussing corporate responsbility, we need to be aware of the fact that pharmaceuticals are the most economic way of treating many illnesses. Therefore if we are concerned about cost containment, we should not concentrate on the price of one product. We should concentrate really on what it costs to treat the certain indication. Under the old system, without the new drug, it may mean that you have to be in the hospital for two weeks before you can be cured. If you get a new drug, even if it is an expensive drug, you may be able to either not go to the hospital at all, or you may get out in three or four days. In other words, there are many costs associated with illness that go far beyond just the cost of the drug. Often an expensive drug will save society and the hospital and the health system in a country a great deal of money.

Paul Maxey expressed the need for new drugs.

Those of us in the ideological world fondly wish that the companies with their research and development would spend a part of their time researching and producing products that would effectively treat diseases in sub-Saharan areas. Those governments and people will never be able to pay for that research and development themselves. Earnings from other products could be used for funding. That would be seen by the world at large as a responsible pharmaceutical industry response.

Hans Wolf suggested the need for incentives in addition to profits.

It seems to me there are two forces that motivate people and companies to do something. One is the sense of moral responsibility and the other is an economic incentive. We have been talking entirely about the moral responsibilities of companies to do things and I think we probably don't go far enough. But we haven't talked at all about what sort of incentives the society can provide to get companies to promote the common good. American industry has expended tremendous resources and innovation on the space program because there was an incentive to do so. It seems to me that governments have a similar opportunity to provide an incentive for research in the areas you just cited. We ought to think about how we can motivate governments to do that.

Philip Ellsworth:

I would like to take a double deduction for every dollar spent on tropical disease research.

Hans Wolf:

There are tax incentives, there are research contracts, there are all sorts of rewards that can be given to motivate people to do something. We learned in Eastern Europe that unless there are economic incentives, things don't happen.

Jacqueline Corrigan questioned the time period covered by patents.

Regarding the length of patent protection in the U.S., there is a seventeen-year patent protection. You were talking about twenty years for the GATT. Other people are talking about different terms. We also have the issue that trademarks can actually, in effect, extend the patent. Is there a median that might meet some of the concerns of the NGOs and the developing countries for a shorter patent term, recognizing that, in effect, it can be lengthened by the trademark?

Tom Carney explained considerations affecting the patent time period.

Many times when a pharmaceutical product is being developed, it is in the development process ten years before the patent is issued. So by the time the product gets on the market, there are only seven years or so left. There is a precedent and a law of regulation where some patents can be extended today for an extra three or four years if they are important and if there has been a delay as a result of FDA action in getting it on the market. So I think the twenty years is just an effort to try to make up that slack, particularly in the pharmaceutical industry, for those products.

PART 3

The Kenyan Experience
First World Medicine
in a Third World Setting

The role of pharmaceutical firms in a country is best understood as a critical component of total health care. As clearly demonstrated in the workshop interaction presented in Part I and Part II of this volume, the delivery of that health care in the poor countries of Africa, Asia, and Latin America is in desperate straits. The Kenyan field work was undertaken in order to ground our discussion in a specific situation, to understand more fully the interaction between pharmaceutical corporations and the broader health care issues in the context of a specific country.

Kenya was chosen as the study site because the government there has demonstrated a greater openness to First World influences than many others in Africa. Moreover, First World medicine is well established as an option for dealing with ill health. Beyond that, the study group participants had a close previous association with Kenyan missionaries.

Part III begins with the centuries-old practice of traditional healing, moves to use of First World medicine introduced around the turn of the century, and then to the present structure of pharmaceutical distribution and its meaning for multinationals. In the field reports, there is an attempt to present the circumstances as lived by the Kenyans and observed by our field team with a minimum of value judgments.

In the first paper Violet Kimani draws us into the practice of traditional medicine. A recognized authority on Kenyan traditional medicine, Kimani traces its physical and cultural role from the concept of causation of illness through diagnosis and treatment. Kimani's respect for traditional medicine and its potential contribution in overall health care is evident.

John Thorp takes the next step — the incorporation of First World curative health care in Kenya. Following an anthropological view of the Kenyan socio-economic background, Thorp describes the government and the missionary facilities which, along with a small number of private hospitals and clinics, constitute the First World medicine of Kenya. He details the structure and problems in managing the government's extensive system of health care — accounting for two-thirds of the nation's health facilities — and the church-related institutions. Specifics about a rural mission hospital portray the depth of the problem in providing medical care to Kenya's remote areas.

Against this background of traditional and modern health care, we turn to the distribution of pharmaceuticals. Gerald Moore outlines the use of essential drug kits by the Kenyan government as an attempt to reach the remote areas. Moore was the consultant to the Kenyan government on this project. Joan Devane, S.C.M.M., presents the pharmaceutical distribution program which she initiated and manages for Christian Health Services of Kenya. Her comments sharpen our awareness of the distribution issue and the potential for private voluntary organizations.

There are two sets of respondents to the Kenyan case. One from Africa and the other from industry. Thomas McDermott, C.S.C., and Mutombo Mpanya respond to the Kenya discussion from an African perspective: McDermott as a missionary, Mpanya as a native African. The industrial response reflects the meaning of the Kenyan situation and similar developing country conditions for the multinational manager. Susan Crowley focuses on infrastructure, quality control, marketing, and information flows. Steven Bauer addresses the "inescapable realities" molding research-based pharmaceutical strategies.

The discussion summary is a compendium of the participant interaction following the Kenyan papers and responses.

The final section in Part III, by Lee Tavis, presents the findings from the Kenyan field interviews across the private and governmental delivery systems in Kenya. The data are outlined as presented by the informants followed by an analysis of the issues. Tavis concludes with the implications for the developmentally concerned multinational pharmaceutical manager.

Traditional Medicine

VIOLET N. KIMANI

A variety of health care systems exist and function to serve the health needs of communities in contemporary Kenya. A sick person has various options to which he or she may turn for the management of the illness. The patient's pattern of seeking health care will be determined, to a large extent, by the nature of the illness, the perceived severity, and the concept of causation and meaning of the illness as well as the availability and accessibility of the health care resource.

The range of options available includes self-treatment with simple, homemade preparations and remedies; shop medicines; consultation with trained Western-oriented health care providers based at institutionalized facilities such as hospitals, health centers, and dispensaries; and seeking the services of traditional health specialists.

Each of these options can be broken down further into specific specialities and institutional levels. Self-treatment, for instance, is used here to refer to simple remedies such as salt solutions taken to relieve an upset stomach, chewing roots and leaves to ease constipation, etc. These ailments do not require the services of a specialist. The majority of mothers know how to prepare these remedies for their unwell children. The shop medicines include all the pain relievers: panadols and aspirins, antimalarials, and a variety of cough syrups stocked in most grocery shops and kiosks. Anyone can buy these items over the counter since no prescriptions are required. The chemist shops are in another category and, therefore, not included with shop medicines.

The Western-oriented health services range from the dispensary at the lowest level to the hospital at the highest level. In between are

Violet N. Kimani is a professor in the Department of Community Health at the University of Nairobi. She has worked with many communities across Kenya on their beliefs, practices, and the current status of traditional medicine for over a decade.

219

health centers and cottage hospitals. The government owns roughly 60 percent of these, while the various churches own about 30 percent; the rest are privately or municipally owned. Church health services charge a small fee, private health services charge a large fee, and government health services are free.

Traditional health care is not institutionalized. In this paper, a traditional healer refers to anybody, male or female, who practices any form of preventive, curative, rehabilitative, or promotive health care and who has no recognized qualifications in terms of scientific, Western-type medicine. Traditional midwives are included in this category. She or he may be a full-time or part-time practitioner. Traditional medicine has distinct specialities such as divination, herbal, surgical, orthopaedic, fertility, psychosocial, and cultural therapy. The healers extract most of their medications from plant, animal, and mineral substances available within their environment, and these will be referred to as herbal medicines. It must be noted that some of the medications are only potent in ritual therapy in accordance with a community's belief system. A scientist trying to establish their pharmacological value would, therefore, become rather skeptical.

Traditional health care is by no means static. In the urban environment, traditional healers tend to become generalists who cover problems pertaining to the habits and social expectations of heterogenous populations (Good, Kimani, and Lawry). They charge high fees in monetary form for all their services. In the rural environment, the healers are more often specialists in one or two areas such as divination and the preparation of herbal medicines or anti-witchcraft protection and fertility. They serve the community for a reasonably small fee which may be in cash or kind, according to the patient's ability to pay. Traditional health care has been with the people since the beginning, but Western-oriented health care was introduced into Kenya around the turn of the century when European missionaries and colonial administrators penetrated the country.

Unfortunately, the colonial authority did not attempt to understand the sociocultural significance of traditional healing or even distinguish it from magic and witchcraft. All forms of traditional health care, prophecy, divination, religious supernatural and ancestral forces were all categorized together as witchcraft and, therefore, evil. As far back as 1925, the witchcraft ordinance was passed in Kenya to deal with the harmful power of witchcraft. Christian followers were discouraged from any association with traditional beliefs and practices. These misconceptions were indoctrinated into the minds of Kenyans, especially the well educated and the Christian, so that even today, when they wish to consult a healer, and actually do so, they are never open about it. Some even deny knowledge of its very existence. Studies conducted in both rural and urban areas show that an individual's background in terms of level of education, religious orientation, occupation, and economic status do not necessarily hinder the use of traditional health services when a real need arises (Good and Kimani). During political campaigns, some candidates are known to try anything to get elected to Parliament. They consult fortune tellers and perform oathing rituals to bind people to vote for them.

CONCEPT OF CAUSALITY

When an individual falls sick, the immediate kin, and sometimes the community, take a collective responsibility to seek health care and identify factors of causation so they may take precautions to prevent recurrence of the illness. Based upon the community's socioreligious beliefs, the effects of the supernatural and ancestral world and the world of the living are interrelated. The underlying factors must be corrected even after an illness has been appropriately managed at the biological level. For instance, diarrhea may be caused by drinking bad water, but the community may argue that the particular individual, or his or her family, may be getting punished by God or the ancestors for social misconduct such as theft, unfaithfulness, or lack of respect to one's parents.

Among the Tharaka people of the Meru district in Kenya, the concept of disease causation embraces two major levels: natural illnesses and illnesses of interrelationships (Volpin). Tharaka people believe that Western biomedical health care is more effective in the management of natural illnesses, while traditional health care is better at dealing with diseases of social interactions. Therefore, people will use both Western and traditional health services for the same or different illnesses to cater to both the natural and the social implications. The traditional healers (*Mugao* [singular], *agao* [plural]) report that they have no conflict with Western biomedicine.

The Pokot people from the Rift Valley province of Kenya view the causation of illness as a dynamic phenomenon, embracing various planes of reality. It is possible, among the Pokot, that one and the same illness may be perceived as caused by natural physiochemical processes, social, and spiritual forces, all focused on the patient's condition. A disease is, therefore, caused by a chain of events (Nyamwaya).

The Akamba people of the Machakos and Kitui districts are monotheistic and recognize God (*Mulungu* or *Ngai*) as the creator and preserver of all living things. *Mulungu* is an impersonal, distant force beyond the daily affairs of ordinary people. Some diseases, however, are attributed to him. The spirits of the ancestors (*aimu*) figure much in the religious beliefs and behavior of the Akamba people's well-being and everyday living. The spirits can cause diseases, especially chronic ones, infertility, madness, and misfortunes. Through divination an Akamba traditional healer (*mundu mue*) contacts the *aimu* to learn the hidden cause of the illness so that he may, in turn, advise the patient appropriately (Good). The *aimu* illnesses may be manifested physically in the individual who breaches social order or who behaves inappropriately to his or her child or to other direct family members.

Other causative factors can be traced to witchcraft and sorcery (*uoi*) and through physical contact, as in infectious diseases. The Akamba recognize allergy as another cause of some illnesses. Among the Agikuyu of central Kenya, the concept of disease and illness causality embodies beliefs in:

1. Natural and God-given illnesses — these include seasonal changes, accidents, and vector-borne, water-borne, and other biological infections.
2. Supernatural, spiritual, and ancestral forces and the consequences of breaching social order and religious-based obligations; infertility, some forms of mental disorders, chronic poverty, and series of calamities and misfortunes may result.
3. Strained social relations, dishonesty, conflicts, tensions, and jealousies with kin group or members of the community may also be responsible for sexually transmitted diseases, madness, infertility, and death as a result of sorcery and witchcraft (*urogi*).
4. Individual bodily weakness, heredity, lack of resistance, and allergies are reported as the causes of many of the contagious diseases such as tuberculosis, frequent coughs and colds, and even asthma.

The belief systems of all the above communities, and of many other African communities not cited here, show that disease causality among Kenyans encompasses physical, metaphysical, and personalistic theories. The community interviewed reported that the majority of diseases and illnesses are community based and are all preventable through environmental sanitation, social harmony, and obedience to religious and other supernatural obligations.

DIAGNOSIS AND TREATMENT

The individual who decides to seek the services of a traditional health care practitioner often gets advice from family and friends as to the most reputable healer. Rarely does the sick person consult the services of a healer alone; he or she is accompanied by a relative or close friend. The healer listens to the patient and takes a detailed history of the illness and social background. For instance, the healer may ask for the name of the patient's clan and that of the spouse. The belief behind this is that the different clans portray various personalities and attitudes, and an individual is a product of that clan.

The healer, especially one based in a rural community, should have an expert and updated knowledge about all the cultural beliefs and traditions. Some clans are not allowed to intermarry and, if such regulations are ignored, the individual and family concerned may experience health problems. Only the healer would be in a position to sort out the root cause of the problem and prescribe a corrective course of action.

Among the Agikuyu, the healer (*mundu mugo* [singular], *andu ago* [plural]) is the most highly respected person in the community. Traditionally, he would have received his "calling" from God (*Ngai*). Quite often he would be said to inherit the aptitude for healing (*ugo*) from a close relative (Good, Kimani and Lawry).

A child destined to become a *mundu mugo* is sometimes said to have been born holding divining counters (*mbugu*) in his hand. In later childhood or adulthood, the "calling" to the profession is manifested through a series of events, misfortunes, calamities, or even dreams, directed either to the candidate or to members of his family. When the signs of *ugo* have been verified by several experienced *andu ago,* the candidate is initiated into the profession through a solemn ritualistic ceremony lasting for three days. A major part of this ceremony involves taking an oath to observe the ethics of the profession. If he should break this oath the consequences would be instituted by the supernatural, so a healer is very unlikely to cause harm to the community.

Divination of a *mundu mugo* involves saying prayers to God, asking for his divining gourd (*mwano*) to be blessed so he can accomplish successfully the task before him. He shakes the *mwano* and pours out the counters (*mbugu*). He scrutinizes the number that fall out, as well as the pattern formed by the *mbugu,* and confirms his interpretation of this pattern through asking the patient and her or his companion(s) more questions. He may repeat this several times to be quite sure. Once he is satisfied with his diagnosis, he prescribes herbal remedies to manage the physical aspect of the illness. He may prepare the medicines himself or refer the patient to a specialist herbalist for the prescriptions. Usually a *mundu mugo* possesses the required skills and knowledge to manage all the aspects of healing by himself. Referral of patients to another colleague is done only in rare cases. Depending upon the nature of the illness, the *mundu mugo* may prescribe a number of substances. An inventory of some of these substances and their effects on selected illnesses is given in Table 1. Once the biomedical condition has been managed, the healer turns, in the case of some illnesses, to ritual healing which may involve a sacrifice to appease the supernatural, psychotherapy, ceremonies of reconciliation with the wronged party, and prayers. The herbal medications are taken only by the individual patient but the ritual usually also involves the patient's family.

ICHAGAKI SUBLOCATION: MURANG'A DISTRICT

The health-seeking behavior of a rural community in the Murang'a district of central Kenya, one of the districts inhabited by the Kikuyu, was observed between April and June 1987. A sublocation is the smallest administrative unit in a district. Kenya has forty-two districts, varying in size and population density.

The Ichagaki community is approximately one hundred kilometers northwest of the capital city of Nairobi. A tarmac road connects the sublocation to the city but the service roads within the sublocation are unpaved. There are about 261 people per square kilometer and orthodox health services are within easy reach. A rural health training unit, one of only six in the whole country (one in each province), is nearby at Maragua. The district hospital is six kilometers away from this community along a tarmac road. A system of dispensaries and clinics under the management of the church, government, and private doctors is within a radius of three to ten kilometers. The church dispensary is in the Ichagaki Catholic Missionary Center and the privately owned clinics, as well as two pharmacy shops, are in Maragua. Other shops in Maragua and smaller markets stock a wide range of pain relievers, antimalarials, cough syrups, and antacids. Several traditional healers are based also in this community.

One of the objectives of the investigation was to establish the community's awareness and use of the various types of health services accessible to them. Judging from the outpatient attendance at the various health units and the reports from the health personnel at these units, it became evident that there was much use of the orthodox health facilities in the area. The health personnel reported that the average daily outpatient load was between 400–600 at the Maragua rural health unit alone. The dispensaries and missionary clinics had an average daily load of between 100–150 patients. As observed in an earlier study of traditional health care in a low-income housing estate in Nairobi (Good and Kimani), the majority of patients were women and children, especially women of child-bearing age.

Government and church-owned facilities offered both curative and preventive health care, free of charge. The preventive services included immunization, health education, and maternal health services. The consumers tended to prefer curative to preventive and promotive health services.

From the consumers' own reports and observations at the tradi-

TABLE 1

Medicinal substances	Disease/illness condition
Surgical operations	Drain boils
Uvulectomy	Chronic coughs and tonsillitis
Purgatives & emetics to induce vomiting	To release constipation and food poisoning
Steaming with boiled eucalyptus leaves	Feverish conditions, measles, headaches, severe malaria
Lemon juice mixed with black tea	To treat diarrhea
Dried droppings of lizard (put into infected ear)	Otitis media
Mother's milk (squeeze into infected eye)	Ophthalmia neonatorum (infantile eye infection)
Yellow leaves of ihūrūra (boil in water, cool & put into infected eye)	Conjunctivitis
Cutaneous incisions	Dizziness & chronic headaches
Suture with thorns and fibre of *mutundu* bark	Open fresh wounds

tional healers' "clinics," about one third of the community had sought the services of a healer at least once in the recent past, either for themselves or for a relative. The illnesses they had presented to the healer included infertility, polio, general bodily pains and malaise, joint pains, and amaemia (described as generalized edema, a condition believed to "turn the blood into water"). Abdominal pains and a succession of deaths in a family were other problems whose cures were sought from a healer. Besides the herbal and other medicinal prescriptions, the community reported that only the healer could identify the underlying causative factors, perform curative and preventive rituals as well as provide advice to be followed by the afflicted family to avoid recurrence and remove social strain.

The respondents felt that collaboration of the two major systems of health care, orthodox and traditional, was overdue. The time had come for health providers to exchange professional knowledge and arrange for patient referrals between the two systems.

To assess the people's knowledge of the morbidity patterns in their environment, in-depth interviews about endemic diseases and their causes were conducted with all the adults in each household visited. The reported causes appear to have been both biological and social. Some of the perceived causes may not be scientifically correct but the reasons given are based on the people's observations. The responses are summarized in Table 2. While there was no dispute that a link existed between malaria, mosquitoes, and water, cerebral malaria was sometimes referred to as "familial malaria." The ancestor spirits may intervene in a case of misconduct and moral faults such as disrespect to one's parents.

TABLE 2

Reported Endemic Diseases and Causes

Endemic Disease	Rank	Perceived Causes
Malaria	1	Mosquito bites, drinking water from unfamiliar spring
Pneumonia	2	Advanced malaria
Respiratory infections	3	Cold wind, seasonal weather changes
Abdominal pains	4	Bad water and bad food
Sexually transmitted diseases	5	Sexual dishonesty
Malnutritional disorders	6	Poverty
Traffic accidents	7	Witchcraft
Cerebral malaria	8	Disrespect of parents
Ophthalmia neonatorum, "Maitho ma nda"	9	Infant's eyes infected in the womb

Asked how the community could collectively prevent malaria, it was reported that spraying against mosquitoes, keeping the compound free from tall grass and bushes, draining stagnant water, and observing social obligations were all interrelated factors. Biomedicine from orthodox health facilities was efficacious in treating malaria but the services of a healer were necessary to rule out the possibility of cerebral malaria. Many other illnesses were viewed in a similar manner but malaria is used here as an example.

Close observation of the small community described above showed differing behavior in seeking health care: many options were available and used.

A category of therapists who seem to take advantage of the situation for their personal gain exists in both rural and urban areas. They are neither scientific nor traditional specialists but tend to borrow from each system in an unscrupulous manner. Some are fortune tellers, palmists, and astrologers who use impressive titles such as "professor" and "doctor" and who advertise their services extensively through the local media. Others administer injections and push antibiotic capsules acquired through illegal means. They give wrong advice to their clients, such as to use a little powder from the antibiotic capsule to treat almost anything from open wounds to fever and abdominal aches. This category is not included under traditional health care, but its existence is noted.

Since traditional health care is so important in the minds of Kenyans, anyone interested in the development of health care in Kenya cannot afford to ignore it. Although the examples used here are limited to one rural community, earlier studies among many other Kenyan communities reveal a similar picture. Traditional healers could be useful in filtering and referring patients to the institutional health facilities. A study of the role of traditional healers in ophthalmology in Kenya showed that they all could diagnose cataract but reported that there was no known traditional cure for this condition (Kimani and Klauss). If the healers were educated as to the possibility of cataract operations in hospitals, they would then refer many such conditions to the hospitals.

SELECTED REFERENCES

Good, C. M. 1987. *Ethnomedical systems in Africa,* New York: Guilford Press.
Good, C. M. and V. N. Kimani. 1980. "Urban Traditional Medicine: A Nairobi Case Study." *East African Medical Journal* 57, no. 5.

Good, C. M., V. N. Kimani, and J. M. Lawry. 1980. "Gukunura Mundu Mugo: The initiation of a Kikuyu Medicine Man." *Anthropos* 75.

Kimani, V., and V. Klauss. 1983. "The Role of Traditional Medicine in Ophthalmology in Kenya." *Social Science and Medicine* 17, no. 22.

Kimani, V., and J. Olenja. 1987. "The Effects of National Programs of Nutrition and Primary Health Care on the Health-Seeking Behaviour of Families. Unpublished report.

Nyamwaya, D. O. 1979. "Societal Response to Illness: The Pokot of Kenya." Institute of African Studies, University of Nairobi, Paper No. 127.

Volpin, D. "The Concept of Health and Illness among the Tharaka of Kenya." Conference Paper, University of Nairobi.

Modern Health Care in Kenya

JOHN P. THORP

SOCIOECONOMIC CONTEXT

Kenya's population of 20 million persons (Mwagiru & Njue 1986:42) inhabit 224,000 square miles of ecologically very diverse land in East Africa. Of this population 90 percent is directly or indirectly dependent upon agriculture, and 87 percent resides in the rural area of the country (Mwangiru & Njue 1986:125,42). Two-thirds of Kenya's territory is arid or semi-arid; approximately 75 percent of the population lives in the remaining one-third of the country which is agriculturally productive. These areas (see Figure 1) are concentrated in the southwestern third of the country and along the seacoast.

The critical factor in agricultural productivity in Kenya is the presence of water, most of which is provided in the form of rain by the Indian Ocean monsoons both along the coast and at the higher elevations in the south central and southwestern sections of the country. Coffee and tea are the major cash crops along with some large-scale wheat farming (see Figure 2). In the prime agricultural areas known in the colonial period before 1963 as the "White Highlands" (see Figure 3), corn and dairy farming are the major forms of production for local consumption. Beans, peas, and potatoes round out the traditional diet. Cattle herding occurs in areas of lower agricultural productivity.

At the national level Kenyans produce enough food to provide

John P. Thorp is the department head of social sciences at Ferris State University. A cultural anthropologist, Thorp has conducted studies in Bangladesh and the Philippines where he served as the anthropologist for the field research on the role of a multinational agribusiness in the southern reaches of the island of Mindanao undertaken in 1978 by an earlier study group of the seminar, "Multinational Managers and Developing Country Concerns."

Figure 1   *Kenya: Population Distribution*

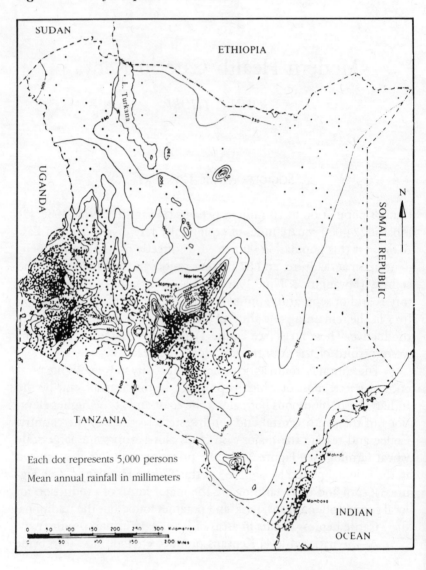

Each dot represents 5,000 persons
Mean annual rainfall in millimeters

Figure 2   Kenya: Distribution of major cash crops

KEY

Rice	
Pyrethrum	
Sugar	
Cotton	
Tea	
Coffee	
Wheat	
Cashew Nuts	

Figure 3   *Land use in the former 'White Highlands'*

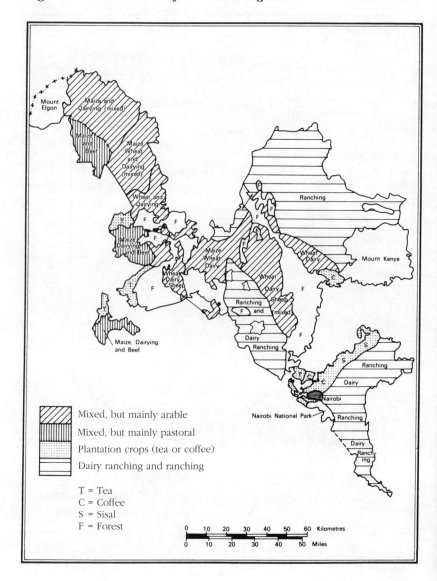

sufficient nourishment for the entire population. However, reports (Mwabu & Mwangi 1986:776) indicate that one-third of all Kenyan households are food poor. Although being food poor is not limited to the quarter of the population who inhabits the semi-arid and arid regions of the country, this segment of the population does live with regular food scarcity as a result of having to support itself through nomadic pastoralism.

British colonialism established the administrative structures in the country and instituted the pattern of greater government interest in those areas with the most naturally productive resources. Administratively the country is divided into eight provinces and forty-one districts including the municipalities of Nairobi and Mombasa (see Figure 4). Since 1984 the districts have become the focus for routine administrative decision making and development activities.

The districts range in size for Marsabit at 30,146 square miles to Kirinyaga at 555 square miles which are roughly comparable to South Carolina and Los Angeles, California. The eight districts of the Central and Western Provinces represent only 4 percent of Kenya's total land area, but they have 27 percent of the country's population. The smaller the districts, the higher is their agricultural productivity, their population, and the level of government services such as schools and health facilities. The extent of the economic and social infrastructure in the districts of the Central Province and the relative prosperity of the populace is in marked contrast to the arid and semi-arid districts. The low level of development in these areas certainly qualifies them to be categorized as typically "Third World." They are at a distinct natural disadvantage even in comparison to an indisputable Third World country such as Bangladesh. However, in Kenya the areas of high agricultural productivity and population concentration evidence a degree of prosperity that makes the appellation "Third World" at best questionable in their case. As Third World countries go, Kenya is relatively well-off, but its population is growing at a very rapid rate (4 percent annually) which cannot but threaten the current levels of differential prosperity in the various regions of the country.

MODERN HEALTH CARE

In the First World people presume that being "healthy" is the normal state of affairs. When someone is not, the sick person seeks a

Figure 4   *Present provincial boundaries as proclaimed at Independence, December 1963*

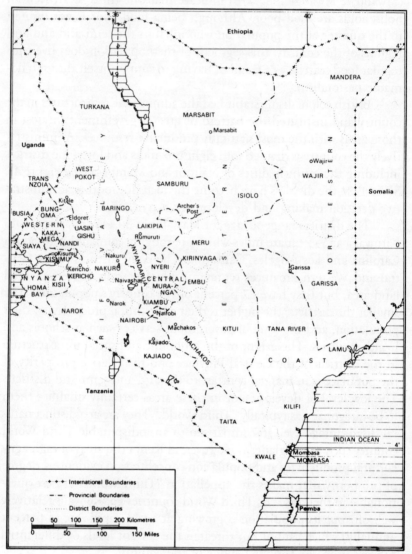

medical cure for whatever disease is afflicting his or her biological organism. Western medicine translates ill health entirely into bio-chemical terms and emphasizes the biological aspects of this human condition (Helman 1985:923). The delivery of health care is organized hierarchically with the "expert" at the top of the hierarchy of health workers, and diagnostic procedures and treatment are technologically dependent (Eisenberg 1977:14; Good et al. 1979:147). People in the Third World live in much closer proximity to the forces of nature, such as drought, without the technological controls or barriers available in the First World. Instead of being the norm, therefore, being "healthy" in the Third World is an ideal to be striven for. Illness is a more pervasive condition which must be managed as part of the entire social context in which it occurs. Typically, illness is not considered to happen to individuals but to occur within social groups. Traditionally relief is sought for the whole community of persons affected by the presence of a sick person. A choice of experts is available to the community whose procedures are largely psychological and ultimately aimed at relieving the social disorder introduced into the community by the sick person's condition. If the condition is not improvable, the community is conditioned to cope with it. Unfortunately, Western observers of Third World societies in Africa usually consider this communal pattern of response to ill health as "witchcraft" or "sorcery," and dismiss traditional healers as "witchdoctors."

In Kenya, modern medical practitioners with their various levels of training have all been accepted as different types of complementary health care "experts" alongside traditional practitioners. By one estimate modern medical practitioners of all categories, however, make up less than 5 percent of the total number of health care workers presently active in Kenya (Nyamwaya 1987). Nevertheless, even with its restricted emphasis on curing disease in the individual sick person, modern medical health care has become an important component in the ordinary Kenyan's way of dealing with illness.

In the face of illness, Kenyans can attempt self-medication by informally consulting with friends, relatives, and/or neighbors. A host of over the counter products are readily available. Prescription drugs are also available to a limited extent from illegal dispensers of various sorts (Wasunna & Wasunna 1974:161–163; Good & Kimani 1980:302). However, if the problem is at all acute or long standing enough, expert assistance is sought. Traditional practitioners, healing churches, and modern medical practitioners separately and concomitantly are utilized.

A handful of private hospitals exist in the larger urban areas, but they serve an essentially European, Asian, and elite African clientele. Further, individual doctors, who may also be employed in the government system, run private clinics in urban areas; but since their fees are high, the bulk of the population is unaffected by this source of modern medicine (Hartwig 1979:124). In large urban areas, at least, the ordinary person also has access to government-trained practitioners (medical assistants, enrolled nurses) who have left government service and have set up their own private, "illegal" practices (Thomas 1975:269). The vast majority of the population, however, utilizes the government and church-related systems of dispensaries, health centers, and hospitals for primary modern health care. These institutions, and especially church-related hospitals are the focus of this analysis.

Medical Institutions

Modern health services originated in Kenya largely to serve the needs of the colonial establishment, both military and civilian. Health services for the ordinary rural Kenyan were almost exclusively provided by the missionary Christian churches before independence, despite numerous colonial plans to assume responsibility for general health care (Hartwig 1979:125; Beck 1981). Since independence, the government has had to create a national system of health facilities almost from scratch to complement the church-related facilities that were already established. Although the system is not yet complete, it is well developed, at least in the most densely populated and agriculturally productive areas of the country.

The hospital is the fundamental unit in this system. These hospitals are organized pyramidally with the 2000+ bed Kenyatta National Hospital in Nairobi as the country's apical teaching, research, and referral unit. Provincial hospitals are second level referral hospitals. District and non-government hospitals are the functional curative institutions in the system. However, Kenyatta and the provincial hospitals also spend a significant proportion of their energies on primary curative care through their out-patient departments.

Non-government hospitals include church-related hospitals, private for-profit hospitals, company hospitals, and military hospitals. Church-related hospitals make up more than 60 percent of these institutions (Government of Kenya 1983:35), and they are the only ones generally accessible to the majority of the population. They participate fully in the government patient referral system through district and provincial hospitals to Kenyatta Hospital.

A system of Rural Health Units (Mwabu 1986:315) which are designed to put basic curative and preventive services within easy reach of the rural population is subordinate to the hospital system (see Table 2). A rural health unit has a health center as its headquarters and four or five dispersed dispensaries. The unit is designed to serve a population of 50,000–70,000 persons. Each health unit is supervised by the doctors at the district hospital. A health center offers in-patient care for ten to twelve persons, and out-patient services. A center is staffed by one clinical officer (non-degreed medical training), one public health officer, two family planning field workers, one statistical clerk, and attendant staff. (If in-patient facilities are absent but staffing is the same, the facility is a sub-center.) In a dispensary, an enrolled community

TABLE 1

Hospital Beds per 1,000 persons, 1983

Province	No. of Hospitals			No. of Beds			1983 Est. Population	Beds per 1000
	Govt	Others	Total	Govt	Others	Total		
Central	13	31	44	1843	1467	3310	2,596,000	1.28
Coast	16	7	23	1881	370	2251	1,495,000	1.51
Eastern	11	17	28	1475	1574	3049	3,027,000	1.01
N.Eastern	3	—	3	228	—	228	428,000	0.53
Nairobi	7	12	19	2882	1461	4343	958,000	4.53
Nyanza	7	30	37	1563	1445	3008	2,825,000	1.06
R.Valley	21	27	48	2665	1804	4469	3,675,000	1.22
Western	5	11	16	694	1165	1859	2,019,000	0.92
Total	83	135	218	13231 (59%)	9286 (41%)	22517	17,023,000	1.32

Source: Ministry of Health 1983a:7.

TABLE 2

Rural Health Facilities, 1982

	Health Centers	Dispensaries
Government	242	872
Non-Government	39	362
Totals	281	1234

Source: Ministry of Health 1983:6.

nurse and a public health officer and attendant staff provide a limited range of most basic curative and preventive services (Mburu et al. 1978:212). Both health centers and dispensaries are provided with ration kits of medicines assembled from a list of forty essential drugs and meant to provide a month's supply of medicines (Moore 1982:197). Both dispensaries and health centers refer more complicated cases to the district hospital, but it is not unusual for a sick person to skip them entirely and go directly to the hospital out-patient department. Nongovernment health centers and dispensaries are staffed in approximately the same way as government facilities at least in regard to curative services. However, their supply of medicines depends upon their relationship with their sponsoring hospital or agency.

The government has developed a large-scale, district-based, integrated system of primary health care institutions with referral institutions for more specialized cases. More than 30,000 persons operate this system (Ministry of Health 1983:8). The government feels the number of people in this system (see Table 3) is significantly lower than it should be and is skewed to the urban population. Seventy-five percent of all doctors work in urban areas where only 14 percent of the population lives (Ministry of Health 1983:8–9).

Personal emoluments and related expenditures are the single largest recurrent hospital expenditure (see Table 4). In 1983 total emoluments including housing and leave allowances, and pension contributions amounted to 58.2 percent of recurrent expenditure. As more

TABLE 3

Human Resource Levels, Needs, and Training Capacity

Human Resources	1983 Level	1988 Needs	Annual Training
Doctors	835	2,100	100
Dentists	79	66	abroad
Registered Nurses	2,347	6,000	200
Enrolled Nurses	7,696	12,000	500
Clinical Officers	1,251	2,720	100
Public Health Officers	374	(?)	30
Public Health Technicians	1,420	4,750	450
Pharmacists	86	320	25
Pharmaceutical Technologists	304	820	35
Laboratory Technicians	525	849	75
Laboratory Technologists	282	429	45

Source: Ministry of Health 1983a:8,51–54.

personnel are trained for this system, an even larger percentage of recurrent expenditure will go to employee compensation. The second largest category, Medical Stores accounted for only 21.5 percent of expenditure.

The government health system is regularly faulted in the literature for being inadequate (Mburu 1981; Kaufman et al. 1982; Mwabu & Mwangi 1986). For the Ministry of Health, however, more troublesome than expanding its system are the problems of actually operating the facilities which do exist. Of most concern are the frequent drug shortages faced by all the institutions throughout the system because of unrealistic budgeting, untimely or incorrect distribution, lack of availability in the supply system, and the circuitous requisitioning system. Furthermore, the government's inability to actually provide complete and free health care is not limited only to drugs. Half the existing rural health facilities are in disrepair (Ministry of Health 1983a:6). A large proportion of the Ministry's vehicles and equipment are inoperative because of inadequate maintenance personnel and spare parts (Ministry of Health 1983a:12). In 1983 (see Table 4) only 2.8 percent of recurrent expenditure went to both operating and maintaining vehicles, and only 0.4 percent went to maintaining medical equipment. New equipment, on the other hand, constituted 3 percent of recurrent expenditures. Shortages of mattresses reduce the number of hospital beds actually useable, and lack of operating tables prevents surgery.

TABLE 4

Recurrent Hospital Expenditures, 1983

	K$000	%
Personal Emoluments	413,637	58.2
Medical Stores	152,945	21.5
Food	38,857	5.4
Transport	20,176	2.8
Elec & Water	25,844	3.6
Linen	6,370	0.9
Stationery	3,159	0.4
Medical Equipment	21,580	3.0
Maintenance	2,665	0.4
Travel & Accom.	9,958	1.4
Postage	4,082	0.5
Other	11,662	1.6
Totals	710,905	99.7

Source: Ministry of Health 1983b.

Stationery can also be in short supply which compromises record keeping, care plans, and drug prescribing. Nevertheless, in comparison to other Third World countries Kenya is significantly above average in the percentage (7.5% for 1978–82) of expenditure in the national budget devoted to health care (International Monetary Fund 1984). The government has an extensive system of institutions with trained staff, but these resources are seriously underutilized. Although medical personnel receive regular salaries and benefits, they are often unable to assist sick people because of insufficient supplies and/or inoperative equipment.

Besides problems within its own health facilities, the government's relationship with non-government institutions is an uneasy one. This is especially true between the government and church-related institutions. General political issues affect this relationship; only the churches and the government span the whole national society and give some functional reality to the term "nation" (Hartwig 1979:124). Clergymen are occasionally outspoken critics of the government. More particularly, problems in the distribution of institutions and uncertainty about continued, adequate government grants to church-related institutions mark the relationship between government and the churches.

Church-related health facilities are self-supporting, fee-for-service institutions, but fees do not cover expenses. Significant outside sources of revenue are necessary. The tradition of government grants to these institutions began in the colonial period and continues today. For most institutions even the combination of fees and government subsidies does not come close to meeting expenses, and outside (usually overseas) contributions are necessary to operate. The churches know they provide a quality product especially to the less affluent which the entire system needs and the government could not duplicate, and they have pressed their case with the government.

In the Ministry of Health's (1983a:32) development plan for 1984–1988 grants to church hospitals were scheduled to remain essentially the same through 1986–87, but they were to be reduced by 38 percent for 1987–88. In 1984 representatives of the churches' national coordinating agencies, the Kenya Catholic Secretariat and the Protestant Church Medical Association, privately petitioned the government to increase rather than decrease their allocations. They argued that their budgeted allocation of only 3.4 percent of the government's recurrent hospital expenditures should be increased. By their estimate church-related hospitals provided 40 percent of all hospital beds excluding Kenyatta Hospital. They pointed out that if they were compensated for their services at the rate the government pays for its own services, they would receive 26.2 percent of recurrent hospital expenses. They also pointed out that their 1983–84 allocation was 11 percent less than 1982–83, but their expenses had risen by 24 percent. They concluded by asking for an allocation of 10 percent of recurrent government hospital expenses. Instead of increasing its support to church-related institutions, however, the Ministry of Health has continued to cut back on its allocations. Indications are that the government has carried through with its plan to reduce subsidies for 1987–88 by 38 percent or more. In all likelihood, church-related institutions will see their government subsidies continue to decline. The government is so hardpressed to support its own facilities at appropriate levels that its current development plan raised the possibility of instituting fees-for-service (Government of Kenya 1983:47–48). With such a radical departure from post-independence principles being contemplated, church-related institutions cannot expect to receive larger government grants. Maintaining the current level of support may not even be possible.

The second area of tension concerns the distribution of institutions. Historically the church-related institutions were the first to be located in rural areas, and with some exceptions the government has built its system around the church-related institutions (Hartwig 1975: 153). However, the church representatives in their 1984 petition to the Ministry of Health also raised questions about government plans for four institutions which were duplicating church-provided services. On the other hand, church-related medical institutions tend to be located in areas where the sponsoring church has large and established congregations of members. Expansion of these congregations results in new medical facilities being established, regardless of other government or non-government institutions already in existence (Opuka 1979). Despite the existence of national coordinating agencies for the Christian churches (Kenya Catholic Secretariat and the Protestant Church Medical Association), local churches are still independent. They can and do make decisions as narrowly in their own best interests as they choose.

Medical Practice

Medical problems are generally the result of either faulty biological equipment, organic competition from "germs," or misuse/overuse of the biological organism. A significant proportion of the causes of morbidity and mortality in Kenya (Table 5) is the result of organic com-

TABLE 5

Cases of Morbidity and Mortality

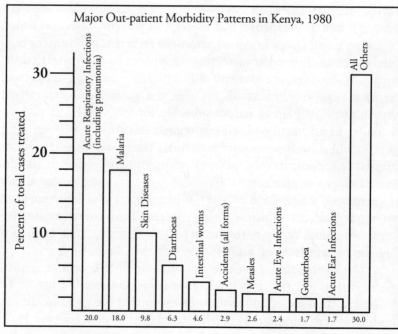

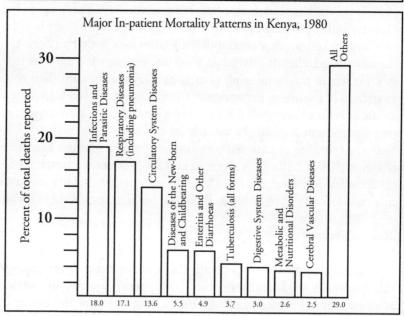

Source: *Ministry of Health 1983 a3.*

petition from hostile organisms. The vast majority of these problems are preventable through vaccination and environmental sanitation. Budget estimates between 1983 and 1987, however, targeted only 6 percent of all recurrent expenditures to preventive services (Table 6). Some movement toward improving preventive services is observable especially through the Kenya Expanded Program of Immunization, Mother and Child Health Care Programs, and Community-Based Health Care programs. Because of institutional inertia, however, for the forseeable future curative medical practice carried out through the hospital system will continue to dominate the medical scene in Kenya.

In the agriculturally prosperous districts of Kenya the complete range of licensed and unlicensed treatment options is available to a sick person and his or her relatives. Although self-medication with legal over the counter medications (or illegally dispensed prescription drugs) is a readily available option, Kenyans prefer consultation with some kind of medical practitioner, and in most cases with more than one practitioner. People can choose between a government dispensary/clinic, pharmacy, traditional healer, private clinic, government hospital, and a church-related hospital. They usually do so on the basis of accessibility, quality, and past experience (Mwabu 1984). Severity, length of illness, and age/sex of the patient are important variables in determining which combination of options will be utilized. The more severe an illness is, the more willing people are to expend time and money obtaining quality care. As Mwabu (1984) points out and our interviews without

TABLE 6

Aggregate Recurrent Budget Estimates 1983–1988

	K$000	%
Curative Services	2,897,323	64
Rural Health Units	439,088	10
Training	407,901	9
Preventive Services	259,948	6
Administration	243,347	5
Research	228,709	5
Medical Stores, Quality Control & Equipment	51,207	1
Nat. Hospital Insurance	27,937	1
Totals	4,555,460	101

Source: Ministry of Health 1983a:32–33.

exception reconfirmed, church-related facilities are considered the highest quality care providers. Positive interaction with staff, same-day service, and the ability to complete treatment by obtaining medication are frequently cited to explain even poor Kenyans' willingness to pay for treatment in church-related hospitals when an illness is considered serious enough.

In the agriculturally less productive districts of Kenya the same decision-making process seems to be operative, but the range of options is considerably restricted. A church-related facility (dispensary/clinic, or hospital) may well be the only available option besides the traditional healer. Even though payment (token though it usually may be) is required, persons who are relatively deprived by Kenyan standards do not begrudge it to the institution because of their faith in the quality of care that they will receive. A brief case study of one such church-related facility illustrates the nature of this quality care.

Ortum Mission Hospital

This hospital is located in the peripheral, semi-arid, and mountainous district of West Pokot which is 3,500 miles square with a population projected for 1988 to be over 200,000. [All general references to the district are from Hendrix 1985.] Nine percent of the land is suitable for agriculture; the majority of this land is located at the higher elevations in the southern and central sections of the district (Figure 5). Another 28 percent of the land is only marginally suited for agriculture because of uncertain rainfall. Forty-four percent of the land is considered rangeland, and semi-nomadic herding of goats, cattle, and sheep is important throughout the district. At the lower elevations and especially in the westernmost section of the district 70 percent of the households are thus engaged. More than one-third of all residents are predominantly pastoralists. This mixed subsistence pattern results in a fairly high degree of mobility throughout the district and even across an international boundary on the part of men and older boys in search of sufficient pasture.

The socioeconomic infrastructure in the district is not well developed. All-weather road communication between the district headquarters at Kapenguria on the extreme southern edge of the district and the nearest sizeable town (Kitale) further south was only established in 1981. By 1983 this tarmac road was extended 73 miles through the southeastern third of the district and on to the next district head-

Figure 5

West Pokot District topography

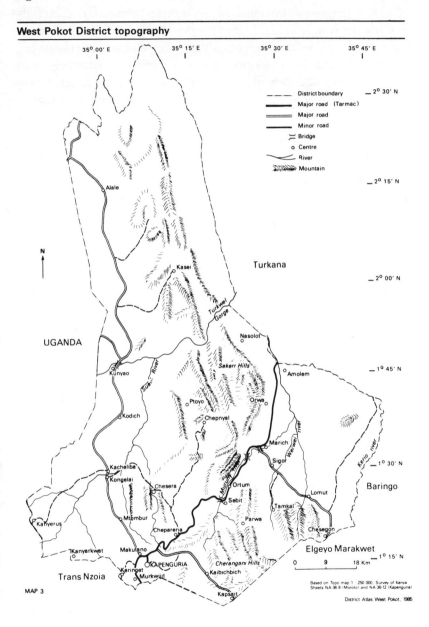

MAP 3

Based on Topo map 1 : 250 000, Survey of Kenya
Sheets NA-36-8 (Moroto) and NA-36-12 (Kapenguria)

District Atlas West Pokot, 1985

quarters. The rest of the 565 miles of road are all unimproved and frequently impassable even in a mint-condition landrover. Regular public transport is only available on 91 miles of these unimproved roads. Electricity is not yet available anywhere in the district. Telephone service is only available in and around the district headquarters. Primary schools number 202, of which the Ministry of Education directly sponsors 19; the remainder are sponsored by the churches. The churches also sponsor four of the five secondary schools and all five of the village polytechnics in the district. According to the census of 1979 only 25 percent of the men and 10 percent of the women have had any formal schooling.

The government district hospital supervises three health centers and seven dispensaries with three more dispensaries under construction. One hospital, one health center, and eight dispensaries with two more under construction are sponsored by the churches. One private clinic operates at the district headquarters. Functional mobile clinics in the district are provided almost entirely by the churches because of a lack of reliable government transport. For example, in 1983 the government mobile clinics saw less than 3 percent of patients attending such clinics. The situation has not improved significantly in 1987. At least 42 percent of the population lives more than four miles (government recommended walking distance) from any service point including mobile clinics. In some parts of the district 85 percent are more than four miles from any medical care delivery point. The average distance from the health centers and dispensaries to the district hospital is 53 miles, with a range between 15 and 100 miles. The average distance to the mission hospital is 33 miles, with a range between 10 and 80 miles (Nyamwaya 1982:208).

A major negative health factor in this district is the precarious nature of the food supply. Drought and livestock diseases over the past decade have caused serious malnutrition to be commonplace, especially among children. One estimate places the mortality of children under two years of age at 216 per thousand, which is more than twice the national average. The general pattern of mortality and morbidity in this district is typical of Kenya as a whole. Malaria and upper respiratory diseases are the two largest problems. Gastroenteritis, measles, eye infections, tuberculosis, sexually transmitted diseases, kala azar (insect-borne parasitic disease attacking liver, spleen, or lymph nodes), and typhoid are common. Cholera is not unknown. Spontaneous abortions and complications in giving birth are common non-infectious problems.

Abscesses needing surgery and seriously infected cuts, bruises, burns, and broken bones are frequent.

Resistance to disease and infection from injury throughout the general population is low, and the presence of individuals who are ill within the basic social unit is common. A significant body of traditional knowledge and practice (Nyamwaya 1982) exists among the population to deal with the presence of illness in the extended family and throughout the clan. An important part of initiation into adulthood is the communication of knowledge about the common herbal remedies. Some individuals develop more specialized knowledge throughout their lifetimes: men as religious healers and women as herbalists and traditional birth attendants. Modern medical practitioners have also come to be accepted as one more complementary source of assistance in the on-going, culturally sanctioned pursuit of self-care. Ortum Mission Hospital is an important contact point for receiving this assistance. That it is church-affiliated is in no small way important because a spiritual level of causation is critical to the indigenous explanation of illness (Nyamwaya 1982:144). Even though most of the people of the district are not Christian, the image of the healer who prays is very familiar.

Ortum (altitude 4000 feet) is located along the Muruny River which is one of the few permanent water sources in the district, and it is surrounded by the Cherangani Hills which rise dramatically to altitudes of 11,000 feet. Ortum is approximately the midpoint of the new and only tarmac road in the district which descends the Cherangani Escarpment from Kapenguria to the plains of the Turkana desert. Ortum Mission Hospital began operation in 1956 as part of a newly established mission outpost of the Roman Catholic church under the administration of European religious. Today, besides the parish and the hospital, the mission center includes residential boys' and girls' primary schools, a residential boys' secondary school, and a village polytechnic. The hospital facilities too have expanded from the original single structure which is still in use as general male, female, and pediatric wards to include a maternity and neo-natal building, surgery and laboratory, and associated staff housing (Figure 6). In 1978 Misereor built an administration and out-patient building, the nursing school, and its associated hostel.

Despite Ortum's remoteness, the lack of electricity, telephones, mail service, and a market only once a week, the hospital is a very busy place (Table 7). Beds in the hospital total 134 which is about average for Roman Catholic hospitals (Kenya Catholic Secretariat 1985:1). In

Figure 6

Ortum Mission Hospital

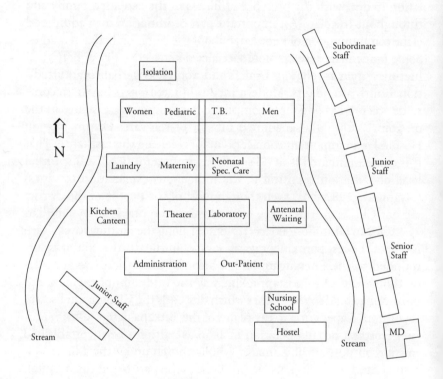

1986 admissions numbered 5,038 which was the largest number ever and a 50 percent increase over 1983 when the tarmac road was completed. All of the wards, except maternity and the special care neonatal unit, regularly have more than one person to a bed. In the pediatric ward sometimes as many as three will share a bed. Not included in these figures are the adults who accompany small children and infants and share space with them. Older children and adults are also regularly accompanied by other family members who camp on the hospital grounds.

The hospital and the nursing school are staffed by 68 persons, 35 of whom are medical personnel. Twenty student nurses also work in the wards as part of their training. Keeping the hospital adequately staffed is a continuous and difficult problem. Doctors are recruited from volunteer organizations in Europe. Five of the eight registered nurses are European and one is from another African country. Only at the enrolled nursing level and in the technical and domestic positions is the hospital staffed by Kenyans. With the exception of the domestic staff and the two paramedicals, all are from other districts of the country; therefore, they do not speak the local language. Turnover of staff is extremely high, especially among the non-local Kenyans, because of the remoteness of the area and the severity of the climate. The entire enrolled nurse/midwife staff changed between 1985 and 1986. In 1986 the number of registered nurses also dropped from twelve to eight. When the hospital succeeds in recruiting non-Kenyans, long delays in getting them approved and licensed by the Ministry of Health and the Nursing Council are not unusual. Since the professional staff lives at the hospital, no one is ever really off duty. In comparison to the dis-

TABLE 7

Admissions, Occupancy Rates, Deaths, 1986

	Beds	Admissions	Occupancy	Deaths
Male	16	854	160%	56
Female	12	680	142%	
Pediatric	23	1,775	180%	127
Tuberculosis	13	261	134%	28
Isolation	6	136	84%	—
Maternity	34	1,109	64%	14*
Neonatal	10	223		50
Antenatal	20**			
Totals	134	5038	123%	275

*stillbirths
**self admission, checked by staff only
Source: Ortum 1986.

trict hospital (Table 8), Ortum is woefully understaffed. Nevertheless, morale among staff members is remarkably high despite the workload. All the senior staff interviewed here and elsewhere worked in a mission hospital because they wanted to. A dedication to genuine patient care seemed to motivate staff members. In church-related hospitals patient care is the regular order of business. Informants with experience in government hospitals opined that lack of equipment, medication, and concern compromised patient care in government institutions.

The hospital staff regularly faces a wide variety of diseases (Table 9) and treats seriously complicated cuts, burns, and broken bones, many of which ultimately result in amputation. Malaria has become the most serious cause of disease in the district due to ever-increasing chloroquine resistance. As an over the counter drug, chloroquine is easily available and is regularly used in insufficient dosages rather than taking a full course of treatment. In some cases quinine (if it is available) is now necessary to arrest this disease. Tuberculosis remains rampant as well, but with increasing knowledge more people are seeking treatment. Because of the length of the treatment, however, the default rate of approximately 40 percent is very high. Kala azar is particularly troublesome for the hospital staff. This disease is life-threatening without pentostam to treat it. This drug is extremely expensive (K$1340 per course), and it is frequently unavailable. During the research thirteen persons were slowly dying because of the unavailability of the medication.

More striking than what people suffer from is who suffers. Chil-

TABLE 8

Staffing of Ortum and District Hospitals

	Ortum (134 beds)	District (150 beds)
Medical Doctors	3*	4
Clinical Officers	2	11
Registered Nurses	8	21
Enrolled Community Nurses	3	16
Enrolled Nurses/Midwives	13	41
Phys. & Occup. Therapists	—	4
Public Health	2	1
Pharmacy	—	5
Laboratory & Radiology	4	12
Clerical	5	18
Subordinate Staff	28	68
Totals	68	201

*one more than usual because of a husband and wife team
Sources: Ortum 1968; Kapenguria 1984

dren and infants account for 55 percent of the non-maternity admissions. With the exception of tuberculosis patients, children also stay in the hospital the longest, averaging better than 8.9 days (13.5 in isolation). Children and infants arrive at the hospital when their diseases are well advanced, frequently extremely dehydrated, and sometimes with secondary illnesses such as pneumonia. Further, more than two-thirds of the 275 deaths in the hospital were children and infants. By contrast a slightly larger church-related hospital in the economically prosperous Central Province (see Table 15) experienced only 135 deaths, 27 percent of which were children or infants. This is just one graphic example of the difference between the developed and peripheral areas of Kenya.

The hospital is also responsible for an extensive out-reach program (Table 10), which is at least partly responsible for the steady increase in the number of hospital admissions. Besides the hospital's own out-patient department and Mother and Child Health Clinic, which is responsible for antenatal and postnatal care as well as immunizations, the hospital operates a mobile unit which provides the same services two times a month in ten locations from 6 to 35 miles from the hospital. A Tuberculosis Follow-Up Program tracks patients released from the hospital, and educates ex-patients' relatives and neighbors about the

TABLE 9

Morbidity Statistics 1986–1983

	1986	1985	1984	1983
Malaria	2,164	2,188	1,758	1,368
Upper-Resp.	1,266	1,005	457	688
Gastro-Intes.	917	847	1,281	851
Tuberculosis	484	225	239	259
Measles	328	304	142	166
Kala Azar	143	59	132	193
Typhoid	135	84	1	—
Venereal Dis.	108	105	122	13
Meningitis	55	49	59	63
Trachoma	39	36	53	16
Inf. Hepatitis	20	11	13	18
Chick. Pox	20	1	1	—
Brucellosis	19	2	—	—
Tetanus	13	7	10	2
Bilharzia	2	2	—	—
Polio	1	—	—	—
Influenza	—	73	14	3
Mumps	—	3	7	34
Whooping Cough	—	35	—	14

Source: Ortum 1986.

disease. In the process other cases are also identified. A Community-Based Health Care Program is also in place in six communities. Groups of ten to twenty families create their own volunteer health committee which chooses a volunteer to be trained as their community health worker. Each volunteer then educates his or her families about the causes and ways of preventing common diseases. The program staff initiates the process of health committee formation, trains new volunteers, and offers refresher courses for active volunteers. The goal of the staff is to initiate and make the program functional in at least one new community each year. Finally, 1986 marked the first full year the hospital operated a dispensary at Chepareria which is a major population center in the district. Adding this dispensary increased the number of patients seen by modern medical personnel 65 percent over 1985.

The expenses associated with supporting the various activities and programs are substantial. In 1986 personal emoluments made up 55 percent of all expenditures (Table 11). This is approximately the same percentage that government hospitals expend on salaries (Table 4) and is to be expected since the government sets the pay scales for all medical personnel. These scales are currently being adjusted upwards. At Ortum the 1986 expenditures were 16 percent higher than 1985, and 1987 expenses in this category increased by 24 percent. As in government hospitals, Medical Stores is the second largest category of expense. However, a significantly smaller percentage is spent on medicines here than in the government budget: 11 percent in comparison to almost

TABLE 10

Outpatient Services 1986

Ortum Outpatient	Attendances	Re-attend	Totals
Male	2,800	958	3,758
Female	2,021	546	2,567
Children	4,799	987	5,786
Antenatal	570	1,899	2,469
Mother & Child	1,017	397	1,414
Mobile Unit			
Adult & +5 Child	1,299	1,739	3,038
Children −5	1,238	2,698	3,936
Antenatal	930	1,670	2,600
Mother & Child	2,698	1,739	4,437
Chepareria Dispensary			
Adults	8,578	3,680	12,258
Children	4,086	1,023	5,109
Totals	30,036	17,336	47,372

Source: Ortum 1986.

22 percent by government. A combination of factors suggest themselves as an explanation. Besides malnutrition, one extremely knowledgeable informant estimated 70 percent of the district's medical problems would be eliminated by safe water. Another informant referred to "soap and water" as the basic medication needed in this environment. In most cases basic medications are extremely effective. Penicillin and chloramphenicol by one estimate are the two most used drugs. Pharmacy records also indicate significant tetracycline use. Visual inspection of pharmacy stocks indicate a reliance on generics produced outside of Kenya. Careful buying of a limited list of pharmaceuticals produces the desired results in this physical and social environment. A final comparison with government hospital recurrent expenditures concerns operating vehicles and maintaining equipment. Ortum spends 11 percent of its outlay in these two categories. Government hospitals on average expend only 3.2 percent on maintenance and transportation (see Table 4).

Funding for the hospital's activities comes from four major sources: overseas contributions and donated services, government grants, patient fees, and training fees from the nursing school (Table 12). In 1986 overseas income and donated services accounted for 52 percent of income, government grants for 23 percent, patient fees for 11 percent, and nursing school fees for 9 percent.

For fiscal 1987 income was seriously reduced. Most significantly, overseas contributions declined by 41 percent because of fewer success-

TABLE 11

1985, 1986, and (partial) 1987 Expenses

	1985		1986		1987
	K$000	%	K$000	%	K$000
Personal emoluments	1,309	50	1,523	55	1,890
Medical Stores	345	13	310	11	514
Food	261	10	272	10	327
Transport	187	7	160	6	173
Electricity and Water	133	5	150	5	133
Linen	108	4	68	2	70
Stationery	98	4	104	4	135
Maintenance	95	4	130	5	104
Travel and Accommod.	42	2	29	1	33
Postage	3	—	9	—	?
Other	27	1	23	1	24
Totals	2,608	100	2,778	100	?

Source: Ortum 1986.

ful grant applications. In the 1984–1988 Development Plan the Ministry of Health indicated it was going to reduce grants to church-related hospitals by 38 percent. The grant to Ortum actually went down by 48 percent. Patient fees did increase for 1987 by 39 percent largely because of greater effort to actually collect out-patient fees and by charging for drugs according to the following schedule:

Penicillin	250 mg.	K$ 0.50 per cap.
	500 mg.	1.00 per cap.
Chloramphenicol		15.00 per inj.
	tabs	50.00 per course
Gentamycin		10.00 per inj. (child = 4.00)
Ampicillin		2.00 per cap.
Crystapen		4.00 per inj. (child = 2.00)
P.P.F.	inpatient	40.00 per course
	outpatient	50.00 per course
Eye ointment		5.00
Ear drops		10.00
Hydrocortisone		17.00 per inj.
Blood transfusion		50.00 then 30.00 per
IV fluids		50.00 then 30.00 per
Outpatient Department		5.00 per consultation
Inpatient admissions		50.00 per week

NOTA BENE: *double for National Health Insurance*

TABLE 12

1985, 1986, and (partial) 1987 Income

	1985 K$000	%	1986 K$000	%	1987 K$000
Overseas Income	1,106	44	1,231	43	723
Donated Services	254	10	269	9	380
Government Grants	651	26	665	23	345
KCS Grants			66	2	147
Fees: Out-Patients	45	2	65	2	104
Clinics	28	1	23	1	19
In-Patients	129	5	157	6	246
Maternity	47	2	68	2	66
Training School Fees	191	8	246	9	166
Local Income	37	1	25	1	63
Other Income	41	2	5	—	90
Nat. Hosp. Insurance	5	—	15	0.5	26
Totals	2,534	101	2,835	99	

Source: Ortum 1986.

Two things are remarkable about this schedule. First, the NOTA BENE at the bottom means that if anyone has the obvious ability to pay for service, they are charged to subsidize those who do not have secure monetary income. (National Health Insurance is available only to those who earn K$1000 or more per month.) Second, on the basis of a very fragmentary and cursory comparison of Central Medical Stores' prices, wholesaler prices, and retail prices in the Central Province, the medication prices in this schedule are higher even than retail in the Central Province. For the most part the hospital purchases its drugs wholesale from commercial pharmacies in Kitale (50 miles) and Eldoret (75 miles) rather than Nairobi (275 miles). Significant transportation costs figure into the prices the hospital must pay.

The actual collection of fees falls far short of what this schedule would produce if everyone paid in full. In 1986 on the basis of total in-patient days, admission fees should have produced K$334,257 without drugs or laboratory charges. The hospital actually realized only 47 percent of that amount. New patients at the hospital's out-patient department and at the dispensary totaled 22,854. This should have generated K$114,270, but the hospital only realized 58 percent of that. Although the number of in-patient days and out-patient attendances for 1987 are not available, they were not significantly greater than in 1986. Even if the hospital had realized full fees in 1987, this increase would not have made up for the reduction in the government grant.

Fees do not and cannot support the level of patient care available in this hospital. Overseas contributions and donated services are essential to operating this institution. How long the ex-patriate religious order of women who have traditionally supplied the registered nursing staff for the hospital and nursing school can continue to do so remains to be seen. Without their presence in the hospital, their contacts with European voluntary agencies, and their fund-raising expertise, quality patient care would not occur at Ortum Hospital.

Most important of all is their presence. Informants employed in this and similarly administered hospitals elsewhere in Kenya were unanimous in believing that the Sisters' presence was essential to the continued provision of quality patient care. One informant gave two examples contrasting care at Ortum and at the district hospital. A former hospital employee who became pregnant out of wedlock bled to death during childbirth at the district hospital because of a lack of blood for transfusions. If she had come to Ortum and the ordinary transfusion pack was not available, she would have been transfused syringe-by-syringe full as long as needed and donors were available. Second, district hospital staff are now reluctant to deal with any patients without rubber gloves (which are not available) because of their fear of AIDS. At Ortum, on the other hand, careful attention and close interaction, especially in pediatrics, are expected. During the research several children were critically ill and not all of them were expected to survive, but they did because of the intensity of the care they received. Due to staff vigilance one child was even resuscitated in the middle of the night.

Ortum Mission Hospital is located in a difficult environment which has been particularly harsh during the decade of the 1980s because of drought. Even without the drought, caring for patients whose language few understand and whose customs as pastoralists are entirely foreign even to the Kenyan staff is very demanding. To provide this care with compassion needs the example of the dedicated service and conviction provided by the Sisters. One of them gives expression to this spirit in the following poem.

> I saw drought
> On the face of the earth,
> Vast stretches of brown earth
> Or raw red dust.
> No cloud in the sky,
> Unrelenting sun, scorching sun,
> Scorching sun.
>
> I saw famine
> On the famished herd
> Weary herd, licking the ground,
> Glad to find a twig, a leaf, a weed.
> Dumb beasts 'neath the sun.
> Unrelenting sun, scorching sun
> Scorching sun.
>
> I saw hunger
> In the silent stare
> Of the thin man.
> No words between us
> Words are not food 'neath the sun
> Unrelenting sun, scorching sun,
> Scorching sun.

I saw my heart
Dried too, helpless.
"God," I cried, "do not forget
This earth you made,
Now in pain 'neath the sun
Unrelenting sun, scorching sun
Scorching sun."

. . . .

I saw hope
In the rainbow span,
God's promise to everyman.
Joy of cloud, tears of rain
Watered earth to yield again 'neath the sun
Gentle sun, sobered sun,
God's own sun.

Ortum, Mutomo, and Consolata-Nyeri Hospitals

Quality care comes at the price of great personal dedication which is willingly paid at all the church-related institutions visited during this research. Church-related hospitals, however, do not all face the same challenges in providing this care. Considerable difference exists between hospitals in peripheral areas and those in prosperous areas. A comparison of Ortum with one other "peripheral" hospital and with one "prosperous" hospital demonstrates significant issues in the provision of modern health care in Kenya.

Mutomo hospital in Kitui District, a peripheral area east of Nairobi, displays approximately the same profile as Ortum in terms of facilities, expenditures, and income (Table 13). Ortum and Mutomo

TABLE 13

Facilities and Services, 1986

	Ortum Hospital	Mutomo Hospital
Beds	134	150
Medical Staff	55	61
Support Staff	33	37
Gen. Admissions	3,929	4,590
Mat. Admissions	1,109	995
Out-patients	47,372	43,515
Deaths	275	220

Source: Ortum 1986; Mutomo 1986.

hospitals are approximately the same size and have equivalent staffs. Mutomo does have a slightly higher rate of general admissions. At least two variables are part of the explanation for this. First, communications within Kitui District are not as difficult as they are in West Pokot which makes it easier to transport patients to Mutomo hospital. Second, the drought in West Pokot has forced a significant but unknown number of men and boys to drive their herds into Uganda to find pasture. Ortum's patient population is, therefore, at least temporarily reduced.

The expenditure profiles of these two hospitals (Table 14) are very similar with the exception of the amount spent for pharmaceuticals. Mutomo spends twice as much as Ortum for medicine. Why this is so is at least partially explained by the fact that Mutomo, although located in an economically peripheral area of the country, is not as isolated from the socioeconomic prosperity of central Kenya as is Ortum. The cost of transporting medicine to Mutomo is, therefore, less. However, a more complete explanation probably lies in the way the doctors feel they are expected to practice medicine by a more socioeconomically aware population.

Mutomo and Ortum (Table 15) have almost the same income for 1986. However, the sources of this income differ in two areas: overseas contributions and patient fees. Overseas income for both hospitals is essential for providing the current level of quality care. Overseas income was higher at Ortum in 1986 because of their successful pursuit

TABLE 14

Expenditures for 1986

	Ortum Hospital K$000	%	Mutomo Hospital K$000	%
Emoluments	1,523	55	1,594	54
Medicines	310	11	743	25
Food	272	10	236	8
Elec-water	150	5	144	5
Med. Equip.	—	—	—	—
Transport	160	6	79	3
Travel	29	1	12	.4
Linen	68	2	18	.6
Postage	9	—	39	1
Stationery	104	4	—	—
Maintenance	130	5	27	1
Other	23	1	49	2
Totals	2,778	100	2,946	100

Source: Ortum 1986; Mutomo 1986.

of a large development grant. Mutomo obtained no such grants but made up the difference through patient fees. Almost 40 percent of its total income is generated by fees, even though the area is not economically prosperous. Ortum is trying to increase its collection of patient fees, but it will be a long time before this source of income is comparable to Mutomo's collection of fees. In 1987 Ortum experienced a significant decline in its overseas income because of reduced grant support. Ortum's budget deficit will only increase unless it can increase its overseas monies. Mutomo and Ortum illustrate the dependence of peripheral, church-related hospitals on overseas assistance to provide quality care. However, when these hospitals are compared to a church-related hospital in an economically prosperous and more densely populated region of the country (Table 16) striking differences are obvious. Consolata-Nyeri has almost half-again as many beds as either Ortum or Mutomo, almost twice the staff, but 15 percent fewer general admissions, and almost double the maternity population of the peripheral hospitals.

The way Consolata-Nyeri spends its money is also different from the two peripheral hospitals. Consolata's emoluments are not significantly higher than the peripheral hospitals because the major increase in its staff size is at the subordinate level, and it has twice the number of nursing students. What Consolata spends on food, however, is five times as much as either Mutomo or Ortum spends. The difference is

TABLE 15

Income for 1986

	Ortum Hospital		Mutomo Hospital	
	K$000	%	K$000	%
Overseas	1,231	43	782	27
Donated Serv.	269	9	173	6
Gov. Grants	665	23	704	25
Church Grants	66	2	—	—
In-patient Fees	157	6	567	20
Out-patient Fees	65	2	277	10
Maternity	68	2	257	9
Clinics	23	1	—	—
Nat. Hosp. Insur.	15	.5	21	.7
Training School	246	9	40	1
Local Income	25	1	—	—
Other Income	5	—	32	1
Totals	2,835	99	2,853	100

Source: Ortum 1986; Mutomo 1986.

TABLE 16

Consolata-Nyeri

FACILITIES AND SERVICES, 1985

Beds	206
Medical Staff	92
Support Staff	71
Gen. Admissions	3,605
Mat. Admissions	1,661
Out-patients	43,004
Death	135

Source: Kenya Catholic Secretariat 1985.

EXPENDITURES, 1986

	K$000	%
Emoluments	2,793	32
Medicines	3,409	40
Food	1,134	13
Elec-water	161	2
Med. Equip.	93	1
Transport	133	2
Travel	30	.3
Linen	46	.5
Postage	44	.5
Stationery	143	2
Maintenance	528	6
Other	83	1
Totals	8,603	100

INCOME, 1986

	K$000	%
Overseas	34	.3
Donated Serv.	324	3
Gov. Grants	987	10
Church Grants	—	—
In-patient Fees	2,020	20
Out-patient Fees	1,845	19
Maternity	1,026	10
Clinics	—	—
Nat. Hosp. Insur.	3,193	32
Training School	108	1
Local Income	15	.1
Other Income	213	2
Totals	9,928	100

Source: Kenya Catholic Secretariat 1986.

really even greater than this because food prices are generally higher in the peripheral areas than in the prosperous areas. The most striking difference of all is in the amount Consolata spends on medicines. Consolata spends five times as much on drugs as Mutomo and ten times as much as Ortum! Like Ortum and Mutomo, the bulk of Consolata's drugs are foreign generics, but Consolata has a larger volume of more kinds of drugs than either of the peripheral hospitals. Some name-brand, non-generic drugs are also available. Consolata pays less for its drugs because of its easy and direct access to Nairobi dealers. A small part of the difference can be accounted for by the regular practice of surgery at Consolata, and only occasional surgeries at Mutomo, and infrequent surgeries at Ortum. The more complete explanation for this phenomenon, however, seems to lie in the way the doctors at Consolata practice medicine. The doctors at Consolata are resident Kenyans and ex-patriate Africans rather than foreign volunteers. They have access to recent medical information, and they have regular and direct contact with Nairobi-based drug representatives. Unlike foreign volunteers who conceptualize themselves as practicing emergency medicine, these doctors are earning a normal living at being physicians. Because of the economic resources of the general patient population in the area, they are not concerned about whether their patients can afford to pay for the drugs they prescribe at the hospital pharmacy. The resultant practice of medicine in this situation is simply more chemically intensive than in the peripheral hospitals.

The final and most important contrast between Consolata and the peripheral hospitals is that Consolata shows a budget surplus with little overseas income. Patient fees and National Hospital Insurance provide 80 percent of its income. Of the three hospitals it also receives the largest government grant, almost 30 percent larger than Ortum's. Even without this grant Consolata would still have a budget surplus. Quality care here is measured not only in terms of the dedication of the personnel providing it, but also in terms of the comfort of its facilities. People who have regular cash income can afford comfortable, quality care. They expect it, and they are willing to pay for it.

DISCUSSION ISSUES

Tension exists in Kenya between the government system of medical institutions and the church-related system. At the local level, however, and on a case-by-case basis cooperation and mutual assistance between institutions and individuals does occur. Nevertheless, church institutions regularly provide quality care, and government institutions can only do so occasionally. The church-related institutions believe they have earned greater government support for doing what the government says it should be doing. With a fairly extensive system of facilities and personnel that is seriously underutilized despite significant expenditures, how much should the government be expected to do for the church-related system? Should the government, for example, be expected to increase its subsidies to cover the revenue currently raised in church institutions by patient fees? Or should the government institute fees in its own institutions in order to provide quality care, so that church resources could be otherwise utilized?

Church-related institutions raise an even thornier issue when discussing quality health care. In Catholic institutions, at least, the presence of religious women in institutional administration is viewed by Kenyans as essential to the continued smooth operation of these institutions. At the very least in any Kenyanization of these institutions, religious women (or men) are viewed as essential to avoid the bureaucratic competition for precedence which occurs within government institutions often at the expense of patient care. European orders of religious are no longer able to guarantee continued staffing of these institutions. One group has attempted to bolster its staffing by recruiting a South Asian order of sisters to assist and possibly replace them. How can Kenyan religious women be recruited into these institutions? Since they run their own, more modest medical institutions, there is no doubt they are capable. Associated with shifting administrative control of church-related institutions is the reality of most institutions' dependence on overseas contributions and donated services. What will happen to the money if Europeans are no longer present in, and in charge of, these institutions?

Modern medicine, like modern political structures, has been introduced and is largely controlled by a modernized, urban-based, sociopolitical elite. As the government of Kenya is itself aware, the practice of modern medicine is largely structured for the benefit of this elite and their immediate subordinates by the concentration of medical personnel and the highest quality institutions in urban areas. Medical care is available in the rural areas, but the premodern traditional system of healing continues to function. What responsibility do modern medical practitioners have to improve their treatment of patients by relearning the strengths of the traditional system? To what extent can traditional healers complement their traditional skills with modern knowledge and techniques? To be modern does a culture have to repudiate its past? As Third World countries go, Kenya is relatively well-off. However, Kenya is at or approaching a crossroad. Population is expanding at a rate of more than 4 percent a year which is one of the highest rates anywhere. The primary, agricultural resources of the country are already fully exploited by the known technology. Modern medical health care is contributing to the increasing human pressure on these resources by keeping more people alive. Curative medicine predominates over preventive medicine; but as greater preventive measures are taken, even more persons, especially children, will survive. The demands on the physical and social environment can only increase. Is modern, First World medicine contributing to the quantity of life rather than the quality of life?

REFERENCES

Beck, Ann. 1981. *Medicine, Tradition, and Development in Kenya and Tanzania 1920–1970.* Waltham, Mass.: Crossroads Press.
Eisenberg, Leon. 1977. "Disease and Illness: Distinctions between Professional and Popular Ideas of Sickness." *Culture, Medicine and Psychiatry* 1:9–23.
Good, Charles, and V. Kimani. 1980. "Urban Traditional Medicine: A Nairobi Case-Study." *East African Medical Journal* 57(5):301–316.
Good, Charles, et al. 1979. "The Interface of Dual Systems of Health Care in the Developing World: Toward Health Policy Initiatives in Africa." *Social Science and Medicine* 13D:141–154.
Government of Kenya. 1983. *Development Plan 1984–1988.* Nairobi: Government Printing Office.
Hartwig, Charles. 1979. "Church-State Relations in Kenya: Health Issues." *Social Science and Medicine* 13C:121–127.
———. 1975. Health Policies and National Development in Kenya. Ph.D. Dissertation, University of Kentucky.
Helman, Cecil. 1985. "Communication in Primary Care: The Role of Patient and Practitioner Explanatory Models." *Social Science and Medicine* 20(9):923–931.
Hendrix, Hubert, ed. 1985. *District Atlas West Pokot.* Kapenguria: Arid and Semi Arid Lands Development Programme.
International Monetary Fund. 1984. *Government Finance Statistics Yearbook,* Vol. VIII. Washington, D.C.: International Monetary Fund.
Kapenguria District Hospital. 1984. "Yearly Report." mimeo.
Kaufman, Arthur, et al. 1982. "Kenya: A Case Study in Third World Medicine." *Journal of Family Practice* 14(3):609–610.
Kenya Catholic Secretariat. 1985. "Statistics of Facilities/Staff/-Services." mimeo. Nairobi: Medical Department, Kenya Catholic Secretariat.

————. 1986. "Yearly Report." mimeo. Nairobi: Medical Department, Kenya Catholic Secretariat.

Mburu, F. M. 1981. "Implications of the Ideology and Implementation of Health Policy in a Developing Country." *Social Science and Medicine* 15A:17–24.

————. 1979. "Rhetoric-Implementation Gap in Health Policy and Health Services Delivery for a Rural Population in a Developing Country." *Social Science and Medicine* 13A:577–583.

Mburu, F. M., et al. 1978. "The Determinants of Health Services Utilization in a Rural Community in Kenya." *Social Science and Medicine* 12:211–217.

Ministry of Health. 1983a. *Development Plan 1984–1988.* mimeo.

————. 1983b. *Appropriation Accounts.* Nairobi: Government Printing Office.

Moore, G. D. 1982. "Essential Drugs for Kenya's Rural Population." *World Health Forum* 3(2):196–199.

Mutomo Mission Hospital. 1986. "Yearly Report." mimeo.

Mwabu, Germano. 1986. "Health Care Decisions at the Household Level: Results of a Rural Health Survey in Kenya." *Social Science and Medicine* 22(3):315–319.

————. 1984. A Model of Household Choice among Medical Treatment Alternatives in Rural Kenya. Ph.D. Dissertation, Boston University.

Mwabu, Germano, and W. M. Mwangi. 1986. "Health Care Financing in Kenya: A Simulation of Welfare Effects on User Fees." *Social Science and Medicine* 22(7): 763–767.

Mwagiru, Wanjiku, and P. Njue. 1986. *A Modern Geography of Kenya.* Nairobi: Mwassco Publications.

Nyamwaya, D. 1987. "Traditional Medicine in Kenya: An Overview." Presentation at Seminar on Participatory Action Research Joint Project on Primary Health Care Tharaka (Kenya), Dept. of Community Health, University of Nairobi, June 25, 1987.

————. 1982. Health in West Pokot. Ph.D. Dissertation, University of Cambridge.

Ojany, F. F., and R. Ogendo. 1973. *Kenya: A Study in Physical and Human Geography.* Nairobi: Longman Kenya.

Opuka, S. 1979. "The Distribution of Rural Health Facilities: A Case Study of Mumias and Butere Divisions, Kakamega District." Research Paper, University of Nairobi.

Ortum Mission Hospital. 1986. "Yearly Report." mimeo.

Thomas, Anthony. 1975. "Health Care in Ukambani, Kenya: A Socialist Critique." In *Topias and Utopias in Health,* ed. S. E. Ingman and A. E. Thomas, 267–281. The Hague: Mouton Publishers.

Wasunna, A., and M. Wasunna. 1974. "Drug Trafficking of Non-addictive Drugs through Unqualified and Unauthorized Persons in Kenya." In *The Use and Abuse of Drugs and Chemicals in Tropical Africa,* ed. A. F. Bagshawe et al., 161–163. Nairobi: East African Literature Bureau.

Pharmaceuticals in Kenyan Government Health Care

GERALD D. MOORE

There are very few countries in sub-Saharan Africa which do not have problems with drug supplies in the public sector and Kenya is no exception. The root causes of the drug supply problems in Kenya, as in other African countries, are (1) shortages of foreign exchange and (2) a free health care system.

I am not saying that health care (including drug treatment) should not be free for the less well-off in a government-run national health service, but that a free system, unless well-managed, controlled, organized, and budgeted will always run into problems with the funding and supply of its main components such as drugs, especially if the necessary allocations of foreign exchange cannot be assured. In other words, wherever a free drug treatment system operates, there is practically no limit to the demand for drugs but there is a limit to supply, and that limit is the amount of foreign currency available to pay for the raw materials or finished pharmaceuticals.

In Kenya, for the past twenty-odd years, health care in government hospitals, health centers, and dispensaries has been virtually free. In-patients and maternity cases are charged a small fee to help cover food costs, but all care, including drugs, for in-patients as well as out-patients, is free. "Free medical care for all" sounded good politically

Gerald D. Moore has been a technical officer for the Action Programme on Essential Drugs of the World Health Organization since 1984. Following seventeen years in the pharmaceutical industry where he worked with generic drugs in Third World countries, he joined the Kenyan Ministry of Health as an advisor. He introduced the essential drug kit system. With the WHO, he has been working with essential drug programs in a number of developing countries.

in the 1960s and, in those days, with fewer health stations and many fewer people to treat, it did not seem an unreasonable objective. But, in the mid-1960s the population of Kenya was 9 million. Since then, it has been increasing an average of 4 percent a year and it is now 20 million. Unless something happens to reduce the growth—and despite one of the longest-running family planning programs in sub-Saharan Africa, the population has continued to rise at one of the highest rates in the world—it will be 33 million by the year 2000 and 73 million 20 years after that.

Perhaps drug supplies would still be able to keep up with this heavy increase in demand if the government put enough into the Ministry of Health's budget, if drug needs were accurately forecast and planned for, if they were used more or less accurately and conservatively. But when you have a system where there are inefficiencies in all those areas, it becomes very difficult for any administration to cope with the needs of a population that is doubling every twenty years and which is not directly contributing to the cost of the drugs it is consuming. However, important steps have been taken by the government over the past ten years to try to maintain an adequate and free supply of pharmaceuticals to the national health service. I want to review a few of them.

RURAL HEALTH DRUG SUPPLY SYSTEM

A new method of supplying drugs to rural health units—health centers and dispensaries—was developed with assistance from the World Health Organization and the Danish and Swedish aid agencies (DANIDA and SIDA) during 1979–80. This involved selecting a limited range of essential drugs suitable for the types of cases seen in such units and the level of health workers treating these cases; procuring the drugs according to tight specifications; packing them in strong cartons (kits) in quantities to cover the treatment needs of a given number of diagnoses; and distributing them, under strict security, according to patient workload.

This system has been operational nationally for the past eight years, and reports indicate that it is relatively effective and economical. Today, there are very few shortages of drugs in the rural areas. Health workers and patients are happy with the system; it cuts out a lot of waste, loss, and damage. Cost of drugs per capita per annum is running at about US$0.50 which is much less than it was before the system started.

It is not the perfect system — sending out fixed quantities of some forty items can lead to build-up of stock of some drugs and shortages of others — but at least it gives the health care units the basic drugs, month after month, enabling health workers, with a little careful training, to treat 70–80 percent of the cases seen in such units. The population, 75 percent of whom live in the rural areas, is able to use the facilities close to where they live, usually within seven kilometers, and not take the twenty-five kilometer trek to the nearest hospital.

IMPACT ON THE PHARMACEUTICAL INDUSTRY

With this new system the Ministry of Health was able to solve some of the problems of drug supplies to the rural areas, though with massive support from external aid agencies. Although popular with health workers and patients, however, the system met with considerable resistance from some sections of the pharmaceutical industry. There were fears the limited selection of drugs would reduce sales and restrict promotional activity. No longer would the industry's sales representatives be free to roam the length and breadth of the country, promoting and selling pharmaceuticals which were sometimes of doubtful necessity and almost always at prices higher than those of the Central Medical Stores.

Such fears, particularly among the speciality pharmaceutical houses and especially those importing finished goods, were valid. There was no justification for rural health units to purchase large quantities of high-priced tranquilizers, antidepressants, cephalosporins, or beta-blockers. Rural health workers are, for the most part, untrained in such diagnoses and treatments, and are advised to refer such cases to the next higher level, the district and provincial hospitals.

Branded chloroquines and penicillins also began to lose their market share as generic, unbranded items at less than half the price of the speciality products took their place. Almost expired items, often sold at a discount, failed to generate any more interest. Drugs labeled in French, German, or Spanish, and often undecipherable to the average health worker, gradually dropped out of circulation.

There was, therefore, a significant change in the pharmaceutical market, but not necessarily a decline. On the contrary, the overall market for pharmaceuticals increased with the introduction of the new system. Where before the Ministry of Health had difficulty in allocating adequate funds for rural health, and where at least 25 percent of units were closed at any one time for lack of drugs, almost overnight about US$2 million poured into the country. These funds came partly from the two leading Scandinavian aid agencies, DANIDA and SIDA, and partly by the Kenyan government through the donor/government agreement. Those pharmaceutical companies that adapted to the new ball game did well; those that did not lost out. The new ball game was for low-priced, good quality, basic generic pharmaceuticals, labeled as such, with maximum shelf lives, in high volume, and with payment guaranteed.

Under the impetus of the new system, the local pharmaceutical producers (including affiliates of transnational corporations) which until then had languished under import discriminations, doubtful manufacturing practices, and questionable quality-control procedures, began to get their act together. Suddenly, there was a golden opportunity— a ready-made, high-volume market and a good possibility of actually getting paid!

The Ministry of Health, with assistance from WHO, DANIDA, and SIDA, encouraged this development. Local companies were screened and advised on methods for improvement. At first, only one local producer measured up to WHO's standards but, by the third year, at least two more had their houses in order and were producing to acceptable standards.

Now there are at last five pharmaceutical companies in Kenya, manufacturing a wide range of essential drugs as generics. Mostly, their business is in the domestic market with government, church, and private health units, but export business also is increasing. In the past three years markets such as Uganda, Tanzania, and Malawi have been supplied from Kenya. So far, however, interregional trade has been hampered by currency, banking, and transport difficulties. The advent of the East/Central/Southern African Preferential Trade Association (PTA), an African economic community, may help resolve some of these hindrances to trade. The setting up of a central bank clearing house mechanism to deal in local African currencies will help companies export without having to demand U.S. dollars in payment and will aid governments and private companies within the region in obtaining supplies by their not having to pay in U.S. dollars, pounds sterling, or other hard currencies. It is slightly ludicrous when, as in previous years, a pharmaceutical company in Kenya insists on payment in U.S. dollars for a shipment of aspirin to its next-door neighbor Tanzania.

The switch in emphasis by the government of Kenya, as well as several other African governments, to basic essential drugs for their national health services has given considerable encouragement and support to producers of such drugs, whether in Kenya or abroad. In addition, it has improved the standards and quality of locally manufactured goods and brought the prices down significantly. Much higher volume has also increased total sales value.

DRUGS IN THE HOSPITALS—DISTRICT FOCUS AND ITS IMPLICATIONS

In mid-1985, the government of Kenya decided that drugs for hospitals would no longer be bought centrally by the Ministry of Health but would be the responsibility of each district. This decision formed part of the decentralization policy of the government, to encourage more responsibility in the districts for their social and economic development. The new policy was known as the "district focus" policy. In principle the idea was good and there were many obvious benefits to the country. But when it came to the supply of drugs and medical supplies, it quickly became clear that the districts were just not set up to handle the responsibility thrust upon them.

There are forty-one districts in Kenya, each with at least one district hospital; some also have one or two sub-district hospitals. The idea was that each district hospital, in coordination with the local district administration, would, almost overnight, be responsible for obtaining its own drugs and medical supplies. The Central Medical Stores in Nairobi, now changed in name to the Medical Supplies Coordinating Unit, would help in the task by floating tenders and gathering quotations. This information would be passed to the districts which would then be on their own to negotiate supply and payment terms with individual suppliers.

Anybody who has had the good fortune to visit Kenya and who has traveled outside the normal tourist tracks knows that some district centers are in remote places. Some can take two to three days to reach, and then only in the dry season by road. Otherwise you have to go by air, and landing strips in Kenya have a habit of being covered by wildebeeste, zebra, and sometimes elephants—not the sort of thing you want to see in your windscreen when you are in final approach.

Telecommunications are improving, but even today it is still hard to reach some district hospitals except by radio through the local police post or non-governmental organization (NGO) missions. Letters can take longer to travel from Turkana to Nairobi than from New York to Nairobi.

It is not hard, therefore, to envisage the predicament of such district hospitals when told to go out and buy their own drugs, including those only obtainable from overseas suppliers. What happened was that the tender quotes obtained by the coordinating unit in Nairobi were largely ignored, either because manufacturers were not in a position to produce and supply forty-one districts individually or because the district administrations found it easier in the end to buy from the local corner chemist who, by sheer chance, had suddenly opened up outside the hospital gates. The only hitch was, the prices were two or three times higher than those through the medical stores, but it was so easy just to walk across the road. The result? The hospitals' budgets bought less than half the drugs they should have. Put another way, hospitals ran out of money and drugs about half-way through the financial year.

When the extent of this crisis became apparent to the Ministry of Health, urgent feelers were put out to more international health agencies and donor agencies. WHO was able to enlist support from two governments, the Federal Republic of Germany and the Netherlands. Soon, a range of essential drugs was coming in, specially selected and packed for use in hospital out-patient departments, partly purchased by the aid arm of the Federal Republic (GTZ), and partly by WHO on behalf of the government of the Netherlands. Together, this action supplied the total hospital out-patient drug needs of ten of the districts.

In addition to covering the short-term requirements of hospital out-patients, this program has allowed the Ministry to test the concept of essential drug packages in hospitals. Experience so far shows that hospital out-patient departments deal with cases similar to those in rural health units and they can, with one or two more items, operate with very much the same range of essential drugs as such units. This will have useful consequences for the Ministry's planning and budgeting of drug supplies.

It now appears that the government has reversed its position regarding drug supplies to hospitals. Henceforward, authority to incur expenditures will be withdrawn from the districts and taken back to the Ministry's headquarters. The Central Stores in Nairobi will be re-instated as the sole procurement and budgetary agency for Ministry drug and medical supplies. By the end of August 1987 a new, centrally directed tender and request for quotations was already published. It seems, therefore, that the Ministry will take back responsibility for its drug supply system. This should lead to immediate improvements if (a) drug needs are accurately estimated and budgeted for; (b) procure-ment, as far as possible of good-quality generics, is carried out under strict supervision; and (c) hospitals continue to implement the pro-gram of rational usage introduced in the ten pilot districts under the emergency situation.

To help the Central Stores cope with its regained responsibilities, a move will be made to new, larger, and more modern storage facili-ties. Considering that the existing facilities were once the barracks of the British Army in 1935, the move is considered timely.

COST RECOVERY

All these efforts by the Ministry to cope with the ever-increasing drug needs of the population can somehow be likened to throwing a quarter of the national health budget over Niagara Falls — it is a one-way stream, nothing comes back, and you have got to throw over more every year just to keep in the same place. It has been estimated that if the government were to charge for out-patient visits, as the church medical units do, a small fee of 10 Kenyan shillings (about US$0.60) it would cover all costs for drugs, dressings, and medical disposables. But, since the mid-1960s, the policy of the government has been free health for all, including treatment, and it has been difficult for the Ministry to explain what that means in terms of cash, and how to get enough of it. So the drain goes on, despite the fact that drugs remain one of the only free services provided by the government; all the rest, water, education, etc., became fee-paying long ago.

Recently, moves were made to search for solutions to the problem. It is possible that the scope and membership of the Hospital Health Insurance Scheme may be expanded and perhaps made compulsory and include cost of drugs. It seems likely that Kenya will consider charges for medical care in government health institutions, similar to what has been implemented recently in Zambia.[1]

OVERUSAGE

So long as there is no restraint on drug usage or no system of cost recovery, demand will continue to exceed supply, and every year the Ministry will be borrowing from the next year's allocation just to keep afloat. Perhaps more in Africa than in many other parts of the world, people love drugs; they love to give them and they love to receive them. How this situation has developed, nobody quite knows. Perhaps it stems from the traditional healers and their potions and mixtures. Perhaps the pharmaceutical industry has been more successful in their promotion than we thought. Whatever the reason, the chances are that if you, as a Kenyan patient, walk into a health center, a dispensary, or hospital out-patient department with a simple cold, you are likely to come out with three or four different drugs in your hand and one in each buttock, all provided with the compliments of the government. We are not so much better in our so-called Western societies but the difference is, we — or our insurance companies — pay for the drugs. In many African countries, including Kenya, where they can least afford it, the government pays.

There are certain mitigating factors, however. A new National Formulary is in the final stages of preparation and will list 250–300 essential drug items by generic names. This will become the basis for the government's drug supply system and will help rationalize drug procurement, distribution, and usage.

The Ministry of Health in Kenya has come a long way in overcoming some of the problems in supplying free drugs for all. But until there is more restraint in the use of such drugs, by health workers and the public, and until there is some mechanism to allow the Ministry to recover some, if not all, of the cost of such drugs, it seems likely that each year the Ministry will run into severe financial difficulties in supplying those drugs.

MANAGEMENT

Running a drug supply system such as Kenya's is similar to running a multimillion dollar business, for that is what it is. US$10–15 million dollars in drugs, dressings, medical supplies, and equipment will pass through the Central Stores' operations in any normal year; they have to be planned for, bought, stored, and distributed. As many items still come from abroad, Central Stores somehow has to acquire the banking and international trading expertise of a highly organized multinational company. As some of the basic infrastructure for such an operation is still lacking, such as telex facilities, photocopying machines, calculators, etc., it becomes very difficult for even the most motivated of staff to perform efficiently. But the signs are that the system is improving. The Ministry has adopted fully the principles of essential drugs and is operating at both hospital and health center levels with lists of such drugs. New methods of distribution have eliminated much waste and loss. Procurement of generics, as far as possible, is now based upon international competitive bidding. Specifications of quality, date of manufacture, packaging, labeling, and delivery are stricter. The local manufacturing industry is geared up to produce low-cost generics of satisfactory quality. Drug costs per capita are going down. Health workers are more accurate in diagnoses and are knowledgeable about the drugs they use.

CHURCH MEDICAL SERVICE

In this respect the experience of the Church Medical Service in Kenya may provide some important pointers. The Catholic and Protestant church medical facilities in Kenya look after the health of around 30 percent of the population; in some remote areas it may be more. These facilities charge for the services they provide; they have to, otherwise they would not be able to operate such a program. Moreover, it is generally believed by the Kenyan population, and this applies to all but the poorest of patients, that a service you pay for is worth something. What you get for nothing perhaps loses some of its value. This is, of course, an important factor in the healing process. In addition, charging helps cut down the number of unnecessary visits and prescriptions which may be a considerable burden on a free health service.

The Church Medical Service in Kenya has existed side by side with government facilities for many years. Although charges are made in the one and not in the other, there are no signs that church medical facilities are being abandoned by patients. This must mean that most people are willing to pay something for the treatment they receive.

To make their services more cost-efficient, the Catholic and Protestant medical secretariats in 1986 got together to form a new central purchasing, storage, and distribution unit. It is based in Nairobi and staffed by approximately thirty people. The objectives of the unit are to provide lower-cost, good quality drugs to church medical units through bulk purchasing, screening of manufacturers for good manufacturing practices, more rational storage, and distribution. The unit also will shortly commence a refresher training program for prescribers in rational drug usage. The Church Medical Service, in building up the new supply system, has fully adopted the principles of the national essential drug program and operates with some 250 drug items selected from the Kenyan essential drugs list and WHO recommendations. All drugs are purchased as generics and labeled only by generic name. The unit serves in a trading capacity, buying at the lowest cost and selling, with a small margin to cover overheads and operating costs, to member medical units. From a start in 1986/87, the unit is now turning over 40 million Kenyan shillings per annum, equivalent to US$1.7 million.

The Ministry of Health fully supports this medical service and provides assistance in the form of annual financial grants, training, and technical services. There are signs that the Ministry is studying the new church operation closely to see if there are areas where the church's experiences could be of benefit to the government's drug supply system.

Summary

Kenya, like most developing countries, is a long way from major sources of drugs, either finished pharmaceuticals or raw materials. At such a distance it is difficult for the Ministry of Health to keep up-to-date with market developments, prices, or supply sources. Procurement, therefore, may not be achieved in the most cost-efficient manner. Delays may be experienced in deliveries, due to lengthy negotiation times, shipping hold-ups, or poor communication with overseas suppliers. Bureaucratic procedures in obtaining import licenses, foreign exchange allocations, or opening letters of credit may also slow down deliveries. These potential obstacles have to be considered in advance otherwise drugs will be in short supply or out of stock. Demand has long been estimated by the method of previous consumption which, in a country with a rapidly growing patient population, can lead to underestimations. A new program of morbidity-based estimates, assisted by WHO, may help overcome this problem.

All drugs, whether locally produced or imported in finished form, cost the country foreign exchange. The Ministry's needs must be budgeted for out of the national reserves. Sometimes it may be difficult for the Ministry to obtain the share it needs in the face of the government's other requirements. Foreign exchange in Kenya depends very much upon exports of coffee and tea and imports of tourists. Changes in the world market prices of coffee and tea, or changes in tourism patterns, directly affect the Kenyan government's ability to provide its population with drugs or with any commodity that has to be paid for in foreign exchange.

Therefore, even though health care (including drug treatment) may one day directly or indirectly be financed more by the population itself, the supply of drugs in government as well as in private medical facilities in Kenya depends mainly on the available foreign exchange; and that depends upon how much Kenya earns from its exports. The same situation exists in most other countries in the developing world where imports have to be paid for in hard currencies. So, if we want to help Kenya obtain the drugs it needs, let us drink Kenya's coffee, tea, or go and look at its animals. Let us provide information and access to the best world market sources of supply. Let us try to ensure that the pharmaceutical industry supplies the drugs that Kenya really needs—essential drugs—as low-cost generics, and takes the pressure off trying to sell its high-priced specialities. Let us continue to help local industry increase its standards, capacity, and technology to produce essential drugs cheaply but well. Let us continue to provide training expertise and opportunities to Kenya's health workers. Let us pray that, with better and sufficient drugs, the people of Kenya will grow healthier and stronger.

NOTE

1. Following the presentation of this paper in the October 1987 workshop, a program of charging for drugs in the Kenyan national health system was initiated and subsequently dropped.

Pharmaceuticals in Kenyan Christian Health Services

JOAN DEVANE, S.C.M.M.

The Mission for Essential Drugs and Supplies (MEDS) is an essential drugs procurement service for the Christian health services in Kenya whose health units cover 40 percent of the health care in rural Kenya. The goal for MEDS is to procure and hold in storage a sufficient supply and range of essential drugs and supplies for resale on a nonprofit basis to the church health units and manage in such a way as to build a revolving fund to maintain the operation in financial viability.

OVERVIEW OF MEDS

MEDS has two thrusts: one is medical supplies, the other is training. A priority of MEDS is to establish essential drugs as the first-line choice of treatment in the churches' health services in Kenya. This concept was introduced to the government rural health units by the Ministry of Health in 1979, and later to the district hospitals. The Ministry of Health is in the process of revising its own essential drugs list within the context of its national drug policy.

In the beginning MEDS was met with a variety of negative emotions and attitudes. The hospitals have always had a choice in what drugs to use and, at the district and provincial levels, the doctors also have choices. If a drug is not available through the government, the

Joan Devane, S.C.M.M., is the founder and general manager of MEDS in Nairobi, Kenya, a joint ecumenical project between the Kenya Catholic Secretariat Medical Department and the Protestant Church Medical Association. An African missionary and pharmacist for thirty years, she has served in hospitals and health centers across the country.

doctors and Ministry of Health professionals will write prescriptions for the patients to go to private chemists. There is a large element of choice at the level of doctor prescribing, so introducing an essential drugs program into the church hospitals, where the element of choice is much larger or more freely exercised than in the government, initiated the need for education. MEDS provides seminars for review and prescribing and encourages the understanding of an essential drugs program itself.

There has been skepticism on the part of some of the doctors about the value of generic drugs. Some have had bad experiences with generics whose quality had not been monitored. MEDS has had to confront this doubt both in individual contacts with the hospitals and in training seminars for nurses and other health care professionals where stress is on both the administration of drugs through good prescribing and through good management in the hospitals.

The MEDS training program offers refresher courses for review and updating in clinical diagnosis, prescribing, and drugs management. Prescribing and management of drugs supply training is necessary due to overprescribing, either through inexperience or response to patient demands for "a capsule for every complaint." It is not uncommon for a patient to be given five or six different medicines. This "poly pharmacy" undermines patient compliance. This is a waste of medicines in a country where drug shortages are a chronic problem.

Since 1988, thirty-two seminars have been conducted for the medical and paramedical staffs of the rural health units. Approximately 600 persons have participated in these five-day residential seminars; the target for the next three years is to train 1,000 more staff personnel. Integral to an essential drugs program is the enhancement of the staff's understanding of the role of essential drugs, conviction of their value, their essentialness therapeutically, and the affordability of the program for the patients, the health agencies, and the countries. The need for a rational use of essential drugs applies to all countries from those in the United States where the cost of health care has risen by 42 percent in the last five years[1] to a Third World country such as Kenya where the average income per capita per annum is $380[2] and the inflation rate in 1989 was 19 percent.

MEDS HISTORY, LOCATION, AND OPERATIONS

MEDS began with a staff of one in 1987; then grew to the present staff of thirty Kenyans, professional pharmacists, administrative personnel, nursing professsionals, and two warehouses. From a central location in the industrial area of Nairobi, MEDS purchases, stores, packs, and dispatches to hospitals and health units throughout the Republic of Kenya, an area almost the size of the state of Texas.

Most local shipping to hospitals is by public carrier, lorries, and buses to towns nearest the hospitals. In turn the hospital personnel come to those towns and collect their goods.

Since July 1990, MEDS has occupied new premises—two adjoining warehouses which have offices at the mezzanine levels. This new location is in the industrial area, about ten miles from the center of the city of Nairobi. The space of more than 15,000 square feet is more than double the area of the former premises of MEDS.

The warehouses have 540 pallet locations, packing and dispatch areas, a special storeroom for flammable liquids, a large refrigeration area, and adequate loading areas. Having adequate operations space has facilitated efficiency and also made provision for internal security more practical. To protect these facilities from thieves who operate in large groups, MEDS has installed a radio alarm system which will detect entry through the most usual routes.

Scope of MEDS

MEDS operations involve purchasing, stock maintenance, processing individual orders as received from hospitals and health units, delivery, and all the administration of processing clients accounts, screening orders, and monitoring quality for forty-four hospitals and 400 miscellaneous bedded units, health post dispensaries, and mobile units as well as other private voluntary organizations. MEDS uses an interfacing stock and account computer program. Also manual stock card records are maintained. In the last six months of 1990, MEDS handled over one thousand orders. Some were for a few items, others involved several tons of pharmaceuticals and supplies. Nearly one hundred tons of goods are packed and dispatched each month from the MEDS warehouses.

MEDS also supplies medicine to some nonprofit nongovernmental agencies such as Flying Doctors Services (AMREF), United Nations Children's Fund (UNICEF), Kenya Association for Welfare of Epileptics, United Nations Development Program (UNDP), and the Population Council. At the time of the writing of this paper, MEDS was preparing 1,500 kits of essential drugs for the Bamako[3] pilot scheme in Kenya. The Ministry of Health and the World Health Organization's AIDS Control Program requested MEDS' services to distribute to the church health services those supplies and equipment allocated to them by the national AIDS Control Program.

FINANCE

The church health units in Kenya, which number over 500, are autonomous in terms of management and financing. Autonomous is not synonymous with independent, as many are financially strapped and barely able to continue operations. Most have variable and unpredictable sources of income. Some charge a service fee which includes drugs; some charge for the pharmaceuticals, hoping to meet operating costs of the salaries and nursing care. Success depends on whether the area has cash in circulation, which in turn is contingent on adequate rainfall and collection of payments for the coffee crop and the pyrethrum yields. In the desert and semiarid areas, there is little money in circulation. Consequently, church health services are nominal or free. When a fee for service is imposed, it is not realistically relevant to the operating costs of the hospitals or the actual drugs costs. Some hospitals are partially supported by donated services of senior staff, or subsidy from their sponsoring board. Formerly the church health services received some government subsidy in the form of revenue and capital grants. However, in the last few years this has dwindled drastically.

Financing of drug costs is a problem in Kenya for both the government and the churches. For the last twenty years, health care including drugs has been free in government institutions. In December 1989 the Ministry of Health introduced a system of cost sharing. Patients in hospitals and health centers were charged a minimal fee for services which included drugs. However, there were many problems and after only eight months the system was discontinued.

OPERATING OBJECTIVES

MEDS has several objectives: (1) buy economically through bulk purchasing, (2) purchase drugs from Kenyan manufacturers whenever possible, and (3) maintain adequate stock to ensure constant supply.

The latter objective was formulated with the hope of achieving a Kenyan organization that could eventually sustain itself within the local economy.

MEDS tries to meet these objectives despite the fact that some have inherent contradictions: (1) locally produced generics are often more costly than imported goods, and (2) maintaining a constant supply is subject to a number of factors including local market availability, delays experienced by local manufacturers in getting raw materials, and world currency fluctuations. For instance, the reunification of Germany influenced the currency, the raw materials for pharmaceuticals, and the finished products.

Even though local Kenyan producers manufacture a wide range of essential drugs, the country is not fully self-sufficient. Of MEDS's present stock of 158 items, 70 percent are purchased in Kenya and 30 percent are imported. Injectables are not manufactured in Kenya. Some products are locally manufactured without the facilities or the financial ability to test or monitor quality.

The policy of buying from local Kenyan producers whenever possible is directed to the development of the pharmaceutical industry in Kenya. The policy saves Kenyan hard currency although on a national basis the savings is mitigated by the high proportion of raw materials imported by the local suppliers. Moreover, locally manufactured generics are more expensive than imported generics. Still, sound local pharmaceutical production is central to the advancement of health care in Kenya.

There is a problem with quality. Few Kenyan producers have adequate testing facilities either for their imported raw materials or their completed products. Beyond that, the Kenyan government requires the use of some local raw materials that do not meet quality standards. For example, the use of local starch is required. There is excessive moisture in this starch and it is difficult for local manufacturers to achieve the precise degree of moisture elimination. The finished product then deteriorates prematurely.

With few dependable laboratory facilities available to MEDS, it is necessary to depend on foreign testing and quality assurance methods outside the laboratory. MEDS initiates orders and reorders only from those firms that have proven dependable — about four of the over twenty-five in Kenya. A good deal of quality assurance is possible through knowing the manufacturing practices of individual producers, keeping apprised of credibility and integrity in business relationships, monitoring the packaging and condition of goods received, and performing periodic checks of stock conditions.

MEDS buys 70 percent of its stock items locally. Thirty percent must be imported. For imports, there are financial constraints due to the uncertain availability of foreign exchange. Although drugs are listed as one of the items given top foreign exchange priority, the actual amounts available for allocation are influenced by world market fluctuations, whether it is coffee, tea, or the unrest in the Middle East. Kenya is totally dependent on imported oil. Availability of foreign exchange affects not only direct importation of finished products but also that of local drugs whose production depends on imported raw materials.

MEDS had initial donor funding for its first three years of operation. This was used for establishing a drugs revolving fund as well as operations and training. This was a source of foreign currency for imports, as well as for buying a basic drug stock locally.

This reserve is practically exhausted. MEDS is seeking further donor supplements to the revolving fund for the purchase of imports. MEDS does not need further funding for local drug purchases because these are bought and resold to the hospitals in Kenyan currency.

There is another potential saving in foreign exchange with goods bought from within Africa under the Preferential Trade Area (PTA). Currently MEDS buys liter infusions from a Zimbabwe firm which manufactures under license from Baxter. In August 1990, MEDS obtained approval from the government of Kenya to pay for a new consignment in Kenya shillings. Previously, hard currency was required.

Import permits are valid for only three months. There is a problem associated in matching duration of validity to shipment arrivals. If there is a delay in the shipment's arrival, renewed government authorizations must be obtained before goods can clear customs. A delay of weeks or months at the port can endanger the drug stability and shorten the timeframe of usage. The Kenya Ministry of Health specifies a shelf life of three years for injectables. This is desirable for ensuring against time deterioration. However, this presents a difficulty in maintaining fresh stock if there are ordering or shipping delays.

For overseas suppliers, the MEDS orders may be too large to supply fresh drugs and too small to fit a new batch into a tight production schedule. MEDS orders may be for thirty or forty different items. It is an advantage to have quantity sufficient to fill twenty-foot containers because the Kenya port of entry at Mombasa only accepts these containers. On occasion, a MEDS order has been included in a container of mixed commercial imports held several weeks in Rotterdam until the container was full. When this occurs, the shipment is several weeks late in arriving in Mombasa. Even when a shipment leaves Hamburg or Rotterdam promptly, it can be delayed by maritime accidents, port congestion, or transport availability. For example, one ship with a MEDS container sailed past Mombasa to Tanzania, unloaded other cargo, and returned to Mombasa many weeks later. All of this can affect the stability and shelf life of products.

In theory, a sea cargo shipment should arrive within three to four months from the time of ordering to its port clearance. Reality has been six to nine months. MEDS needs optimum shelf life extent because it is a stockist, not an immediate user. Therefore, for drugs with two to three years shelf life, MEDS is forced to import by air cargo.

AVAILABILITY OF DRUGS

The local pharmaceutical field is plagued by stock "outages." For example, at the time of the writing of this paper, a certain injectable has been unavailable in Kenya for several months from any of the usual importers. MEDS has no supply at all and is awaiting a delayed shipment. The Medical Supplies Coordinating Unit (MSCU) of the Ministry of Health experiences similar frustrations.

Another challenge in maintaining a constant supply of essential drugs is that of accurately forecasting stock needs. This applies to both local purchases and imports. Due to epidemics of tropical diseases and changing prescribing patterns of medical staffs, demands are unpredictable. In 1990 there were severe epidemics of meningitis and cerebral malaria, and an outbreak of plague. In 1989 cholera was epidemic and an outbreak of meningitis which followed the path of the Ethiopia epidemic continued into 1990 like brushfires throughout Kenya. Just when emergency purchases of antibiotics are made and adequate stock is ensured, the prescribing pattern of treating meningitis may change, and MEDS is left with an excess of stock which has a limited shelf life. At the same time, there may be a shortage of drugs for the new treatment.

One redeeming factor is that professional relations improve with a sharing of such drugs. Rather than allow stock to expire MEDS has shared some pharmaceuticals with MSCU and Kenyatta National Hospital whose patient loads are large enough to allow speedy usage of short-term shelf life products. MEDS has also "loaned" stock to some local manufacturers when they have had emergency demand orders.

The availability of drugs specific for tropical diseases fluctuates. Some of these fluctuations are due to changing patterns of diseases as in the last twenty years with the increase of chloroquine usage for malaria treatment and the subsequent decline in the usage of quinine. There is beginning to appear an alarming spread of choroquine-resistant malaria, and MEDS is experiencing difficulty in finding manufacturers of quinine. For the injection especially, it is difficult to locate suitable suppliers. Kenya experienced severe outbreaks of "highlands" malaria in 1990 with scores of deaths in the Kericho and Uasin Gishu districts. For MEDS, the stock of quinine injection was adequate for nine months on routine orders. With this epidemic, however, the supply was depleted in four weeks, before an emergency air shipment from Europe could replace it.

GLOBAL AFFORDABILITY VERSUS NEED

The relatively limited production of drugs for tropical diseases is related to the low volume of sales even though 50 percent of the world's illnesses are due to tropical diseases.[4] The Third World represents 75 percent of the world's population of 5.2 billion people, yet only 21 percent of the world's drug consumption in terms of U.S. dollars.[5] This market demand in the Third World may be an index of available cash with which to purchase drugs, rather than an index of the actual need of the sick who cannot afford a treatment which may be more than a month's wages. A few facts follow to elucidate the unaffordability of necessary medicines for the poor of Kenya. Workers' salaries in the rural areas range between $30 and $80 per month which is about $1 to $3.50 per day. The local wholesale cost of some vital drugs is:

Rabies vaccine	$36 per course
Antisnake venom serum	$22 per dose
Insulin	$50 per month
Biltricide (praziquantal)	$2 per treatment
Pentostam injection	$100 per treatment

The two latter drugs are for conditions prevalent in the desert and semiarid areas among nomad people who do not have a cash economy.

Some vital drugs are still under patent and the generic form is not yet available. These examples show that costs of drugs for tropical diseases are inversely proportional to the income of those who most need them.

The local wholesale prices of the Kenyan subsidiaries of the multinational pharmaceutical firms are often higher than the prices of the same brand products of the parent multinationals on the European or U.S. market. Albendazole and Pentostam are examples. Companies explain this high cost differential in terms of the expensiveness of opening a new market for a product or detailing expenses. Yet the cost of a brand product in Kenya can be five times higher than its cost in Europe, as is the case with Albendazole. There are opportunities for the pharmaceutical firms to invest some of their profits in the Third World especially by helping make critical drugs more easily available. Some multinationals are presently engaged in this effort.

Another example of what could be done is MEDS' revolving fund for investments aimed at making lifesaving drugs available to the rural people of Kenya. This effort is small and is used specifically to subsidize the cost to the hospitals of phenytoin sodium, the drug most widely used for epilepsy. MEDS would like to make more items accessible, especially rabies vaccine, antisnake venom serum, and pentostam.

MEDS would welcome contributions from multinationals to this fund. The larger the capital, the more effective will be the fund. The principle of the fund is the investment of the capital while the interest from it plus income from the nominal sale of drugs is used for the purchase of drugs. The sale of drugs would be 5 to 10 percent of the cost. This continues in a cycle, as a revolving fund. Five to 10 percent seems a ridiculously low markup. But the disparity between the need for the drugs and the resources of the church hospitals is absurd.

SHARED RESPONSIBILITY

The dialogue of this group presents an opportunity for information concerning progress and problems, creative exploration of mutual concerns, and an invitation to share blessings of skills, capital, research and development, and expertise in design and production. It also presents a challenge to accept an even greater responsibility for the poor and the disadvantaged. This seminar itself is a blessing by offering an occasion to share concern about these proportions and disproportions, and the potential for the greater acceptance of responsibility by corporate America.

NOTES

1. *IO CU Newsletter,* No. 6, 1990 (190).
2. Kenya shillings 8750 per annum = US$380, *Daily Nation,* October 8, 1990.
3. The Bamako Initiative was presented earlier in the section on essential drugs.
4. *International Development Forum,* July-August, 1990.
5. *IO CU Newsletter,* No. 6, 1990 (190).

Response from Africa

H. THOMAS McDERMOTT, C.S.C.

I lived in Dandora, a World Bank project on the edge of Nairobi, about a mile long and a half a mile wide, and at this point populated by about 75,000 people. It is a kind of a planned slum, a project where the government and the World Bank offered a water core and then had a lottery system where some of the lucky ones were allowed to build houses around this water core. It really was a place of hope, particularly for those who came from the worst slums, because it was a place where there was safe water and an opportunity to build permanent housing.

In this project we had a large maternity hospital or clinic ready to receive many women giving birth. It was owned by the government and built by the World Bank. Unfortunately, for all of the nine years I was there, this hospital stayed empty. We slowly watched the grass grow up around it because there was no money for staff. It was frustrating for all to see one large building in the middle of the compound which had no people in it. Each morning a government clinic at one end of the project would open with its staff of one doctor, several nurses and several kinds of aides to receive the various health problems of the neighborhood. It was popular in the sense that there were long lines. However, the people were often frustrated because the response was minimal, the range of drugs was very, very limited, and in fact, the clinic was troubled by a kind of corruption where the attendants, before you could even see the doctor, generally required a certain amount of bribery to let you move through the system. Any serious illness was referred to the national hospital across town.

H. Thomas McDermott, C.S.C., is on the campus ministry staff at the University of Notre Dame. He has recently returned from nine years of missionary work in Uganda and Dandora, a World Bank housing project outside Nairobi, Kenya.

The national hospital is a massive institution, one of the largest in Africa, a place of much noise and confusion, and a place again where people would often be referred and come home very frustrated. The source of the frustration is that, even if they would see the doctor after a long wait, typically he would give them a small piece of paper to go to the pharmacy for medicines. The drugs would not be available in the hospital and must be sought in the private markets.

We had private practitioners, people who called themselves doctors. I never knew quite how qualified they really were as doctors, but apparently some of them are. We had a wide range of medical services available because Kenya loves petty capitalism. There was a wide variety of other small, private clinics that were available where people had to pay a large amount of money relative to their income and where it was never clear how much adequate diagnosis was going on and what kind of drugs were being dispensed.

The most popular place for people of my parish church to go for health care was to cross a small river into the next parish, another quarter of a mile away, to go to a private dispensary run by a group of missionary sisters. This was particularly for the poor, so the poor would always come and ask us to give a small note of recommendation so they could talk to the Sisters. They knew they could trust the Sisters, who they knew didn't tolerate bribery, and so that was the place where most people hoped to go.

Across the spectrum of choices that were available, the typical person in our neighborhood would be very happy to have a chance to get in line at the private missionary clinic and have an opportunity to see, not a doctor, but one of those Sisters they could trust. For one reason, the Sisters were reliable; people actually believe they cared about them. The people had seen results from the Sisters' diagnoses and the kind of medicine dispensed seemed to match the needs of the people. Second, the people were treated with respect. It was very clear to them that they were not abused and they were given a kind of dignity which they deeply appreciated.

I had a similar experience in Uganda, where I lived for a shorter time, and out in the rural areas. There the Sisters received an essential drug kit provided by the United Nations. Uganda has been disrupted much more in the last twenty years than Kenya and thus it is less able to service its people in these various areas of health and education. Thus the missionary clinics there were even more popular.

The first point I want to make then is that, from my experience, there is a clear preference among the people for a place where they can go knowing they would get reliable and respectful care. They understood that to be, at least in our context, the mission place administered by the Sisters.

The second point is to highlight the relationship of the available health care to political stability. For some twenty-seven years, Kenya has been independent and is often cited, particularly in recent years, as an example of a well-developed sub-Saharan African country where more facilities are available in terms of education and health and there is less political turmoil than in many of its neighboring countries. But, as Sister Joan said, Kenya has many economic difficulties underneath the pleasant façade of downtown Nairobi. There are attractive, new skyscrapers and fancy hotels and the headquarters of the United Nations. (I think it is the third-largest United Nations' city in the world.) There are many diplomats and multinational executives visibly present in this apparently affluent city. However, underneath the façade of the downtown area, there are the surrounding slums of the city.

As the general economic climate for the developing world has become more difficult, Kenya has felt the pinch. In recent times, the people are feeling more and more squeezed economically as employment is more difficult to find. The government's inability to balance its own budget because of the growing cost of importing oil and other things, has caused it to be under pressure from the IMF. The World Bank advisers have asked the government to stop giving free education and also to stop the long-time policy of providing free medical care.

In the last several years, we have had developing in our neighborhood small Christian communities, groups of adults who meet together to pray and then to do a bit of social analysis, reflecting on their own experience. In those small groups, as people began to talk more and more freely about their own day-to-day experience, a clear sign to them that they were being squeezed and were being abandoned was first the fact that parents were expected to contribute a certain amount of money for their children's education each year. By American standards, this amount wasn't so much but to people who are working in the informal economy it was an extensive amount of money. When the government announced recently that to enter the national hospital you would have to pay an entrance fee of 50 shillings or 100 shillings—which is a few dollars—people began to say, "Look who has to suffer. Look what is being cut out. And we are the ones who are being left behind." A mother with several children who had someone sick was no longer able to obtain free medical care. People feel more and more squeezed and abandoned. I personally experienced, in reflection and conversation with our people, that these government policies occasioned a turning point. People began to turn in their evaluation of the government and they began to feel a growing kind of anger that they were the ones who were being abused by the system.

Previously in Kenya there was a commonly held idea that all one needed was to have one smart child out of all those in the family who would rise through the educational system, get a job in some multinational bank, and lift the whole family out of poverty. It was almost like waiting to win the lottery by having a smart child. This notion seemed to have served as a safety valve for all of the social pressures. When people stopped believing that education was available and equal for their children and when it appeared that the political leaders no longer cared about the health of the poor, we began to experience a growing anger and political instability.

Response from Africa

MUTOMBO MPANYA

The discussion about pharmaceuticals reminds one of an African saying which goes something like this: Trying to take a short cut one may
sleep in the forest. This is comparable to the notion of cutting corners
or haste makes waste. Many of the issues we are dealing with on this
topic are encapsulated in this saying.

My remarks are about how Western pharmaceuticals can best contribute to the improvement of health in African countries. They will
sound different because of a particular African experience that I bring.
But for me the difference is an opportunity to present another perspective and create perhaps a potential for cross-cultural learning and
discovery.

In Africa I worked in several countries including Kenya, Zaire,
Tanzania, Senegal, Mali, Ghana, and Cameroon. My experience has
been in the area of food and nutrition studies, community health financing schemes, logistics of pharmaceuticals, and economic development projects. I also worked on environmental issues and their implication for health.

It is important to acknowledge the work that is being done in
the area of health by different "social partners" including the governments, private voluntary organizations (PVOs) and multinational
corporations. Often African governments are portrayed as corrupt and
inept, which is true in some cases. However, it is also true that these
governments are working under very difficult conditions with limited

Mutombo Mpanya is director of the international environmental studies program at World College West. Originally from Zaire, he worked with international development agencies in several African countries for fifteen years before coming to the
United States where he has been associated with the Center for Research in Economic
Development at the University of Michigan and the Helen Kellogg Institute for International Studies at the University of Notre Dame.

resources of finances and personnel. PVOs have always played an important role in the provision of health care in African countries, especially with respect to the poor sections of the population such as those in remote areas. Historically, PVOs have not emphasized the training of the local administrators; most of medical personnel at the top level tended to be expatriates. Perhaps this was due to the fact that a number of PVOs receive support for their medical work mostly when the work is done with some Western "missionary" personnel. In that case Africanization of hospital administration could lead to reduction in outside funding. It is important to notice that things are changing now; Africanization is underway. Multinational corporations also have done a great deal for the health care in Africa. In many African countries, companies had set up dispensaries and hospitals for their local personnel. This has been the case in Zaire, Zambia, and Zimbabwe. Those multinationals working on pharmaceuticals have kept their business in the African markets in spite of the difficulties associated with doing business on the continent. It is also true that part of the reason for staying is that they are making some money. So, a lot of work is being done by multinationals, PVOs and the African governments to improve the health status of African people.

Having acknowledged the good that is being done, it is important to ask the major question about the use of pharmaceuticals in African countries. Namely, to what extent do pharmaceuticals contribute to the health status of African people. One should not look at the health problems in Africa as lack of pharmaceuticals so that their provision will constitute the ideal solution. The answer to the above question seems to be that pharmaceuticals alone contribute very little to the improvement of the health status of the people. For pharmaceuticals to make a meaningful contribution they need certain medical, economic, social, cultural, and infrastructural conditions which do not exist at present in most of Africa. Pharmaceuticals are like any other technology, their performance depends on the broader context in which they are used. Take, for example, an American-made pickup truck. One could get 150,000 miles of life in the United States; however, the same truck may get only 50,000 miles in most African countries. The reason being that the road conditions, the availability of spare parts, the quality of maintenance services are all different. It is the same, I would argue, with the pharmaceuticals; they make a contribution to the health of the people only if certain conditions are met.

I remember when I was in high school a friend had a urinary

infection and he got some medication from the dispensary. The medication was to be taken with a lot of water. But we were in a dry season in a place where water was scarce, even during the rainy season. People went for a whole day without drinking and drank only sometimes in the evening. This situation was not unique to this area; it is common to many places in Africa. So my friend took his pills with very little water, thinking that the pills alone would help. His problems got worse. He went to see the nurse again, and the nurse told him that he *had* to take the pills with a lot of water; the pills alone would not help. So it is important to know under what conditions the pharmaceuticals are helpful and whether these conditions exist where they are being used.

In general these conditions have to do with economics, physical infrastructure, and the local conception of medicine. From an economic point of view African countries have been for a long time now in a crisis. Since 1960 one could say that the economic growth has been very slow or stagnant. The prices of their traditional sources of income — minerals and cash crops — have been low and decreasing. Following the increase in the oil price many of these countries developed serious balance of payment problems. In the 1980s the debt crisis was so severe that in some countries debt payments took close to 50 percent of export earnings. Overall the actual income of the people has been reduced by about 4 percent a year since the mid-1960s. Under those conditions it is very difficult to see how people can buy pharmaceuticals. If they do, it would be at the detriment of food which is also needed for good health. Only a small minority of people can afford to buy pharmaceuticals — generally speaking — and that small minority can hardly be called the people of Africa.

From a physical infrastructure point of view most of the African countries are still rural even though urbanization has been increasing over the last several decades. Many communities live away from health facilities which are located mostly in urban centers. Transportation networks to reach rural people are not well developed. Roads are often dirt roads with very difficult terrain which can be "impassable," especially during the rain season. Rail transportation can be very slow because of the poor quality of the rail system, lack of spare parts, and lack of cars. Air and water transportation face similar problems. Overall, the transportation infrastructure has a small and unreliable capacity due to a lack of equipment and ultimately lack of financial resources. Also, the conditions of high temperatures and high losses in certain cases may make it difficult to deliver the pharmaceuticals where they are needed.

Perhaps the most important element in the African context in determining the contribution of pharmaceuticals to the health status of Africans is the Africans' own conception of medicine. Even though there are a lot of Western influences in the African medicine one would say that for the most part African conceptions of health and diseases have kept a strong traditional element with more emphasis on the social and psychological factors than on the biological ones. Africans know that social stress can weaken the body and make people sick. They will try, therefore, to reduce social tensions in order to improve individual health. Africans will look at a malaria crisis, for example, as more likely to be caused by a quarrel in the family rather than just by a parasite in the blood. As a consequence, they will deal with the sources of disharmony in the community while they are treating the specific symptoms of the malaria. This way of thinking is quite different from the Western medicine which emphasizes the specific biological process instead of social causes.

Another aspect of the African traditional medicine is the democratic character of the medical knowledge and practice — its accessibility. In general, common people medicate themselves frequently using common plants and procedures and providers of health care services are close by in the community. This means that medical knowledge is passed on in families from generation to generation. I remember that growing up I was taught to identify more than a half dozen medicinal plants to treat cough. Healers could be paid in kind. Often they wait until the patient has recovered. This is quite different from the Western pharmaceutical knowledge which is highly specialized and requires a lot of financial capital. Africans have tended to make the medical knowledge more accessible physically (logistics), intellectually (education), and economically. For Africans, pharmaceuticals begin to contribute to their health system only as they begin to be available for people to use them in their own self-healing.

Finally, another characteristic of the African traditional medicine is that it is inserted in a spiritual context which gives meaning to death. In the Western world, dead people are dead, generally speaking. In Africa things are somewhat different. Most cultures, including my own Luba culture, believe that dead people can come back to life and be born again. This is particularly true for small babies and older people who are perceived as getting closer to joining their ancestors. Generally, Africans believe that the community of the living constantly interacts and exchanges members with the community of the dead. This conception of death can help people cope quite well with illness and with the limitations of the medical technology and it gives a different sense to the grieving process (in case of death). This is not to say that Africans prefer death to life, but rather that they experience death differently and this may have a special impact on the way they may want to use pharmaceuticals in the treatment of certain illnesses.

People sometimes are skeptical about African medicine because they think that it is superstitious and ineffective, especially in the light of the current African life expectancy as compared to the life expectancy of industrialized countries. This perception may not be altogether wrong; however, it does not take into consideration some of the most effective cases of this kind of medicine. Just to give an example, I had a friend who was a Ph.D. student on a scholarship from the Ford Foundation. His wife was expecting their third child. He had failed the first round of comprehensive exams and was under the threat of having his scholarship cut off. He had also taken a job in case he would be without income from the Foundation. As he was approaching his second round of comprehensive exams, he began to develop a neck pain for which the doctors could find no remedy. At some point it was suggested that they should operate on him. As we were talking about his neck pain in a gathering of Africans, we inquired into his sleeping postures. He revealed that he did not sleep well at night. He had nightmares; he dreamed that he was drowning in the ocean and could not swim. We also found out in the course of the conversation that he had not told his wife that he failed his comprehensive exams and had taken a job. It was clear to all of us that my friend's pain may have been related to stress. We advised him to begin by telling his wife what was happening. We asked him to write a letter, with the help of his academic advisor, to the Ford Foundation explaining his difficulties and promising to succeed in his second round of exams. We also suggested that he drop the job until he heard from the Foundation and he should concentrate only on the preparation for his comprehensive exams. Shortly after all this was done, his neck pain went away. He passed his exams and got a good job with an international agency in Ethiopia.

This example is similar to some of the ways in which African medicine works. Of course, not everything can be cured like this neck pain simply by relieving social stress. There are severe bacterial infections that African traditional medicine cannot cure. But limitations are part of every medical approach. The point, however, is that the Africans look more readily to the socio-psychological system that produces illness than just to a specific biological function. In this conception, pharmaceuticals can be perceived as a part of a broader social health strategy rather than just medication to deal with a problem in the body.

In conclusion, I will make three points. First, it is clear that pharmaceuticals alone cannot make a major contribution to the health status of the African people. They would be an incomplete solution. Pharmaceuticals need to be provided with a context of economic development which would allow for their distribution through a modern infrastructure and at the same time give the people an increased income and a level of education to buy and use the products properly. Short of this, one has to look at the traditional health care and see what aspect of that system may be compatible with the use of Western pharmaceuticals. One should add that it is not the responsibility of multinational corporations, PVOs, and academics to single-handedly develop Africa; however, it is essential that these groups think in terms of overall development and its relation to the use of pharmaceuticals.

Second, it is important to avoid presenting pharmaceuticals in the African countries as associated with Western charity. This puts too much emphasis on doing good, forgetting the fact that when the right conditions are not there pharmaceuticals can harm people. We know cases of poor people who could not afford antibiotics, buying them one dose at a time, or people who were hurt by medications that were outdated because they could not read the labels. Also, it is not fair to give the Africans the idea that they are living in a world of tribal kinship where brothers and sisters from PVOs, multinationals, and academics have the obligation to care for their African kin. In fact, it is about time for the Africans to understand that the world of international affairs is guided by the hard ball of economic gain and self-interests. This is not to say that there are no individually generous people. Rather, the emphasis is on the fact that such a generosity should not become an impediment to the Africans developing their own developmental context to improve their own health.

Third, if the goal is to help improve the African health status, then African experience has to be taken into consideration and their voice heard. After all, Africans by now have had some knowledge of what works and what does not. PVOs, multinationals, and academics ought to find a way of legitimizing this experience and incorporating it into their reflection, thus enhancing the chance of better decisions about the medical systems in African countries—or in other Third World countries.

When I listen to the discussion I feel that it is all Western and it is all self-confident. There is a very little "epistemological" humility. Because of the power you have, you can intervene in the world of the Africans in such a way that your solutions are likely to be implemented even though those solutions may have a much poorer fit with the African realities. It will be helpful to all of us if you make room for the African views so that together we may find better solutions to problems of health and development. Trying to sell pharmaceuticals without thinking of the developmental and cultural context would be like taking a short cut. As Africans say, trying to take a short cut one may sleep in the forest.

Response from Industry

SUSAN CROWLEY

Is a company responsible for improving basic infrastructure in a Third World country? We have heard very poignant descriptions about the enormity of the problems in Kenya and that these are typical of much of the Third World, but we have also heard about the very limited ability of corporations to effect changes that will have a lasting impact.

Certainly, philanthropy can, and should be, part of the mix of corporate activities in these countries. The industry's approach has been to carefully select projects which present a good chance for success. The model established by the Washington-based agency, Africare, to improve pharmaceutical distribution in The Gambia and also in Sierra Leone—both with funding by the Pharmaceutical Manufacturers Association—has won plaudits from the World Health Organization, the World Bank, and others. As a follow-up, PMA member companies have underwritten a full-time pharmaceutical specialist position at Africare. Hopefully, with the new staff member in place, the Gambian and Sierra Leonean projects will be replicated in a number of other countries.

One of the problems most frequently raised at this seminar is inadequate quality control. Merck and other multinational pharmaceutical firms are taking steps to address this problem in practical terms by supporting a collaborative effort organized by the World Health Organization and the Council of the International Federation of Pharmaceutical Manufacturers Associations to provide quality control training for Third World pharmacologists in our facilities in Europe and the United States. To date, over sixty Third World trainees have completed training programs in company laboratories and manufacturing plants.

Susan Crowley is the director of public policy management for Merck & Co. With a background in Latin American banking, she has been involved in the management of international issues since joining Merck in 1981.

For example, a Kenyan spent four months training in Merck's quality control laboratory in England and is now employed in Kenya's Health Ministry quality control laboratory. Most of the companies represented in this seminar have also participated in this program with favorable results.

Another question voiced during these discussions was whether pharmaceutical companies—by virtue of being in the health care business—have a greater responsibility than firms in other sectors to ensure appropriate marketing practices. We affirmatively acknowledge this special responsibility and are carrying out a range of activities to fulfill it. One of the activities proven most successful is the selection of specific health education projects. For example, the Warner-Lambert Company has developed Tropicare, a purely philanthropic noncommercial health training and education program in place throughout Africa. A number of PMA member firms also support health education programs that emanate from a hospital in Soweto, South Africa, that may provide a model for the rest of the continent.

But, philanthropy is not a paradigm—it cannot be mounted on a scale sufficient nor sustained long enough to make a dent in the problem. Perhaps the most important contributions of multinational pharmaceutical corporations are provided through mechanisms of business. One of the most valuable contributions of pharmaceutical firms in this regard is the provision of critical information about the proper use of important new therapies to patients, doctors, nurses, and health care workers through labeling, background documents, and medical symposia. This information, essential for conducting business, also serves a real need: It brings to the attention of health care workers and physicians the fact that new therapies exist, and it provides them with information on their appropriate use.

Response from Industry

E. STEVEN BAUER

There are some inescapable realities concerning multinational corporate strategies and the pharmaceutical industry. Corporate strategy cannot be simply stated. Corporate strategy is the natural outcome of the perception of an industry within the overall configuration of the world in which the industry lives and functions. Thus, it may be useful to outline some aspects of the role of the pharmaceutical industry—what it is, what it is not.

This research-based pharmaceutical industry must be differentiated from other participants in the pharmaceutical industry such as a spot trader operating from Zurich, seeing what he can get from Czechoslovakia or Hungary at a given moment, or what a generic producer somewhere in England or Holland has to offer, and then approaching Kenya in order to win a bid. Remember that research-based pharmaceutical corporations spend 10 to 15 percent of their turnover on research and development annually. That is similar to sitting at a roulette table for a lifetime, one cannot afford to leave because so much money has already been spent. The research-based pharmaceutical industry, when stripped of its glamour, multicolored advertisements, and annual reports, is the provider of medicines or therapeutic substances to the health care system—a system the industry does not operate, control, or determine priorities for. The research-based pharmaceutical industry serves the health care system. It provides what the system seeks.

It responds to perceived needs by providing new or better therapies, prophylaxes, or disease management. Occasionally it perceives

E. Steven Bauer is the retired vice president of corporate and government affairs for Wyeth International Limited. He speaks from a broad background of managing in the Third World as well as teaching and research in areas such as cardiovascular diseases.

needs before they are recognized. Sometimes when a new or better or different compound is discovered, those who need it or want it the most have not been aware of the need or the product's usefulness until it was presented or developed. Those in the pharmaceutical business know many cases where products were invented, developed, and marketed for one purpose and those products had much more useful purposes that were not originally recognized. That is the serendipity portion of the research-based pharmaceutical industry.

The industry responds to the medical needs of people. For example, every company in the pharmaceutical industry is devoting increasingly larger amounts daily to every conceivable aspect of AIDS. Before AIDS, there were the vaccines for childhood diseases. Someone once said, "The industry is weird. People accuse industry managers of making every possible dollar out of every possible opportunity. And then they invent vaccines that prevent kids from catching these diseases so they cannot sell the drugs to treat those diseases. The industry cuts off its nose to spite its face." The contributions to vaccinations for the prevention of childhood diseases in the last ten to fifteen years has been staggering. The eradication of smallpox is an example. There was a time when typhoid was a 35 percent lethal disease in the developing world; today it is the rare case of typhoid which if treated within reasonable time after onset cannot be treated effectively. Glaucoma, one of the largest single causes of blindness in the world, can be effectively managed with modern-day therapy. The role of the research-based multinational pharmaceutical corporation is that of being supplier of these products.

The new, improved pharmaceuticals of today are the generics of tomorrow. And the generics of tomorrow will increase as the period of patented coverage shortens while the period of research and development prior to marketing lengthens. So from the time of invention at the chemist's bench or in the test tube and the registration of the first patent to the time that a new product is marketed can be twelve years or even longer. Seventeen years is the customary length of a patent; in some countries because of the long approval process, even more years can be added to the process. If there are five years of patent protection for a marketed new pharmaceutical product today, it is the exception.

It takes the pharmaceutical industry approximately two years to create a market for any new product. Meanwhile for the investment of fifty cents anyone can buy a copy of the patent from the patent office and start working in any lab to produce the product more cheaply.

The subject of generics leads to the related topic of a central drugs list. When the World Health Organization first published, and in subsequent editions since, its List of Essential Drugs, it was made clear that it was a model, not an ideal, but a pattern to be followed, something to be used or adapted for a minimum of medical care for the entire population of a given country, but particularly, of course, for those underserved, those who do not ordinarily receive the benefit of even the minimum of modern medical care. It was a minimum list for all populations of the country. The Essential Drugs List was never intended to be the total or maximum therapeutic armamentarium of a country. Thus, any proposal to limit available pharmaceuticals to an essential drugs list is to reduce the treatment for anyone in that country to the lowest common denominator. It does not improve the treatment for anyone, or as the Chinese would say in their lovely proverbs, "It only cuts the tops off the flowers." If only 220 drugs are available, more cheaper drugs can be purchased in a country and hence, hopefully, a larger number of people could benefit. This is an argument of expediency, not of medical treatment. It is an argument of expediency to avoid making a basic policy decision on how available funds should be spent or allocated. The tradeoff is whether a country should approve a new 747, a new fleet of Mercedes stretch limos for governmental officials, or new weapons systems. If a country decides that among its priorities is improved health care for its population, then it is not in the imposition of an arbitrary list of 220 drugs only. (The list published by the WHO increases yearly, it began with around 106 products, it is now 220, the next edition may be more.) If a country wants to provide good medical care for its people, it must be through developing a medical infrastructure. We have heard how the Kenyan government is attempting to tackle this through a system from the center to regional area hospitals to clinics to health stations with the training of more people to care for a larger number of those in need. But if there is no room at the top to grow, if better treatment or better therapy cannot be evaluated at Kenyatta Hospital, then it will never filter down to the districts into the clinics and health stations. And so this artificial "calling a halt" to the improvement in therapy for people is a serious detriment to improving the long-term health care of a country. It may do something for the Ministry of Finance this year because its officials can tell the Prime Minister how they have once again slashed the Health Ministry's budget, but it does not do one thing for treating people who are ill.

Are corporate strategies fixed? Are they permanent? Are they absolute in the pharmaceutical industry? They are not. This industry is in constant change. At times it leads, often it follows science and technology. It stays alert to the needs of patients and listens to what the health professionals define as their needs. It strives, where possible, to meet those needs in terms of products, product forms, and delivery systems. This change is in an evolving role. It is led by the evolution from inorganic chemistry to organic chemistry to biologicals to biochemistry to recombinant DNA; who knows where it will lead next? To state it more succinctly, the research-based international pharmaceutical industry is not like coal mining. It is not involved in the simple extraction of a raw commodity, loading it on railcars, and delivering it to the nearest furnace. With each package that goes out the door of a research-based international pharmaceutical firm, goes a potential life-or-death issue.

The issue of liability suits has been raised as a major detriment to policy decisions. Multinational corporate managers are aware of their responsibilities to patients and health care professionals without threats of litigation. In fact, it is probably not commonly known that the pharmaceutical industry actually invented quality control and quality assurance long before any other industry or production system adopted or adapted any similar subsystem. The industry has taken those requirements and standards seriously for a long time. In the industry, for each company, there is only one standard for quality control and quality assurance, whether in domestic plants in the United States or in Britain or anywhere else in the world, including the many plants in the developing countries. There is only one standard quality manual in the corporation. That manual is translated into many languages, but it is the same manual and it is updated every month and updated on a worldwide basis.

Thus, upon reflection, perhaps the multinational pharmaceutical corporate strategy is not a single document. Perhaps it is a set of cardinal principles, standards, criterias, and ethics which when taken as a whole becomes that elusive corporate strategy.

Discussion Summary

Michael Reich opened the discussion with a critique of the attitudes of industry.

John Kenneth Galbraith reminds us that there are basic issues surrounding the definition of a private corporation. He talks about the private corporation as not being private. He sees it as a public institution, part of society, and one that should be integrated through various mechanisms to promote public responsibility. In a sense he dismisses the notion that a corporation is or should be privately controlled.

The tenor of some industry representatives at this meeting is quite different. Their message seems to be, "Leave us alone; as corporations we know what to do. On investment, we will put our money where we think it is best; that may not be the Third World if certain measures transpire. On quality control, do not bother us with complaints; we can control ourselves. We have our own code of ethics, and it works well. Trust us; we know it is working. On philanthrophy, we will give you a little money for some activities, but we will decide what should be done. As corporations we respond to needs—the needs of technology, health professionals, and patients. We are aware of our responsibilities without litigation. We do not need litigation to do good deeds. We know what good deeds are. Litigation just reduces our efficiency. We can regulate ourselves without a code. And while we enacted the code, perhaps responding to some pressure, it really was not necessary."

This set of attitudes raises fundamental questions about how corporations relate to governments and to private voluntary organizations and consumer agencies. This kind of message does not seem to address the issue of what has been described as developmental responsibility. Designing corporate strategy to overcome these attitudes and achieve social responsibility in Third World countries represents a strategic challenge for the industry and individual firms.

305

Steven Bauer responded:

That is true. Those persuaded against their will remain of contrary opinion still. Multinational pharmaceutical corporations are constantly involved, both in the communities and countries where they are located, in what can be broadly termed "the social responsibility issues and roles" for a corporate citizen. Particularly in the Third World, however, involvement must be approached with caution so as not to infringe where pharmaceutical corporations have no right and where they would be seriously out of place were they to do so. Yet, it is easy to sit on a university campus in the United States and tell corporations what they ought to do in a Third World setting. However, Mpanya and Kimani tell us it is *their* country. We are invited to be there by their governments and their policies, but we are not there to interfere or to tell them even by implication what to do.

Rosemary Sabino raised the question of attitudes of activist groups.

As I have listened to the voices of managers of pharmaceutical companies over the six-year span of this study group, there has clearly been a shift in their agendas. Efforts have been made to correct abuses that were the result of the largeness of organizational structures. At the same time, the pharmaceutical industry seems to be moving toward withdrawal or minimal presence in Third World countries because of the hassle of doing business there — limited profitability and/or public image in the United States or in other countries. In spite of these pressures for withdrawal, they continue to try to contribute to overall health care in the areas where they operate. However, in some situations, there is never enough. There is always more to be done. This attitude is new in the business community.

On the other hand, there does not seem to be a changing strategy in the activists' groups. Much time and energy is expended in human and financial resources to produce abrasive confrontational behavior that will do finger pointing at the business community. But, there is still sickness and disease. Do the activists need to shift their focus?

Regina Rowan responded:

Just as Steven Bauer made a distinction among the different kinds of components in the pharmaceutical industry, there is a need to distinguish among the various activist organizations and their agendas. For some activists, including myself, the agenda has not ever changed. My agenda has been one of asking questions, trying to do it in a way to garner information, and to listen. I have made great efforts to open dialogues.

One change is that real dialogues are evolving. Corporations are starting to respond by seriously accepting questions, answering them honestly, and entering into productive discussion. Philosophical issues are at stake and listening is occurring.

It is dangerous to label people. A bootleg company from Eastern Europe would not be used to categorize the entire pharmaceutical industry. Therefore irrational activists from the fringe spectrum must not be used to label all activist organizations.

Dennis McCann stressed the need for cultural autonomy.

Both multinational pharmaceutical corporate managers and activists have acknowledged their tradeoffs. In thinking about issues and agendas, both corporate and activist, we need to stop and listen again to Mutombo Mpanya and Violet Kimani. They are calling for cultural autonomy but we are not listening. It is not on our list. They, for example, might even accept greater levels of infant mortality, or they might accept lower life expectancy in order to maintain the integrity of their cultures. They both seem to say, "Do not interfere." Both managers and activists must follow host governmental leads, accept the situation created by local society and government, and work within those parameters. Otherwise time and energy are expended in efforts to try to outflank governments to accomplish what "they ought to be doing but are apparently not doing."

Violet Kimani pointed to the need to help Third World governments within their own priorities.

When Kenya attained independence, three major needs were identified. The first was literacy. The objective was to give education to as many people as possible, both children and adults. The second major need was health. It was stated: "to fight disease," because there was an abundance of health problems. The third major need was poverty; the need for economic development.

The political objective for health care was to make it freely available to all. The Kenyan government did not consider it necessary to provide first-class sophisticated, First World health care, but health care must be made available to all citizens. The government has made a great effort to provide free health care for everyone.

When everything is free, there are no limitations. The system is doomed to failure. This is the kind of a problem where multinationals could provide some guidance.

Mutombo Mpanya emphasized the importance of cultural diversity.

Three points deserve emphasis. First, African people are generous. Second, we are ecumenical in every sense of the word; we accept things that come to us. Third, if anything distinguishes Africa, it is the variety of cultures. All the people are allowed to be where they are because any cultural development must fit its own ecological environment. Every culture has its own kind of rationality. It is extremely important to understand that. God in her own wisdom has created this variety as a way of helping humanity survive.

The Western culture is particularly monolithic and imperialistic, but not necessarily in a military sense. Reductionism, which reduces variety in the system, also reduces the ability of the world as a whole to survive. What happens if we all become Americans? Now, similarly, what will happen if the whole world depends on a single pharmaceutical company? We may lose the ability to survive. This is what is happening in Africa today.

The changes that came with the initial acceptance of Western ways demonstrated our openness to the world. We did not know how far the changes were going to go and how difficult they were going to be. But once embarked, the ability to keep that variety, that dexterity of strategies, is lost. Westerners came to Africa to fix things. They did not fix them, and worse yet, they seem to have made things worse.

We have accepted Western strategies, we are Westernized. Look at me. I am a Westerner. My clothing is Western, my education is Western, I speak a Western language. We took Westernization seriously. We are serious people.

Some say, "Things are not working because the Africans do not have management skills." However, many of our leaders took all the Western courses. The thinkers in our countries have been educated in the West. Perhaps it is important to include in those strategies the African insights, the African experience, because those people, having lived in that context, having gone through Westernization, having carried over all of their own traditions, have accumulated some kind of wisdom as a totalization of experience, which is relevant in any projection, in any planning of the future society of Africa. Moreover, Westerners must develop more generosity to incorporate a sense of otherness. Give us just a little bit of space, a little bit of doubt within your own confidence so that we can give, not only to Africa, but to humanity as a whole the possibility of greater diversity and perhaps a better chance of survival.

Joan Devane underscored the need for new approaches.

Multinational corporations must decide if they want to share. If so, the decision must then be made about how it is to be accomplished. If the principle of corporate responsibility is accepted as an ethical response and an obligation, the basic question that was asked many centuries ago is recalled, "Am I my brother's keeper?" If there is an affirmative response to that question, then the next question becomes, "In what way can I share the good things I have received?" There are two considerations. If the companies are making money in Kenya, then they have an obligation to return some of that money. If the corporations are not making money in sub-Saharan Africa or in Southeast Asia, then do they no longer have a responsibility for sharing? The managers present in this seminar are accepting corporate responsibility on moral grounds, whether or not they are making profits in these countries. They are saying, "Yes, we want to share, but it is difficult." It is extremely difficult for private organizations to say to governmental officials, "Look, we want to help but our structures are totally different. We need patience, we need understanding about help, and we need to consult the people themselves as to how they want to be helped."

Kenya has an excellent health plan. However, with nongovernmental organizations, bureaucracy is a problem, making it difficult for government to work with private organizations. In the health services, rather than joint services, there is a parallel development. The Christian churches cover about 40 percent of the health care in the rural areas of Kenya, and participate in the integrated rural health plan of the Ministry of Health. Yet, they develop their own strategy. There is a parallel development and mutual cooperation, rather than integration, which has existed for the last eighty years in Kenya. If corporations are serious about developmental responsibility, they must look at the operations within a country that have freedom and flexibility for incorporating outside assistance and freedom to incorporate the felt needs of the Kenyans.

Americans tend to focus on a problem, decide the way it should be handled, and then consider whether or not to spend money to solve the problem. In Africa, a different approach is often made. This is the circular approach, to fully understand all of the dimensions of a problem before making decisions or taking action. Problem solving is seldom confrontational.

Paul Belford reflected on the differences between Western and African culture.

The Reich and Mpanya comments tie together. The relationship between the government sector and the private sector in Europe is different from the United States. There is a substantial difference, not just a nuance. In Europe there is a presumption of governmental interference in corporate activity, whereas in American companies, while there is not a rejection of it, there is not an assumption of it. Multinational firms do not need litigation to be good corporate citizens, but it is good there is the possibility of it. There is not an executive in the American pharmaceutical industry who believes the Food and Drug Administration is absolutely essential.

Pharmaceutical corporations belong to the most regulated industry in the world. Basically, the understanding is that regulation is sound and good and we proceed in it. But, Mpanya is saying the African experience of the West was initiated as exploitative. Africa had things the people in the developed world wanted. There were some very unpleasant times and there is still hangover. At this point, where do we really want to go? Africa is still tempted to ask, "Do you have something that will cure malaria? Give it to us." It takes them away from a different reality where malaria was part of their life, part of their style.

There are cultural differences. The most technically trained MBA in the world might be Kenya's Minister of Industry, but if no one else in the department thinks in Western concepts, then the MBA might just as well not have been educated in the West.

Mpanya says, "If Africans are left alone, they might not have a high statistical quality of life, but they would be happier with their own style of life." Mpanya might ask, "Is life more important because we can measure how long we live and how many of our children survive?"

Our presumption has been that First World medicine is, in and of itself, good and should be shared. Mpanya asks, "Is that necessarily the case?" It is a very interesting question.

Steven Bauer placed the needs of patients as a high priority.

Pharmaceutical corporate managers consult with the governments of the countries of the world where they attempt to be active and do business, observing and respecting the established procedures and levels of authority. There is active contact both with the medical community and other health workers—pharmacists, nursing professionals especially, hospital administrators, health service administrators—to respond to their needs.

There is no attempt to impose U.S. health care, by any means available, on the health services of other countries. There is a respect for the existing cultures. People, with all of their cultural autonomies intact want their malaria treated, and want their schistosomiasis treated, and want their infants to live. It is possible to structure economic paradigms to create an idea that if some children died and some people did not live long, the total picture might improve. It is difficult to persuade the individual of this logic. So, multinational pharmaceutical managers respond to the wishes of the people in the health care system and those whom they serve—the individual patients. This is a serious agenda.

Wyeth International is a global organization: 12,000 people outside the United States, 400 in the United States in the international headquarters operations of the company. Of those 12,000 abroad, there are four U.S. citizens; all the others are nationals of the individual countries, or Third World country nationals from adjoining countries.

Penny Grewal called for more work on drug quality assurance.

Most corporate executives feel a responsibility to serve the underdeveloped part of the world. The questions are, "How far should this responsibility extend, and what kind of form should it take?"

Ill health is rampant in the developing world. Most of it can be cured either by present technologies or by improving the environments in which people live. It is not in anyone's interest to see children die.

Vaccines are one of the most cost-effective ways of preventing ill health and premature death today. But, that takes time. It is true the environment must be changed.

One of my major concerns at the moment is many drugs available in developing countries are of substandard quality or counterfeit drugs. This problem must be addressed. The pharmaceutical industry has knowledge and expertise in this area. Together with the World Health Organization or with World Bank financing, the industry must investigate ways to help governments screen their products. We need to dialogue about tangible things in areas where we actually can make contributions, where we can make some impact on the medical systems in developing countries.

Considerations for Multinational Managers

LEE A. TAVIS

THE KENYAN SITUATION

Kenya's Role in East Africa

Kenya has been described as the "risky success" of East Africa.[1] Due to political stability, an unusually serious commitment to education across all groups of the society, and a productive agricultural sector (Kenya and Zimbabwe are the only two countries in East Africa with private ownership of farmland), Kenya has continued her economic growth in contrast to the rest of East Africa.

These factors of success, however, are approaching their limit due to a high population growth rate (estimated at 3.9 percent). Kenyan agricultural plots are being divided among an increasing number of male offspring into smaller and smaller less-efficient plots. This represents the majority of the Kenyan people (85 percent of Kenyans live in the rural areas). Manufacturing is not expanding rapidly enough to absorb those who are being forced off the land. Only one in ten high school and college graduates can find work. The government has absorbed as many Kenyans as it can, employing about half the formal (as opposed to rural farm) work force. The larger markets necessary for Kenyan industrialization would need to come through exports to other sub-Saharan African countries.

Lee A. Tavis is the C. R. Smith Professor of Business Administration and director of the Program on Multinational Managers and Developing Country Concerns at Notre Dame. His work focuses on development at the grassroots and the potential contribution of multinational corporate resources to that process.

313

While Kenya has fared better than many other developing countries in terms of international debt, the government borrowed heavily to finance unproductive government-owned enterprises and oil for consumption. Budget constraints have forced the government to let some of these fail. Negotiations are currently underway to sell others. There are few potential foreign investors and even fewer Kenyans with sufficient resources or interest to privatize these firms.

Kenya has been a pocket of relative stability in the often turbulent political scene of East Africa since her independence in 1963.[2] Under the early leadership of Jomo Kenyatta, the Kenya African National Union (KANU) came to dominate the political scene. Following Kenyatta's death in 1978, Daniel Moi was proclaimed president. In mid-1982 Kenya was established as a one-party state by the National Assembly. The first political test was an unsuccessful, bloody coup two months later.

President Moi has consolidated the power of KANU by brokering power and favors among the tribal leaders. The largest tribe is the Kikuyu of Nairobi and central Kenya, followed by the Luo of western Kenya and the Masai of the south. President Moi is a member of the much smaller Kalenjin group. In studying the decision-making process of the Kenyan government, one is reminded of the Partido Revolucionario Institucional (PRI) in Mexico, where dealings within the party are opaque to outsiders.[3]

As a father image, Moi works at engendering great support and nationalistic feelings among the Kenyans and places great emphasis on overcoming the age-old tribal animosities. For example, in the boarding schools visited by the research team, a dominant theme expressed in the welcoming dances was the many ethnic groups represented among the students and how well they get along together. Still, ethnic differences remain a major tension in Kenya.[4]

The most serious threat to KANU and Moi is probably the current call from many sectors for a multi-party system. Stirred by the death of the Minister of Foreign Affairs in February 1990, the resistance to KANU as the single party is getting broader and louder.

Government Philosophy and Controls

The Kenyan government is drifting from African socialism to more of a market-oriented economy. While the Kenyan government is clear and articulate in expressing its philosophies, when it comes to setting and implementing policy at the ministerial level, there is great confusion. As with so many young countries, there is much yaw and gap between policy and implementation. Senior officials will make sweeping statements of policy followed by slow and cautious implementation. Budget realities are often the implementation bottleneck.

Centralized Power. Power resides in the president's office and, through budgets, with the Minister of Finance. There is a great deal of turnover at the ministerial level (an average tenure of about two years) but much less in the lower professional positions.

Ministers have little power. Due to budget realities, there are few discretionary funds. Most of the funds allocated to the Ministry are committed to the direct costs of running the Ministry with few monies available for programs.

In spite of the apparent political disruption associated with the ministerial changes, it did not seem to be a perceived source of risk to the executives interviewed.

Indigenization. An increasingly important component of governmental policies is the so-called "indigenization." This is the drive to draw more African Kenyans into the formal, organized economy. In a negative sense, it is intended to exclude Asians (primarily Indians), both citizens and non-citizens, and along with them European and American firms involved in manufacturing and distribution in Kenya. The government policy was stated well by the Minister for State:

A Minister for State, Mr. Justus ole Tipis, on Tuesday made a strong statement in Parliament where he accused some Kenyans—including MPs—of frustrating the indigenization of the economy.

The Minister pointed an accusing finger at some Kenyans for colluding with non-Kenyans, especially those of Asian origin, to frustrate the process by agreeing to be used as "rubber stamps."

The Minister's statement re-echoes what many genuine businessmen and leaders have all along complained about on this policy where businesses passed over to Kenyans revert back to the same foreigners they were acquired from.

It is clear that all along, the government's intention is to gradually pass over the running of the economy to Kenyans themselves. It is a process that cannot be achieved overnight given the fact that the majority of our people lack business acumen.

It is one of the reasons the government enacted the Trade Licensing Act in 1967 with a view of encouraging more Kenyans to get more involved in trade and acquiring businesses from foreigners without disruption of the entire economy. The goal has been achieved in some sectors, but more still need to be achieved in more sophisticated businesses.

The sad issue—and this is the concern Mr. Tipis expressed—is that after the takeover by Kenyans, some of them mismanaged and the end result they were to be acquired by same foreigners willing to pay more goodwill. This trend needs to be reversed and protection to be given to upcoming indigenous people.

To achieve this goal we need to apply measures through legislations to ensure indigenous people have a fair share in the economy. At the same time, the locals need to be educated on business management and be protected from unfair competition from imported products.

The government has already indicated it will step up the Kenyanization policy in the remaining businesses. Both Ministries of Commerce and Industry are vigorously pursuing the matter to ensure the process moves faster than before.[5]

There is a strong preference given to Africans in granting and renewing the many licenses necessary to do business in Kenya. As suggested by the Minister's statement, however, indigenization is difficult to implement. For example, the Trade Licensing Act required all manufacturers or importers to sell to distributors or wholesalers—they could not sell directly to retailers. This was designed to pull Africans into the distribution channels. As one might expect, retailers became wholesalers and wholesalers became retailers. In spite of legal attempts at enforcement, such as disallowing a wholesale and retail license at the same address, the law has been largely unenforceable.

There is currently a strong emphasis on the promotion of small businesses as a means of drawing Africans into economic activities. The government provides facilities for any entrepreneur who can prove that he or she has four employees. If the noise can be withstood, a person can watch the extensive recycling of metal barrels into stoves and other metal wares in the recycling sheds of Nairobi. Programs to aid small business with bank financing have been established, some with the assistance of the U.S. Agency for International Development and the International Finance Corporation.

In spite of all these efforts, the relative participation of Kenyans does not appear to have increased significantly. The Asians and foreigners are efficient operators. Moreover, they have access to funds—the foreigners to markets in the United States and Europe, and the Asians through family ties and various religious societies.

Nevertheless, indigenization is clearly a long-term policy of the Kenyan government and there will be continued attempts at its implementation.

District Focus. In the mid-1950s the government undertook a major effort to decentralize the Kenyan bureaucracy. It was presented as an attempt to develop centers outside Nairobi and Mombassa. If it eventually succeeds, it will move much of the governmental financial decision making to the forty-seven rural districts, including Nairobi. This follows the British colonial model where the district commissioner was a powerful position.

While there is clearly a philosophical principle of decentralization behind this plan, other motives have been attributed to the move. For example, President Moi has been accused of attempting to move power out of Nairobi, heavily populated with Kikuyu, as part of a broader anti-Kikuyu coalition.

As with any major change in governmental bureaucracies, this one is associated with a good deal of confusion. With senior bureaucrats being dispatched to districts and the associated civil service seniority bumping tied to the lack of clarity and uniformity in procedures, the confusion is bound to invite corruption.

Governmental Regulation of the Private Sector. Kenya gained independence in a socialist context. While all would agree that there has been a movement from governmental control to more of a market orientation, there are numerous regulations still on the books.[6]

Compared to the other countries in East Africa, the private sector of Kenya is not overregulated. Multinationals have more freedom of action than in Mexico and Korea—the countries most recently studied by the Notre Dame Program on Multinational Managers and Developing Country Concerns.[7]

THE PHARMACEUTICAL DELIVERY SYSTEMS

There has been dramatic improvement in the standards of health for Kenya.

The death rate is estimated to have dropped from 20 per 1,000 of the population in 1963 to 14 in 1982, while the infant mortality rate dropped from 120 to 86. Life expectancy at birth improved from 40 years in 1963 to 54 in 1982.[8]

Pharmaceutical manufacturers have played a key role in this success. Drugs are imported and manufactured in Kenya by locally owned and multinational pharmaceutical companies. They are distributed through the government health networks, a missionary network, and private channels.

The market for pharmaceuticals in Kenya is large for the country but not by international standards—about $30 million (U.S. 1985 dollars) to $60 million, as determined in a survey taken by the Kenyan Association of Pharmaceutical Industry.[9] Of this total, 65 percent is purchased by the government on a contract basis and disbursed through its dispensaries, health centers, and hospitals with the remainder moving through private channels: mission hospitals, local chemists, and dispensing physicians. This current balance represents a decrease from the previous government share of 78 percent in 1980.[10]

A considerable number of the government contracts are supplied by local manufacturers. Most of the rest are imported with a few supplied by local multinational corporate producers.

In 1984 the United Nations described the pharmaceutical industry in Kenya as follows:

The pharmaceutical situation in Kenya is characterized by (1) a low level of local production and continued dependence on imports of both raw materials and finished products; (2) substantial expenditures on drugs in both the public and private sectors; (3) predominance of foreign subsidiaries in supplying the country with its drug needs; (4) selective and very flexible regulations; and (5) lack of a well-defined pharmaceutical policy.[11]

Government Health Care

Kenyan governmental expenditures on health are modest compared to developed countries but high compared to other developing nations. See Table 1.

The Ministry of Health offers an integrated rural health network and hospital-based curative care which is usually urban-based. In the government plan, health services are free (via hospitals, health centers, dispensaries). However, medicines and medical supplies (sutures, X-ray film, and so on) are frequently out-of-stock, and the patients must buy them from private services.

Essential Drugs. The government provides generic drugs taken from the World Health Organization's essential drugs list. The Kenya schedule of essential drugs is made available to hospitals. Since 1982 a limited number of them are available to health centers and to dispensaries through a "kit" distribution system.[13] The full list, including all the drugs and the approved suppliers for each, is over 700 items long. We noted only two United States pharmaceuticals on that list, indicating that very few of the pharmaceuticals flowing through Kenyan governmental channels come from U.S. sources produced inside or outside the country.

Government medical doctors are not limited by the list of essential drugs. They can prescribe unlisted drugs, in which case the patient must have the prescription filled by the local chemist at the patient's own expense.

Tendering Procedures. Before the decentralization of the government bureaucracy, the government's drug needs were purchased through tenders issued by "Central Medical Stores" in the Ministry of Health. The most common procedure was to tender each year for a two-year supply with supplementary tenders when necessary. At times, the tender has been for a complete kit to be distributed to dispensaries and health centers. Tenders for complete kits can become very large, effectively eliminating all but the largest producers.

The government of Kenya tender policy in all ministries is to accept the lowest bid. For pharmaceuticals, this has contributed to low-cost drugs and the development of the locally owned pharmaceutical manufacturing industry. It is also associated with poor drug quality, persistent shortages, slow payment, and charges of corruption. The competition of the bidding process forces the local manufacturers to search

TABLE 1

Governmental Expenditures on Health in 1984[12]
(as a percent of total expenditures)

Country Groups		Selected Specific Countries	
World	9.83	United States	11.04
Industrial Countries	11.53	Kenya	6.73
Developing Countries	4.22	Mauritius (highest African)	8.10
Africa	4.37*	Zaire (lowest African)	1.84
Asia	3.05		
Western Hemisphere	4.92		

*Most recent data available is for 1978.

for the cheapest possible imported elements and the barest essential local mixing and packaging.

Quality has suffered in this process. The government has the authority to impose punitive measures on those suppliers who do not meet quality standards. The goverment inspects the factories and can close them if they do not meet the ministerial standards. But, the government cannot refuse to buy from a producer who is the lowest bidder on a contract. There are instances of drugs deteriorating on the shelf, large numbers in storage past their expiration dates, and numerous repeated instances of low potency. These quality shortfalls are not apparent at the time of delivery, only as the drugs are stored and used. The government has limited laboratory facilities and limited access to others sufficient to test samples.

With this discovery lag, it has been impossible to police quality. It takes time for doctors in the field to stumble across a low-quality drug. When they do, they are unsure whether the patient took the full course of the drugs, or the proper dosage. More time elapses as the doctor observes other patients and consults with his or her colleagues. Finally, after field confirmation, reports get lost in the bureaucracy. Seldom are effective penalties imposed on suppliers for low quality, failing to deliver, or other violations of governmental contracts. A producer may be stricken from the bidding list only to turn up on the next round with a new owner and a new name. There have been very few formal court charges of tender violations.

Every firm interviewed was attempting to minimize its government tender business. The managers of most firms, however, believe some minimum level of government sales is necessary to move enough bulk to achieve economies of scale and as a means of presenting the firm's brand to large numbers of potential private consumers.

Government dispensaries, health centers, and hospitals are persistently short of drug supplies. We visited one government dispensary where the nurse had been out of pharmaceutical products for three weeks. The area supervisor responsible for that dispensary had indicated the previous week that there were no shortages or problems with the dispensaries in her district. At another urban area, the health center was typically out of pharmaceutical products every second week of its two-week delivery cycle. The injection room was bare, as they seldom had antibiotics or other injectable drugs (vaccines, however, were available).

The Kenyan Ministry of Health, as with so many governmental

agencies across the world, is a slow payer. There is typically a delay of twelve to twenty-four months. The problem is not as severe for pharmaceutical drugs as for other items supplied on government tenders. In one case, we encountered a firm that regularly ran eight million shillings (20 Ksh/$) in overdue accounts and was suing the government for a debt that was four years old. Fortunately, the court system in Kenya is effective and the government can be successfully challenged.

The Impact of District Focus. Initially, the tendering of drugs was decentralized as part of the government's district focus policy. Under district focus, the decision-making body was the district development committee, chaired by the district commissioner. For each district, there was a tender committee handling all the tenders for the district. Representing the medical needs would be the district medical officer, hospital nurse, or pharmacist sitting with district financial officers and others. With a combination of some districts, there were about thirty-four tenders for all items, including pharmaceutical products.

The suppliers in the district were to be given preference. Licensed pharmacists (120 country-wide, 70 in Nairobi and 20 in Mombassa), wholesalers, and distributors became the preferred bidders. Producers and importers, of course, hurried to establish contacts with these preferred bidders.

District focus did not work for pharmaceutical firms: Some of the districts were in remote areas where simply collecting the documents was difficult; the advantages of scale were lost; the level of expertise involved in the tendering process dropped as hospital pharmacists were not as qualified as those in the higher levels of the Ministry of Health; district pharmacists did not have the same level of experience with alternative sources; and districts would spend their annual allocation of funds for pharmaceutical products in the first three months.

The minimum enforceability of quality standards was seriously threatened by district focus. The single quality check the government has is its knowledge of the supplier. Even though the tendering policy results in the acceptance of the lowest bid, officials are particularly alert to bidders with whom they have had bad experiences.

The effort to decentralize governmental drug tendering was suspended in September 1987. Purchasing was recentralized although the ordering of drugs and paying for them were left at the district level. Thus, district governments are still deciding what percent of available funds will be devoted to pharmaceutical products and what drugs to order. This procedure reintroduces some savings through economies of scale and allows for some centralized monitoring as orders are processed. The limitations of information, expertise, and experience at the district level remain.

Charging for Health Care. Alert to the many arguments that effective public health care cannot be obtained until the patient is required to pay something for his or her care, the Kenyan Minister of Health recently imposed a modest fee for access to government hospitals. Violet Kimani's statement in the discussion summary of this section as well as Agostino Paganini's description of charging for drugs as part of the Bamako Initiative summarize these factors.

The Kenyan people strongly objected to this practice and it was quickly dropped. Father Tom McDermott relates the feeling of abandonment on the part of his parishioners when they were charged for health care. There were other factors at work as well. The Kenyans were asked to pay a modest amount when they visited the doctor. But, then when they took their prescriptions to the government pharmacy, there were no drugs. They paid for something for which they felt they did not receive a benefit. Moreover, the reaction over being charged for health care occurred at a politically sensitive time in Kenya, when the calls for a multiparty system were being voiced loudly. A valid test of charging for health care remains to be tried in Kenya.

The Private Pharmaceutical Sector

There are three sources of drug supply in Kenya—locally owned manufacturers, multinational pharmaceutical corporations producing locally, and imports.

Locally Owned Manufacturers. As noted, local producers have developed primarily as a result of the government tendering process. At this point, they supply a surprisingly strong private market in Kenya and government programs in neighboring countries (Malawi, Zambia, Uganda, etc.). Most now limit their bids on Kenyan government tenders due to the poor payment history.

The largest and most sophisticated local producer is DAWA—a joint venture between a Yugoslavian pharmaceutical corporation, a Kenyan development agency, and a few private Kenyan investors. Initially, DAWA was envisioned as the dominant government supplier with the right of first referral on all government tenders. At the present time, however, it appears that DAWA competes on an even basis with all other bidders. As of June 1991, DAWA was one of the Kenyan government enterprises being offered for sale to the private sector.

Beyond DAWA, there are a number of well-organized producers and some very small firms. Although, the total number of locally owned manufacturers varies, in 1987 it was in the mid-twenties.

Locally owned producers concentrate on manufacture of generics, although their range of compounded drugs is increasing. Product components are imported with local content limited to mixing and packaging. It was estimated that the local value added in this process for government-tendered products was only about 10 percent. Imported components thus become the dominant factor in the price and quality of domestically produced pharmaceutical products.

We were amazed at the number of products offered by these companies. One firm listed over one hundred products in its brochure.

Multinational Pharmaceutical Companies Producing Locally. While most of the large American and European pharmaceutical companies are present in Kenya, few maintain production facilities in the country. As with the locally owned manufacturers, these facilities are devoted to relatively simple products.

Multinationals also differ in that they are components of an international management system. Their facilities and production processes must meet corporate standards and are subject to inspection. They have more complete laboratories than do local producers as a group. Imported production inputs are from sources with which the global corporate organization deals, or which are approved by headquarters.

Market Structure. Multinational firms (local producers and importers) seem to have a clear edge in marketing. Their packaging and advertising are superior.

Most multinational corporations, as well as some locally owned producers rely on detailmen to pull the drugs through the channels of distribution. This is necessitated by the general disorganization in the distribution system and the lack of marketing interest on the part of distributors and local chemists.

Many of the multinationals employ qualified pharmacists as detailmen. These detailmen function as they would in the United States, communicating to the medical profession details of a company's products. This practice is not broadly applauded. Some observers fear that detailmen, more pharmaceutically sophisticated than the paramedical personnel they visit, are in a position to oversell. Moreover, given the shortage of pharmacists in Kenya, employment as detailmen decreases the number available to hospitals and pharmacies. Governmental officials expressed a concern that their good pharmacists leave after training to join the private sector.

Governmental Regulation. The pharmaceutical industry is subjected to the full range of governmental regulations applying to the private sector in Kenya as well as those specific to the industry. In addition, multinationals must meet the requirement for foreign investors.

In 1982 the Kenyan government required the registration of all pharmaceutical products sold in the country. Suppliers were directed to apply for registration but allowed to continue selling while the requests were pending.

The criteria for registration are safety, efficacy, and quality. Kenya does not follow the requirements of the Scandinavian countries where a drug must be demonstrated to be more effective or cheaper than those already approved, although price is a factor in the Kenyan evaluation.

For imports, a consideration is given to whether they will compete with locally manufactured products. For new locally produced products, however, there seems to be little concern over excess capacity.

Many documents are required, including clinical trials. As a practical matter, full compliance requires access to the documentation submitted to countries such as the United States, the United Kingdom, or West Germany. If a product is not registered by country of origin, it has little chance of being registered in Kenya.

To register a locally produced pharmaceutical product, samples produced and packaged on the local equipment must be submitted as part of the registration package. Technically, this requires an investment in equipment and production of at least a limited batch before the registration application. We found no case where registration was denied in situations such as this, and understand that many producers commence distribution with the first sample while the application is pending.

Two committees are involved in the registration process. A technical committee composed of the chief pharmacist at the Ministry of Health, three other pharmacists, and two physicians evaluate the product. For the approval committee, members are nominated by the pharmaceutical society and chosen by the Minister of Health.

The process is slow. In 1987 there were still some applications from the initial 1982 registration that were not cleared. One company waited five years to have any of its less than two dozen products approved. For current applications, the process generally takes from twelve to eighteen months.

Delays can be traced to a technical committee overwhelmed by paperwork and an approval committee that meets infrequently. The technical group in the Ministry of Health which evaluates the application is the same one which approves import licenses. While they are trying to keep the process from becoming a "paper approval," they are buried in that same mountain of paper.

We found no perception of discrimination in the registration process. There are, of course, differences of opinion among the committee and there is a tendency of individuals to give preference to a company or country with which the member is familiar.

All imports must be approved. The process is clear but priorities are determined by foreign exchange limitations. Application is initiated at the Ministry of Commerce, then moves to the Ministry of Health, the Central Bank, back to the Ministry of Commerce, to the Import Management Committee, and then to the Central Bank for funds.

The procedure normally takes two to three months. Due to recent shortages of foreign exchange, the government has been extending that period by asking the applicant to resubmit rather than approve or disapprove.

Pharmaceutical products on the essential drugs list are imported duty free. Active ingredients, provided they are registered with the Ministry of Finance, are also imported duty free. Other products such as starch, talc, or packaging materials are subjected to a tariff. To the extent that components are subject to a tariff, local producers are placed at a competitive disadvantage.

Kenya has a broad system of price controls on basic foods and consumables, including pharmaceutical products. The political motivation is to keep the basic cost controlled.

For pharmaceutical products, the base price is the landed cost for imports (standard importing costs) and the average total cost of production for local manufacturers determined for each application with the components carefully specified.[14] The formula allows for such items as indirect expenses, finance expenses, exchange losses, and an allowance for a cost of equity capital. No explicit marketing expenses are included.

Beyond the accounting for costs, the price controller is allowed a wide range of discretion for consideration of such factors as the interest of protecting the Kenyan consumer and, in appropriate cases, making Kenyan producers more competitive in international markets.

Standard markups are then applied to the base cost to determine the maximum trade and maximum public (retail) price. Once a price is set, changing it can take as long as six months. In some cases, the approval is so slow that companies have discontinued supplying the product.

Within these constraints, shifting import prices causes the greatest pricing problems for producers since such a large share of their product is imported. With the Kenyan shilling closely tied to the U.S. dollar (technically tied to the International Monetary Fund Special Drawing Right), and most of the imports coming from Europe, dollar devaluation relative to European currencies puts great pressure on products selling at their price ceiling.

The policies controlling pharmaceutical product prices have changed substantially in recent years. The government has been deemphasizing price controls on pharmaceutical products. Through its tendering process, the government has been able to keep the prices low for its target group—the poor.

The process of price control has also changed. Now, importers or manufacturers can increase the price to the requested level if they do not hear from the pricing authorities within thirty days of their application for a price increase. For some, this has signaled the end of price controls as they will claim, if challenged, that they applied and did not hear. For others, who still wait, the government can acknowledge receipt, thus meeting the thirty-day deadline, without taking action.

A key factor in the governmental deemphasis of pharmaceutical price controls is that competitive pressures are causing many products to sell below their maximum price at the trade or retail levels. Estimates of the percent of pharmaceutical products selling below their price ceiling range from 25 percent to 40 percent with the more standard generic products experiencing the greatest price competition. In the case of one local producer concentrating on branded generics, all of the firm's products were selling below the maximum.

Systemic Tradeoffs: Price-Accessibility-Quality

The purpose of pharmaceutical delivery systems in any country is to provide informed access to quality drugs at a reasonable cost, particularly for the poor—access, quality, price. There are tradeoffs among these three criteria for each of the three delivery systems of the country. For the government delivery system, there are chronic shortages of drugs, over-prescription is common, quality is low, and the price is free. For the mission hospital system, essential drugs are purchased through the Mission for Essential Drugs and Supplies (MEDS); overall availability is good with some shortages due to international outages or in-country epidemics; over-prescription is not a major problem; drug quality is good although based on judgment more than testing; and the cost to the patient is modest. In the private delivery system, accounting for 10 percent or less of pharmaceuticals delivered, there is a broad range of generic and branded drugs available from domestic producers, international brokers, and multinational producers (domestic and imported); over-prescription or no prescription are problems; quality varies substantially; the price is higher and more variable than at mission hospitals.

Price. The price on government tenders is low. One well-informed source estimated that generics purchased on government tenders were 40 to 70 percent below the price of those sold to private distributors. After considering the savings in production expenses — bulk packaging, large quantities, and the lack of inventories to be maintained by the supplier — it is clear that bids are based on direct cost only, with the overhead allocated to products headed for the private sector.

Further evidence on the price through government channels is available in the products that mission hospitals purchase from the government Central Medical Stores.[15] In a small sample drawn from one hospital, the drugs purchased from the government's Central Medical Stores were consistently less than those purchased through private channels. The largest difference in our sample was 25 percent.

As noted, prices in the private sector are subject to significant competition with the result that many products sell below their price ceilings.

Accessibility. The availability of pharmaceuticals to the Kenyan people is limited by the national budget and access to foreign exchange. These have contributed to the severe shortages for government dispensaries, health centers, and hospitals. In the private sector, however, pharmaceuticals appear to be readily available for those who can afford them. There is a dual tier system at work.

This circumstance is especially critical for the poor in the vast arid and semiarid parts of Kenya where there are no cash crops to generate the currency with which to purchase medicines. In areas such as the Nyeri district where coffee and tea provide buying power, the people are not faced with the currency barrier. In areas such as the Kitui and Pokot districts, with few sources of cash, patients must rely on the limited government sources, on donations from mission hospitals, or on the sale of scarce personal assets such as goats.

Quality. In Kenya, quality is a much greater issue than price. The price emphasis in the tendering process is severe, and there are no ways of effectively enforcing pharmaceutical quality standards.

For local producers, the quality shortfall can occur either with the raw material inputs and/or local production and packaging. Given the price pressures of the tendering process, local producers or importers will submit a bid before they have purchased their raw materials and then scout the European market for these inputs. Raw materials and finished pharmaceuticals float around European markets in abundance, many from Eastern Europe and China. Some are of good quality while others are substandard. Others are near expiration. As the expiration date approaches, prices drop. The Kenya price bidder can thus be encouraged toward substandard and/or expired drugs.

Facilities for quality testing of imported components or finished products are limited. There are facilities at the Kenya Medical Research Institute or in the University of Nairobi for the independent testing of drugs, but nowhere near the capacity needed for a broad-based testing program. Even if facilities were adequate, there would be a shortage of qualified laboratory personnel and the need to insulate the laboratory workers from the outside pressures. For example, in another African country, plagued by substandard and counterfeit drugs, the government laboratory certified 95 percent of the drugs tested as meeting full standards.

With the budgetary and foreign exchange limits on the Kenyan government, full-fledged testing facilities are, at best, in the distant future. Investment in equipment and adequate staffing would cripple the ability to purchase pharmaceuticals. At this point, the government seems intent on imposing the quality assurance burden on the suppliers, although lack of enforcement makes this a most difficult policy.

The quality assurance for local production is also inadequate. Cases can be observed where the facilities for on-line production quality control are located miles from the production site or where exhaust fans at the production sites are mounted backward. Initially, the pharmaceutical plant inspectors were police officers who had no knowledge of the intricacies of pharmaceutical production. This is slowly changing. Beyond that, local producers with adequate testing facilities and the determination to use them incur a cost disadvantage. They then lose the economies of scale associated with government tenders and must offer their products to the private market at higher prices. Thus, in the Kenyan government delivery system, price considerations clearly dominate quality.

In the mission health care system, price considerations are not as dominant. In a number of hospitals we observed the price-quality balance as the subject of continuing tension between the doctors and the Sister matrons. The majority of doctors interviewed were strongly opposed to generics available from local Kenyan-owned producers because of their perceived poor quality. They recognized the differences among these firms but would not take a chance by prescribing any of them. Physicians opted for multinational corporate drugs, locally produced or imported. The other position was taken by the Sister matrons. In the missionary hospitals where drug markups are designed only to cover the direct cost of handling, Sister matrons saw their role as making inexpensive drugs available to the patients. The negotiated price-quality balance seems to depend on the access of patients to currencies (urban centers or cash crops), the background and training of the physicians (Scandinavian countries stress generics while Italy or the United States, for example, do not), and doctors' exposure to government health centers and hospitals where the quality problem is the most severe.

The development of the Mission for Essential Drugs and Supplies is slowly changing the doctor's perception of local producers. The MEDS selection of a few local producers and the continual monitoring of production facilities, shelf life, and patient reaction to these pharmaceuticals, along with some foreign testing, has dramatically improved drug quality assurance in the missionary system.

IMPLICATIONS FOR MULTINATIONAL PHARMACEUTICAL STRATEGY

As a multinational pharmaceutical company approaches a production and/or marketing activity in Kenya, management faces two fundamental policy issues; issues that are best confronted before entry: (1) What are the extent and limits on the firm's economic and social responsibility to the Kenyan people? and (2) What policies will guide the firm's interaction with the Kenyan government?

The first policy relates to what has become known as "developmental responsibility." As it relates to pharmaceutical manufacturers, developmental responsibility is the extent to which a pharmaceutical corporation takes on a responsibility for pharmaceutical production, distribution, and use of its products in an environment where there is little guidance from either the marketplace or the government, and where the firm has little control over the delivery systems.

The second policy, governmental relations, touches on every aspect of the firm's operations in a country such as Kenya where the government is so active in regulating and participating in the marketplace, and for an industry which is one of the most closely regulated across the world, including Kenya.

Developmental Responsibility

As noted in the introduction to this volume, the existence and implementation of developmental responsibility is the fundamental thrust for the Notre Dame Program on Multinational Managers and Developing Country Concerns. Developmental responsibility is the role a manager in the Third World defines for his or her firm within the constraints of markets and regulations. When markets are efficient and regulation is effective, the place of the firm in the local economy is totally defined as the optimization of productivity.[16] In a perfect world, managers are driven by efficient markets (competitive in structure with information flowing evenly to all participants) to maximize productivity. Firms with a productivity shortfall are culled from the efficient marketplace. For governments, while productivity is an important national objective, it is surely not the only one. The other social goals of a society are assured by restrictions on the market participants in the form of effective constraints — governmental regulations that reflect a social consensus clearly signaled and enforced. The market thus drives managers to continually test these constraints in their pursuit of productivity.

To the extent that markets are less than efficient and regulation ineffective, managers have flexibility to pursue their own objectives, for good or for ill. Developmental responsibility calls these managers to a consideration of all those with a stake in the firm's activities — employees, suppliers, customers, owners, communities.

The Kenyan market for pharmaceuticals is not efficient. Consumers often do not have alternative sources from which to select, and information on these sources is limited. To the Kenyan government's credit, competition has been enhanced due to the increase in local producers as reflected by the number of pharmaceuticals in the private sector with prices determined by competitive conditions rather than price controls. Still, the basic conditions for an efficient market are not present.

Regulation is clearly not effective. For starters, the existence of a one-party system raises the question of whether the government represents a social consensus. The mechanisms for enforcing quality standards are not in place — inadequate inspection of manufacturing locations, lack of testing facilities. Enforcement is not effective as evidenced by the fluidity of producers entering and leaving the market (or changing names) and the lack of court cases. Regulatory imbalance is obvious when the government tendering process drives prices so low that its own quality requirements cannot be met. Under these conditions, managers must be wary of pursuing their advantage against weaker market participants, unprotected by governmental regulations. Again, developmental responsibility directs these managers to consider the needs of their firms' various stakeholder groups.

Developmental responsibility is difficult conceptually, and unusually demanding in practice. For a multinational pharmaceutical company producing and/or marketing in a country like Kenya, the stakeholder group in greatest need, with no way of helping themselves and with no negotiating power to garner help, are the poor in need of pharmaceuticals. These people deserve informed access to quality drugs at a price they can afford.

For quality decisions, the multinational pharmaceuticals have taken a clear stance. "We will not jeopardize our global quality standards for any reason." Managers are determined to maintain quality standards far more demanding than those regulated or practiced in Kenya. Multinationals purchase raw materials from known or approved European suppliers, test those raw materials, mix and package in facilities approved and inspected by headquarters staff, and employ final product testing.

As reflected in the workshop discussions of the Notre Dame Program on Multinational Managers and Developing Country Concerns, quality is a non-negotiable, overarching value of pharmaceutical executives. This practice could be viewed as cultural imperialism — the imposition of values from one culture onto another. It is clear that the Kenyan government, and perhaps the people, are sometimes constrained to accept lower quality for lower price. In spite of this, pharmaceutical managers have taken quality as a matter of developmental responsibility.

As well as an issue of developmental responsibility, it is in the self-interest of multinational managers to work for the enforcement of their standards across the industry. This would involve putting teeth into the *ex post* quality evaluation with severe penalties for the owners of a firm who supplies substandard pharmaceutical products. Managers should push for broad testing and training of governmental and private-sector laboratory personnel, using the multinational facilities on a multiple shift basis. A local multinational producer has suggested this scheme, but with little response from the government. On an international scale, the Pharmaceutical Manufacturers Association program of training in Sierra Leone is targeted to this need. A third approach is to push for independent certification of quality. This can be initiated through support of programs such as MEDS — an alternative considered at the November 1990 workshop of the Notre Dame Program.

As for price, the requirement is for efficient production combined with a return to compensate for the risk of invested capital in physical and management structures. In a country such as Kenya, the political determinants of risk tend to be higher than in more mature, developed countries, although the economic dimensions of risk can well be lower due to the lack of effective competition.

A focus on invested capital, however, misses the main point. In pharmaceuticals, the issue quickly reduces to a question of return on research and development expenditures. This is the question in the discussion of intellectual property rights in Part II of this volume.

Informed access is the area of greatest invitation to the developmentally responsible multinational pharmaceutical manager. An informed user is one who receives full information about the product and knows how to use that information in his or her decision making. With pharmaceuticals, the decision is made by the health care professional prescribing or dispensing the drug. MEDS training focuses at this decision point. It needs to be supported.

Developmental responsibility calls pharmaceutical managers to stress published information and the communications role of their detailmen. Just as the multinationals tap the best of the available qualified pharmacists in Kenya for their sales forces, so they must ensure that this talent permeates the drug prescription and disbursement systems across the country. Across the world, one of the greatest multinational corporate contributions to development has been its training capabilities.

The key problems of access are lack of financing to put drugs into the system and the inability to get them through the system without deterioration. Multinationals have participated in making drugs available to the system through donations as discussed in earlier sections. Distribution is an area where multinational operating expertise should be of value, although Paul Belford's difficulty in finding multinational expertise for The Gambia project was disconcerting. MECTIZAN, the Merck drug for river blindness, is an example of an effort targeted to both of these needs. The Merck corporation developed and donated the drug. Great effort has been expended to ensure that the drug reaches the parasite victims with no deterioration or cost.

Interacting with the Government

It is essential in a country such as Kenya, where the government is so deeply involved with so many facets of the market, for managers to crisply choose a strategy for governmental relations. There are two ends to the spectrum of available strategies: power-based and participative.[17]

In a power-based strategy, management decides a course of action and aggressively pursues it into regulatory voids or in confrontation with governmental officials. A power-based strategy does not mean the corporation is necessarily attempting to take advantage of the local populace or of the government, simply that the manager's decision structure does not allow government participation in either the decision or its implementation. In the earlier example of multinational quality standards, the determination to maintain international quality standards in spite of local pressures to drive down the price at the cost of decreasing quality was a power-based strategy.

Participative strategies are based on a close association between multinational managers and governmental officials. Emphasis is on the long-term vision of the society and how the multinational can fit into that future while maintaining its own economic interests. This is a collaborative strategy. Governmental objectives are weighted with corporate objectives in policy decisions. Implementation is also a joint effort. The extension of quality assurance to make corporate laboratory facilities available to governmental testing and for the training of laboratory technicians are examples of participative strategies.

Participative strategies are demanding. They take time and effort. They require a much closer monitoring of the environment. They result in the relinquishment of power.

In a participative strategy, information is shared with the local government. Information is power and once shared, cannot be retracted. Beyond that, full information sharing means sharing the capability of collecting and processing that information with local authorities.

Indeed, in one interview with a senior governmental official, he called for just this kind of participation. He recognized the information processing and control limitations in his ministry, understood and appreciated the multinational corporate expertise in these areas, and indicated that he would welcome the assistance.

In a participative strategy, emphasis is on the clarification of regulatory signals rather than their obfuscation. Clarifying regulatory signals means relinquishing power. In confused environments, it is far easier to exert that power.

A major issue with participative strategies is the legitimacy of the government. If a government is not representing the social concerns of its people, developmental responsibility calls managers to represent these social concerns to the very government that should be espousing them. The bureaucratic equivalent to a politically illegitimate government are those officials who represent themselves rather than the society that employs them. Participative strategies call for extended dialogue and involvement between corporate managers and these officials, with the attendant opportunities for extortion and bribery.

As noted in previous volumes, we believe this kind of collaboration, although rife with risk for both the government and the multinationals, is the most appropriate in developing countries. In theory, it can be demonstrated that a participative strategy is more effective in the long run than a power strategy. The basic argument is that power erodes in negotiations over time and will always lead to zero-sum rather than positive-sum games.[18]

In practice, which strategy is more appropriate for a multinational manager in today's Kenya? Based on current practice, it is participative. In our executive interviews in Kenya, we encountered no power-based strategies, no statements such as, "The government simply must change. We are going to push them." The comments were more, "How do we communicate with the officials? How do we get them to understand what's going to work?"

The Kenyan government is not necessarily an easy one with which to interact. The lack of coordination among ministries creates a major impediment to effective collaboration. Moreover, there seems to be a deep-seated mistrust of the private sector, particularly the foreign component, probably stemming from the country's socialist beginnings.

As noted, we observed a number of miscommunications between business and government. In one case, the offer of multinational corporate laboratory facilities and training was not seriously considered by the government. In another, multinational managers were unaware of the desire for information sharing in the Ministry of Health.

What is labeled "corruption" in the United States is a fact of life in Kenya. One is struck by the number of financial scandals and the space devoted to them in the local press. The notion of a person's public service as separate from his or her private business does not exist and the public service regulations allow the holders of public office to conduct business in their own behalf.[19]

Indeed, the structure of the system, as described earlier, invites corruption: centralization of political power without new parties coming into office to reveal the shortcomings of previous administrations; administrative confusion; governmental agencies organized under the executive rather than the legislative branch; and lack of comprehensive governmental quality testing and effective policing mechanisms.

In the pharmaceutical industry, the charges of corruption in the government tendering processes are commonplace from both the business and the medical communities. There were accusations that influence had been exerted on registration although it was not clear whether the pressure was to approve drugs for which there was an objection, or whether it reflected a frustration with the great delays in the registration process.

The response of multinational executives to these circumstances was similar to that reported in the work of the Notre Dame Program study group, *Multinational Corporations and Host Government Interactions.*[20] Executives indicated that bribery was not a necessary condition for doing business in Kenya. As their counterparts in Mexico and Korea indicated, a no-bribe policy may result in greater delays for governmental approvals or licenses, but they eventually do get accomplished. In some cases, as in government contracts, however, it may mean withdrawing from that market segment.

Interaction with Nongovernmental Groups

The selection between power-based and participative strategies also applies to the interaction among corporations, religious networks, and nongovernmental organizations. There are, however, important differences in the nature of these nongovernmental interfaces.

The activists, although genuinely concerned with the poor, are not formally charged with that responsibility in the same way as the legitimate (or illegitimate) governmental representatives. Activists have their own problems with government interactions. Local religious networks and many other nongovernmental organizations have roots with the poor that few governments are able to achieve. They also tend to have tight international ties, more like a multinational corporation than a host government. It is this unique integration with the poor tied to links with the international scene that provides those organizations with social information networks on an international scale similar to, although less formal than, the multinational corporation's capability in international economic information. For example, the Medical Mission Sisters know what is going on in Kenya. They are inextricably involved with the rural poor through their hospitals and dispensaries; they are managing the pharmaceutical delivery system for these facilities nationally and internationally; they have a basis of comparison with many other countries where they are involved with health care delivery systems; they have an internal information network and a way of interfacing with others. When executives in our seminar ask the religious network members to bring forward problems of drug misuse, it is in full recognition of these informational capabilities.

The World Health Organization is similar to religious networks in terms of the information it seeks, but it is not nearly as involved at the grassroots. In this sense, the WHO is the social equivalent of the multinational pharmaceutical company. As noted in a previous section of this volume, the corporate view of the World Health Organization is changing from suspicion and separation to requests for the WHO to be more proactive.

Expand or Retract Kenyan Investment?

If multinational pharmaceutical corporations are to be developmentally responsible and follow positive participative strategies in their Kenyan operations (as distinct from philanthropic), they must be present in the country. The balance of return over perceived risk must be enough to prevent withdrawal from existing production and marketing activities and to invite new commitments.

The future for economic and political conditions of East Africa is not encouraging. For companies who want to enter or stay in those markets, however, Kenya is still the key. As noted earlier, Kenya, in spite of a rapid population growth set against a fixed amount of land and a slow-moving economy, is surely the best in East Africa. Exports, legal and otherwise, to the surrounding countries are a growth factor in the Kenyan economy. The risk and "hassle" factors are less than neighboring countries.

While the private sector and the multinational component of that sector face myriad regulations, they are not as onerous as those in either Mexico or Korea. There are continuing delays and frustrations over drug registration. The many licenses required to do business in Kenya and to move goods and funds across the borders and the continuing hassle of alien work permits (although few foreign firms have more than one or two European or American managers) were accepted as manageable by those executives interviewed.

At the present time, there are no restrictions on profit or capital repatriation. However, the observed shift to management contracts and technical agreements suggests that many managers do not believe uncontrolled remittances will continue. While Kenya does not have a large debt overhang by Latin American standards, her export performance is tied to international coffee and tea markets, and her debt is largely held by international agencies that are not allowed to reschedule.

Investment is essentially unencumbered. Even though the requirement for joint ventures with parastatals or local investors has been a cornerstone of Kenyan investment policy, it falls in the classification of a policy stressed for political purposes but one which the government is unable or unwilling to enforce. The view of the business community is that any investor who can meet the criteria of labor-intensive, high-use of local raw materials, and export orientation will be welcomed with open arms. The previous Kenyan emphasis on import substitution has disappeared with the new market concepts.

Thus, at this point, Kenya has the best political and economic investment environment in East Africa. It is also one where managers have been able to pursue activities we would call developmentally responsible. Either or both of these environments could change, individually or together, for better or worse, very quickly. As Kenya clearly demonstrates, the invitation for pharmaceutical managers to address the needs of Third World poor for informed access to quality drugs at a price they can afford, while still maintaining the economic viability of the multinational corporation, is a true challenge.

NOTES

1. For an insightful analysis of Kenya, see "Survey of East Africa: East Africa Turning the Corner," *The Economist*, June 30, 1987, pp. 1–18.

2. "Kenya Introductory Survey," *The Europa World Year Book, 1990* (London: Europa Productions Ltd., 1990), 1521–1523.

3. See Kenneth P. Jameson and Juan M. Rivera, "The Mexican Case: Communication Under State Capitalism," in *Multinational Managers and Host Government Interactions,* ed. Lee A. Tavis (Notre Dame, Ind.: University of Notre Dame Press, 1988), 204–238.

4. "Survey of East Africa."

5. "Locals Should Manage their Economy," *The Standard,* Friday, June 26, 1987.

6. See *National Legislation and Regulation Relating to Transnational Corporations,* United Nations Centre on Transnational Corporations. (New York: United Nations Printing Office, 1983), 208–223.

7. Jameson and Rivera, "The Mexican Case." Also see Kwan S. Kim, "The Korean Case: Culturally Dominated Interactions," in *Multinational Managers and Host Government Interactions,* ed. Lee A. Tavis (Notre Dame, Ind.: University of Notre Dame Press, 1988), 173–203.

8. *Kenya: Development Plan 1984–1988* (Nairobi: Government Printers, 1983), 35.

9. Kenya Pharmaceutical Market Survey, July 1985.

10. Mister Masafu of the Kenyan Association of Pharmaceutical Industry (KAPI), personal interview, June 1987.

11. *Transnational Corporation in the Pharmaceutical Industry of Developing Countries,* United Nations Centre on Transnational Corporations (New York: United Nations Printing Office, 1984), 105.

12. *Kenya: Development Plan 1984–1988.*

13. Gerald Moore, the consultant who initiated the kit system in Kenya, presents his experience earlier in this section.

14. *Price Control Act,* The Minister of Finance Legal Notice No. 302, November 24, 1986.

15. At the time of the sample, mission hospitals could purchase drugs from the government's Central Medical Stores at cost plus 10 percent. Since 1989, this access has been discontinued.

16. See Lee A. Tavis, "Multinational Corporate Responsibility for Third World Development," *Review of Social Economy* 40, no. 3 (December 1982): 427–437.

17. Strategies for multinational corporate interaction with host governments is the subject of Volume II in the series, "Multinational Managers and Developing Country Concerns." For a discussion on power-based versus participative strategies, see Lee A. Tavis and William P. Glade, "Implications for Corporate Strategy," *Multinational Managers and Host Government Interactions* (Notre Dame, Ind.: University of Notre Dame Press, 1988), 287–319.

18. Ibid., 293–301, 314n.12, and 315n.14.

19. "Survey of East Africa," 9.

20. Jameson and Rivera, "The Mexican Case"; also see Kim, "The Korean Case."

PART 4

Moral Commitments and Collaboration

The conclusion to this volume captures the current sense of challenge, response, and possibilities for collaboration between activists and multinational pharmaceutical managers. Regina Rowan, S.C.M.M., poses the invitation based upon her work in Venezuelan health care, her involvement with the study group, and her present role as the chairperson of the Pharmaceutical Workgroup of the Interfaith Center on Corporate Responsibility. Al Angel responds from the corporate view. As the past senior counsel and line manager with responsibility for Merck's operations in Anglophone Africa, he brings a broad view to the notion of corporate social responsibility and the potential role of religious networks in interacting with multinational corporations in its implementation.

An Activist Voice

REGINA ROWAN, S.C.M.M.

In April 1985 I introduced my comments on the relationship between the pharmaceutical industry and religious networks as follows:

The establishment of a dialogue is needed at this time. The pharmaceutical industry has found itself in a different and perplexing situation. The industry is being strongly criticized by religious groups and others.

What perception of itself has the pharmaceutical industry promoted? How does the ordinary person regard the industry? The industry is aligned, in people's minds, with other health care providers. A great deal is expected from the pharmaceutical industry.

At the same time there is a real need for the industry to explain itself to the public. The industry must respond. When it chooses not to do that, people reach the conclusion that their concerns are not being taken seriously and the industry is perceived as arrogant and uncaring. At this juncture, the confrontational mode of reacting to each other is established.

An approach to change this mode would be to explore areas of agreement, to enter into "constructive engagement." The setting of a common goal which can be used as a benchmark for discussion is important. Such a common goal would be the provision of safe, therapeutically effective medications available at affordable prices for all. Actions could then be held against the goal for evaluation.

It is important for us to work together and focus on what we can do. Time is short. In developing countries and throughout the world, people are dying while we defend our turf. I call on the pharmaceutical

Regina Rowan, S.C.M.M. is chairperson of the Pharmaceutical Workgroup of the Interfaith Center on Corporate Responsibility. For eight years, she directed the clinical laboratories for the Medical Mission Sisters in Venezuela and also served as the assistant administrator for her community's hospital in Caripito, Venezuela.

industry to begin a constructive engagement in dialogue with its critics. Through this mode, areas of commonality will be discovered and much more can be accomplished.

In the intervening years, two issues have demanded our attention: the conditions in Third World countries, and the ethics of the industry.

PHARMACEUTICAL NEEDS

Countries around the world are facing critical health needs. Drugs are needed to treat major health problems in their populations — tuberculosis, leprosy, and parasitic diseases such as malaria, schistosomiasis, trypanosomiasis, leishmaniasis, and onchocerciasis. Yet these countries do not have the money to pay for the drugs needed.

In order to improve the quality of life one must consider the economics involved in achieving this. Poverty, lack of education, and the lack of infrastructures to address these issues affect the health care available. These issues need to be addressed if the quality of life is to be improved.

There are basic health prerequisites in any community, whether in developed or developing countries. Without these requirements there will not be good health or improved quality of life. These prerequisites include: a regular source of clean drinking water, proper diet, adequate nutrition, sufficient housing, vector control, vaccination programs, more health professionals, and health education.

There is a need for more physicians, pharmacists, and other health care providers to staff a good health care system, especially in rural areas. Many health care professionals are underpaid and overworked, with limited resources of medicines and equipment to care for patients. These professionals want better wages, more equitable working and living conditions, and adequate schooling for their children. They abandon rural areas for urban ones or leave the underdeveloped countries so they can procure more of these benefits. This can result in entire populations without access to a "medical system."

Those who live in developing countries have additional concerns. The training of doctors and other health care providers in Western-type medical systems has created the need for sophisticated medicines with little regard for traditional medicine or home remedies. This has led to a growing dependence on these drugs and the belief in their omnipotence. This dependence, which has been nurtured, has led to many problems such as over-medication, self-medication, and inappropriate medication.

Local health education is critical. It is composed of two parts: the education of individuals (the local people) so they can assume responsibility for their own health, and the education of all those who are part of health care delivery. These types of education will assist in drug use compliance, seeking of medical care, and the avoidance of over-medicating. The combination of these prerequisites and health education are important parts of preventive medicine, which is a necessary complement for the curative role for which pharmaceuticals are used.

Medicines may be carefully manufactured, stored, and shipped by the pharmaceutical companies but the system seems to break down or is nonexistent when these products reach a developing country. What happens when the product reaches the wholesaler or distributor? Drugs are not properly stored, shipped, and dispensed. Vaccines are useless if they sit in a heated warehouse. Improper rotation of stock can result in the use of expired drugs. Precious financial resources are wasted. How does the vital information of indications, contraindications, and adverse reactions reach the health care provider? Companies state they have no control over the drug once it is shipped to the wholesaler or distributor. Yet the need for drug information that is easily available to the health care providers is critical. This lack of information has been a source of contention between the pharmaceutical industry and consumer activists for years.

LOCAL GOVERNMENT RESPONSES

Government regulatory systems to assess the quality of drugs to ensure that they are therapeutically effective and to remove those drugs which are not of that quality are a critical component of any delivery system. There are many companies providing or manufacturing medication. Some of these firms are unscrupulously selling drugs that have little or no therapeutic efficacy. These companies can include national firms as well as those from countries which have less stringent regulations and codes. Substandard producers must be identified and removed.

Many government agencies purchase items they do not need or

which they cannot afford to use. How can the pharmaceutical industry address that problem, or should it?

We need research and development dollars allocated by drug companies to provide the new drugs to treat parasitic diseases. But governmental money to purchase these drugs is lacking in many developing countries and companies cannot afford the expense to develop the new drugs and then give them away.

PHARMACEUTICAL INDUSTRY RESPONSE

Under these conditions, does a multinational pharmaceutical company have an obligation to promote health, improve the quality of life, and contribute to basic requirements such as clean water and proper nutrition because it does business in an underdeveloped country? Do pharmaceutical companies have a greater obligation because they are in the health business? If the obligation does exist, where does it begin and where does it end?

If a company sells products to treat diseases caused by contaminated water, should health education on the need to boil water or to locate sources of potable water be on the agenda of that company? Is it more appropriate to include an active campaign for the use of clean water with the advertising and selling of prepackaged oral rehydration packets to treat infant diarrhea? Would it be feasible to go one step further with these oral rehydration packets and sell the product premixed in clean water? How can all those interested in promoting health and improving the quality of life for the poor in developing countries address these questions?

Alternatively, the pharmaceutical industry needs to make a profit in order to contribute to health care. I have no problem with this. But, the industry must be aware that when people are denied access to health care and medicines because of their cost, when people suffer and die because of lack of resources, the issue of how much profit is being made takes on an entirely different slant.

There is a need to provide medicines at affordable prices. What is an affordable price? What is the tradeoff between affordable prices and corporate profit margins?

These needs for the people, returns for the companies, and notions of responsibility are based on what we have been calling "ethics." What is ethics? What is the ethos that holds a company together? I am not a theologian nor a philosopher but an ethos in a company or in any group, it seems to me, is that moral value that holds a group together and motivates the actions of individual members. When members of any group believe they have "wonderful policies" but the "bottom line" of the group is money—how to make it, how to keep it, and how to spend it—a real challenge exists.

The word "challenge" has many layers. We are going to try to look at some of these. They need to be peeled like an onion. So we are here to peel onions to look at the various layers.

Corporate America is faced with many challenges and one foremost for this group is the challenge of leadership. Most businesses have high ethical standards. No company policy states, "We are in business to harm people. We are in business to disregard the rights of others, to lie, and to cheat. We do not keep promises or contracts. If you disobey the law, our day will be made." However, we must be honest in identifying the ethics that drive us. Not just the corporate body, but each one of you, because you are the corporation. What you are and what you want to do is going to influence that corporation.

Creativity abounds in a multinational pharmaceutical company. A corporation has scientists who spend hours and millions of dollars to develop a product. And everyone in the company feels good about the end result. The advertising people look for the best way to get the message about the product to the public. Marketing personnel work to get the product to the public. All of that effort and creativity is thrown away if the product is not used correctly.

Why should corporations accept this challenge of providing safe, therapeutically effective drugs at affordable prices? The first reason is because it is the moral thing to do. We have no other choice but to do that which is right. It is a moral obligation because we share this planet and we are acting to achieve the common good. That has to be our underlying goal. It does not matter if we get famous for accepting the challenges we are offering to each other; it does not matter if we get rich as a result of it. The important thing is to act on the challenges presented to us here.

Legality should be our minimum standard. Corporate managers should not be saying, "It is legal. If we are obeying the law, we have fulfilled all of our obligations." Go beyond legality. Start with the challenges.

After reflecting on where we have come over the last five-and-a-half years, I conclude by commending companies for the efforts which they have made to provide safe and therapeutically effective drugs. Multinational pharmaceutical corporations do a great deal to promote health and improve the quality of life. I urge them to be creative in finding ways to continue to do so, and in expanding their efforts. I urge them to dream — to dream with their critics and to dream with those who praise them.

We started this seminar with the concept of challenge. Our challenge started with a way to find efficient, reliable distribution and communication channels. The need for education and training was repeated over and over. Look at these needs as angles in a triangle. Medicines are in one angle, health education in another, and drug information is in the third. They go around and around supporting each other. The good practice of medicine is not possible without education. Drug information must be available to use the medicines as well as to build education.

We have talked about the fact that there are not enough medicines in many cases. We have talked about counterfeit and spurious drugs that are available. We have discussed an essential drugs list to treat the majority of common ailments. We have talked about the need to treat tropical diseases. We need to find ways of collaborating to provide the access to adequate health care for all. I suggest we covenant with each other to work to the best of our ability to make this possible. We have made a real breakthrough in looking at these issues. I hope we are going to find ways to continue what we have started. It would be a pity to have all of this good will and this energy wasted. What are we going to do to be partners to continue?

An Industry Voice

ALBERT D. ANGEL

There is a tendency—call it "intellectual imperialism" or "scientific imperialism"—to assume we know all the answers. Mutombo Mpanya cautioned us about this tendency. As we approach the role of multinationals in Third World locations, we must be humble in recognizing that we do not know all the answers.

From a corporate perspective, this meeting revolves around three themes. First, what is the nature of corporate social responsibility—the extent of corporate social responsibility and the constraints associated with it? Second, what are the rules by which companies conduct their core business—the nature of the rules and the role of outsiders in helping corporations determine what those rules are? The third is something very important for outsiders to take into account in their discussions with corporations—what conditions are necessary for corporations to conduct their business? Each of these questions has influenced our discussions.

THE NATURE OF CORPORATE SOCIAL RESPONSIBILITY

I will share some background and questions about Merck's decision to donate the drug MECTIZAN for treatment of onchocerciasis, also known as river blindness, for as long as it is needed to help as

Albert D. Angel is vice president of public affairs for Merck & Co., Inc., president of The Merck Company Foundation, and member of the firm's Management Council. An attorney, he has served as senior counsel for Merck with responsibility for international legal affairs, as well as in line management as the chairman and managing director of Merck Sharp & Dohme, Ltd., in London with responsibilities for the United Kingdom, Ireland, and Anglophone African operations.

many people as possible. This decision was debated among our managers for eight months. We took the question seriously. The discussions consumed enormous amounts of time.

Typically, debates about donating MECTIZAN were preceded by discussions on the value of conducting orphan drug research. In a sense, orphan drug research is a zero-sum game. Merck will spend one billion dollars on research in 1991. Despite this enormous sum of money all potential research projects cannot be followed to completion. Research management must make choices.

That is the reality of our business. For example, a company has two roads to travel in research. One road leads to a potential cure for river blindness in the Third World, the other leads to a useful First World medicine. There will be profits from the product in the First World, there will not be any from the product in the Third World. What should the company do?

At Merck, there was no question about what to do when faced with the onchocerciasis challenge. We did our homework, and we knew that most of the people for whom MECTIZAN was meant were in Africa with some in Latin America and others in certain parts of the Middle East. For the most part, these people had no money.

We discussed the issue at great length with many people, including members of our European Advisory Council. Some were strongly opposed to giving the product away. If a successful, profitable company such as Merck were willing to commit several million dollars in research knowing it would get "zero" in return, what precedent would be set for our competitors who may be less prosperous or who may have similar types of leads?

Many questions must be answered each time a company thinks about its social responsibility. In addition to addressing a present need, a company must project the resulting implications and complications of its actions. With MECTIZAN, for example, even if we were to give the medicine away, how were we to get it to the people who needed it? We learned quickly that there are very few viable infrastructures for drug delivery in the remote areas afflicted by onchocerciasis.

Merck has committed enormous time and resources to the MECTIZAN project. In addition to donating the drug, Merck has devoted millions of dollars to the activity of the MECTIZAN Expert Committee, which evaluated applications for MECTIZAN. Merck has a full-time parasitologist working in Africa to see that MECTIZAN reaches as many people who need it as quickly as possible. We are trying to get everyone to work together on this project, which has surpassed by far anything we have done in distributing other products in Africa.

More than one-and-a-half million people have received MECTI-ZAN at least once. Many have received it for two, three, or four years.

Projects of varying size are underway in all of Central and Western Africa where the disease is endemic. Particularly impressive is the extent to which MECTIZAN has been used in the eleven-country region in West Africa covered by the Onchocerciasis Control Program (insecticide spraying) administered by the World Health Organization.

Even with this progress, eighty-five million people remain untreated. In the First World, if only one-and-a-half million people were treated out of eighty-five million who were at risk, the project would be considered a failure and the product manager would be fired. What is the balance for a socially responsible company?

The MECTIZAN experience has drawn us to a much broader social challenge. Research in tropical parasitology may lead to a drug that could help the four hundred million people who have elephantiasis. That is nearly five times the eighty-five million people afflicted with onchocerciasis.

Merck is moving ahead with the elephantiasis project even though there are other issues of concern closer to home which can fully occupy a socially conscious company; two examples: the AIDS crisis in the United States, and our scientifically illiterate society. The concern about AIDS is evident, but the latter issue is significant in a different way. Everything possible must be done to assure that those emerging from our educational system are scientifically literate. Even if they do not pursue careers in science, all people must possess at least a basic knowledge of science in order to make sound policy decisions for this country in the twenty-first century. You and I can think of other issues which can command massive resources. But, there is a limit to what we can do.

Philanthropy is another critical component of social responsibility. At Merck, a great deal of time is spent thinking about the philanthropic good we can do in Third World nations. Some people ask, "Why should we do anything in the Third World when there is so much to do in the First World?" From the perspective of the poor, there is as much to be done in New York and Manchester as there is in other parts of the world.

There are many questions for which I have no answers and that is one of them. In essence, the question could be recast to, "How much money do you make by way of sales in these countries, and what is the percentage of your philanthropy to those sales?" Merck's sales in the Third World are a very small part of our business, and yet our contributions in that part of the world are proportionally much higher.

Philanthropy has three components—products, money, and people/technology/time. Companies must use their individual judgment, based on the priorities they have set, in responding to the proposals they receive.

We will provide our products free of charge in selected cases. Last year, Merck gave away twenty-eight million dollars worth of drugs. Our company does not give expired goods; we donate in-line products. However, the problem of getting the product from here to there still exists. Berating the donor does not solve this problem. Rather, efforts must concentrate on improving the distribution chain, which includes the private voluntary organizations, to make certain the drug actually reaches its intended destination. In this seminar, examples of good projects have been outlined. Also, problems encountered in getting voluntary organizations to work together have been presented. Corporations have similar problems. Countries, too, have enormously difficult problems.

We will only give our drugs to organizations who have proven they can actually get the medicine to where it is needed, because we do not always have that skill. This means refusing many worthy groups. Our priority is to get products to the patients; thus, we work primarily with those who can achieve that objective.

Merck also provides a great deal of training. In addition to the Africare drug inventory management projects now functioning in three African countries, we have trained quality assurance technicians from Africa in our British laboratories. For the past twenty-five years, The Merck Company Foundation has been awarding fellowships to train people, most from the Third World, to become experts in clinical pharmacology, and then return to their native land. It is impossible to guarantee they will stay and practice in the Third World, but most have returned.

One may ask why we do not expand our programs to address other great needs. Priority setting means every worthy cause cannot be accommodated. Every need cannot become a priority.

A question fundamental to the work of this seminar is the nature of the rules by which companies conduct business, and how people outside the corporation often help the company make certain decisions. Leisinger spoke about "the rules of the road," the various rules companies make for themselves. For example, where, how, and what should govern research decisions? How must marketing be conducted? What are the ethical rules? What are the appropriate levels of return expected? How do we define what return is necessary to justify the risk of investing eight hundred million to one billion dollars a year in research, knowing that many product candidates will fail?

There are certain rules of civility associated with helping a corporation come to conclusions about business. Those who do not believe a multinational pharmaceutical corporation should make profits should not be too surprised if the firm's members do not listen. Also, there is a growing anti-science movement around the world that says, "My cup is filled enough, stop the world, and figure out how we redistribute the existing knowledge for the greater good." We at Merck do not feel that way, however, and thus we tend not to work closely or frequently with those who do. There is an old English saying, "If you are going to sup with the Devil, use a long spoon for fear of infection." We spend much time in our business thinking about morals and ethics, and if we begin to feel that we are "supping with the Devil," (or you think you are "supping with the Devil") we will respond defensively.

The third issue that has surfaced during this seminar is, "What are the necessary conditions for undertaking the research and discoveries that make a difference to health?" There has been much discussion on counterfeiting, intellectual property, and respect for private enterprise. Clearly, there is a direct relationship between Merck's willingness to do business in certain parts of the world and the region's political stability, its level of corruption, and the existence of appropriate rules of respect for our business.

If the rules do not exist, companies like Merck cannot be forced autocratically to do business in such countries. So, you can best help us to do business in certain areas of the world by engaging your interests in helping to develop economic and political stability in those regions.

The related question is whether it is appropriate to expect companies to do business in places where there is no business. There is a worldwide triad of pharmaceutical issues—access, quality, and cost. These issues exist in New York, California, Kenya, and Zaire, albeit at very different levels.

The first is access. If there is not a logistical chain in place that assures that insulin will be delivered regularly—not once a year, but every single time a patient needs it—then practically everything else has to fail.

Another dimension is the maintenance of quality standards. If there is one thing that has come across clearly, whether it relates to supplied services or products, it is that Gresham's Law applies—"That which is of worse quality and cheaper will force out that which is of better quality and more expensive." Gresham's Law is at work today in the Third World drug industry just as it was in the sixteenth-century monetary world of Britain.

Multinational pharmaceutical companies do not have much to offer when it comes to providing low-cost, low-quality drugs in Africa. We take pride in providing products of the highest possible quality at the lowest possible cost (efficient production with an appropriate return) for that high quality. That is far more expensive than the backyard substances produced by individuals, whether in Bangladesh or Kenya, or the products of a supposed pharmaceutical production facility which takes some raw materials out of cans, adds a few excipients, and pounds out a product. Merck will not compromise its ethical or production standards in order to do business in certain countries.

As a result of our standards, there are only certain places where we can do business directly. That does not mean our drugs are not available for those who want to purchase them. There are many countries where we work through distributors, but we will not be there. Thus, a focus on the problems suggests that a firm should not be present in a country where there is no business or where it cannot absolutely assure the quality of the product as it reaches the patient.

In developing countries, both corporations and charitable groups struggle with the same undernourished health delivery systems and the same, well-meaning but misguided governmental policies and officials. Both groups have a common purpose relative to the delivery of pharmaceuticals but their missions and options are quite different. It is appropriate for religious communities to commit and stay. For corporations, however, when minimum standards of distribution and use cannot be monitored, withdrawal may well be the best policy in the long run, both for the firm and, through its pressure on local governments, for the health care delivery system.

A focus on needs leads to a different conclusion. Anyone who looks at world demographics knows that an unbelievably high percentage of the world population is now located and will still be located fifty years from now in places that, by our standards of measurement, have no money.

Yet those parts of the world not only have people who are important resources, but who ultimately will be part of the economic world as well as the physical world. We as global companies must play a part.

We have a group at Merck totally dedicated to determining how we can try to do business in the parts of the world where we currently find it difficult to do business. In fact there is no way we can walk away from what could amount to 70 percent of the world. And we must continually examine how we can do business in places where there is now no business.

In all of this discussion, the key is economic development, and the key of what is coming out of our discussions is priority setting. This involves asking very tough questions.

The canvas for doing good is as broad and as limitless as the eye can see. But priority setting means making choices. It means making the decision to do good *here*, regardless of whether there is a tremendous need *there*. That is the nature of priority setting, and it is difficult. In our social responsibility, we set priorities, and we set priorities on where we do business, depending upon the conditions that exist.

The point has been made that multinationals ought to be clear about their role. Multinationals are *not* clear about their role. They probably never will be. However, it is forums like this that help corporations do a better job in clarifying what they are doing, what they *should* be doing, and what they *can* do.

Participants

Carol C. Adelman

Vice President
Consultative Group on Development

Albert D. Angel

Vice President, Public Affairs
Merck & Co., Inc.
President, The Merck Company
Foundation

Fernando S. Antezana

Programme Manager
Action Programme on Essential Drugs
World Health Organization

James Armstrong

Vice President, Public Issues and Corporate Ethics
Pagan International

Malcolm B. Barlow

Vice President, Industry Affairs
SmithKline Beecham Pharmaceuticals

Walter M. Batts

Multilateral Programs Coordinator
International Affairs Staff
Food and Drug Administration

E. Steven Bauer

Vice President, Corporate and Government Affairs
Wyeth International Limited

Thomas A. Bausch

Dean, College of Business
Administration
Marquette University

Clyde J. Behney

Director, Health Program
Office of Technology Assessment

Ernest J. Bartell, C.S.C.	Executive Director Helen Kellogg Institute for International Studies University of Notre Dame
Paul A. Belford	former Assistant Vice President, International Pharmaceutical Manufacturers Associations President Association Executive Resources Group
Ingar G. F. Bruggemann	Director World Health Organization Office
Thomas P. Carney	Chairman and Chief Executive Officer Metatech Corporation
John B. Caron	Past President, Caron International President, TECHNOSERVE
Octavio de Caso	Director Mexican Health Foundation
Gerald F. Cavanagh, S.J.	College of Business Administration University of Detroit
David M. Charron	Manager, Q.A. Strategic Planning The Upjohn Company
Andrew Chetley	Representative Health Action International
Kevin J. Christiano	Department of Sociology University of Notre Dame
Elizabeth M. Coit	Director, International Programs Unitarian Universalist Service Committee

David E. Collins

President
Schering-Plough HealthCare Products

Aldrage B. Cooper, Jr.

Director, Public Affairs
Johnson & Johnson

Jacqueline A. Corrigan

Analyst, Health Program
Office of Technology Assessment

Roger B. Crawford

Director, Human Resources
Johnson & Johnson

Gwen Crawley

Associate for Health Ministries
Presbyterian Church (USA)

Susan Crowley

Director, Public Policy Management
Merck & Co., Inc.

Roy L. Crum

Director
Center for International Economic and
    Business Studies
University of Florida

Gabriel Daniel

Pharmaceutical Health Specialist
Africare

Richard A. DeGraff

Special Assistant to Chairman
W. R. Grace & Company

Leo A. Despres

Department of Anthropology
University of Notre Dame

Joan Devane, S.C.M.M.

General Manager
Mission for Essential Drugs and Sup-
    plies (MEDS)

Earl W. Doubet

President, Caterpillar Americas
Caterpillar Tractor Company

Giulia Earle

Program Coordinator
International Medical Services for
   Health (INMED)

Alberta R. Edwards

Vice President, Public Affairs
Schering-Plough International

Robert L. Ellis

Associate for Program Development &
   Resourcing
Health Ministries Office, Presbyterian
   Church (USA)

Philip G. Ellsworth

Vice President
Government and Industry Affairs,
   International
Marion Merrell Dow Inc.

Carol G. Emerling

Corporate Secretary
American Home Products Corporation

James J. Ferguson, C.S.C.

Director
Holy Cross Mission Center for Cross-
   Cultural Ministries

Michael J. Francis

Department of Government and International Studies
University of Notre Dame

Yusaku Furuhashi

Ray W. and Kenneth G. Herrick
   Professor
Department of Marketing
University of Notre Dame

Hellen Gelband

Project Director and Senior Analyst,
   Health Program
Office of Technology Assessment

Janet Gottschalk,
S.C.M.M.

International Consultant, Primary
   Health Care
Sector Superior, North American
   Medical Mission Sisters

Denis A. Goulet	O'Neill Professor in Education for Justice University of Notre Dame
Msgr. Joseph Gremillion	former Director Institute for Pastoral & Social Ministry University of Notre Dame
Penny Grewal	Staff Relations to Third World CIBA-GEIGY Limited
Doris Haire	Representative National Women's Health Network
Jean Halloran	Director The Institute for Consumers' Policy Development
Eric O. Hanson	Department of Political Science The University of Santa Clara
Kirk O. Hanson	Stanford Graduate School of Business Stanford University
Howard F. Harris	Vice President, Corporate Affairs CPC International Inc.
Kevin J. Healy	Foundation Representative Inter-American Foundation
James Hennessy	Executive Vice President NYNEX Corporation
Peter J. Henriot, S.J.	Director Center of Concern
Theodore M. Hesburgh, C.S.C.	President Emeritus University of Notre Dame
Michael W. Hodin	Vice President, Public Affairs Pfizer International Inc.

John W. Houck

Department of Management
Co-Director
Center for Ethics and Religious Values
    in Business
University of Notre Dame

Linda L. Hudgins

Department of Economics
University of Notre Dame

Thomas Joyce, C.M.F.

Staff Member
8th Day Center for Justice

Jacob Keli

President
International Trade Exchange
    Corporation

Roger B. Kelley

former Vice President
Caterpillar Tractor Company

Kwan S. Kim

Department of Economics
Helen Kellogg Institute for Interna-
    tional Studies
University of Notre Dame

Violet N. Kimani

Department of Community Health
University of Nairobi

Jay J. Kingham

Vice President, International
Pharmaceutical Manufacturers
    Association

Richard J. Kinney

Director of State and Community
    Affairs
Schering-Plough Corporation

Douglas W. Kmiec

Director, Thomas J. White Center on
    Law and Government
University of Notre Dame

Ved P. Kumar

Senior Pharmaceutical Specialist
The World Bank

Louis Lasagna, M.D.   Dean, Sackler School of Graduate
                               Biomedical Sciences
                               Tufts University

David C. Leege   former Director
                             Center for the Study of Contemporary
                               Society
                             University of Notre Dame

Klaus M. Leisinger   Vice President
                             CIBA-GEIGY Limited

Flynt Leveretts   Representative
                             Health Policy International

William P. Looney   Supervisor, International Public Affairs
                             Warner-Lambert Company

Joseph J. Lovett   Research Associate
                             Mercy Health Services

David W. Lutz   Department of Philosophy
                             University of Notre Dame

Edward A. Malloy, C.S.C.   President
                             University of Notre Dame

Paul A. Maxey   President
                             Allied Medical Ministries for Medical &
                               Healthcare Supplies, Inc.

Dennis P. McCann   Director, Center for the Study of
                               Values
                             DePaul University

H. Thomas McDermott,   Office of Campus Ministry
  C.S.C.   University of Notre Dame

Robert T. McDonough   Manager, Public Policy Planning
                             The Upjohn Company

Donald P. McNeill, C.S.C.   Director, Center for Social Concerns
                             University of Notre Dame

Leona A. Miklas   Director, Regional Operations, Europe/
                                Africa
                             Merck Sharp & Dohme International

Gerald D. Moore   Technical Officer
                             Action Programme on Essential Drugs
                             World Health Organization

Ronald R. Morris   Company Group Chairman
                             Johnson & Johnson

Mutombo Mpanya   Director
                             International Environmental Studies
                                Program
                             World College West

John R. Mullen   Vice President, Corporate Relations
                             Johnson & Johnson

Elisabeth S. Murphy   Family Nurse Practitioner
                             Presbyterian Church (USA)

Patrick R. Murphy   Department of Management
                             University of Notre Dame

Michael J. Naughton   Department of Management
                             Marquette University

Jack S. Newberry   Director, Pharmaceutical Services
                             St. Mary's Hospital, Mercy Health
                                Corporation

Eileen Nic   Project Coordinator
                             Coordinating Committee on Toxics and
                                Drugs
                             Natural Resources Defense Council

John S. North   Manager, International Corporate
                                    Affairs
                                 Eli Lilly and Company

Timothy O'Meara   Provost
                                 Kenna Professor of Mathematics
                                 University of Notre Dame

Michael A. O'Neill   Director, Industry and Government
                                    Affairs
                                 Wyeth-Ayerst International Inc.

Rafael D. Pagan, Jr.   President
                                 Nestle Coordination Center for Nutri-
                                    tion Inc.

Agostino Paganini, M.D.   Manager, Bamako Initiative Manage-
                                    ment Unit
                                 United Nations Children's Fund
                                    (UNICEF)

Robert S. Pelton, C.S.C.   Director
                                 The Institute for Pastoral and Social
                                    Ministry
                                 University of Notre Dame

Linda Pfeiffer   President and Chief Executive Officer
                                 International Medical Services for
                                    Health (INMED)

Lee E. Preston   College of Business & Management
                                 University of Maryland

Michael L. Privitera   Director of Public Affairs
                                 Pfizer International Inc.

James T. Rahilly, C.S.C.   Missionary, District Representative
                                 Holy Cross Mission Center for Cross-
                                    Cultural Ministries

Jean Daniel Rainhorn, M.D.

Takemi Program in International Health
Harvard School of Public Health

Nelson Reavey-Cantwell, M.D.

Global Medical Director
Merrell Dow Research Institute

Michael R. Reich

Director, Takemi Program in International Health
Harvard School of Public Health

Frank K. Reilly

Bernard J. Hank Professor of Business
University of Notre Dame

Juan M. Rivera

Department of Accountancy
University of Notre Dame

Susan E. Robertson, M.D.

Medical Epidemiologist
Centers for Disease Control

Regina Rowan, S.C.M.M.

Chair, Pharmaceutical Workgroup
Interfaith Center on Corporate Responsibility
Medical Mission Sisters

Norlin G. Rueschhoff

Department of Accountancy
University of Notre Dame

Nicholas L. Ruggieri

Director, Washington Affairs
Johnson & Johnson

James B. Russo

Director, Government and Public Policy
SmithKline Beecham

Leo V. Ryan, C.S.V.

Department of Management
DePaul University

William Ryan

Chief Counsel
U.S. Senate Committee on Labor and Human Resources

Rosemary Sabino, R.S.M.   President and Chief Executive Officer
                            Catholic Health Association of
                                Wisconsin

David E. Schlaver, C.S.C.   Editor and Publisher, Ave Maria Press
                            University of Notre Dame

Brian S. Schuster   Assistant Counsel
                            Miles Laboratories, Inc.

Leroy L. Schwartz, M.D.   President
                            Health Policy International

S. Prakash Sethi   Associate Director, Center for
                                Management
                            The City University of New York

Robert L. Shafer   Vice President, Public Affairs and
                                Government Relations
                            Pfizer, Inc.

J. Robert Shaffer   Director, International Public Affairs
                            Sterling Drug Inc.

Sybil Shainwald   Representative
                            National Women's Health Network

Walter W. Simons   Executive Director
                            Industry Council for Development

Roger B. Skurski   Director
                            Center for the Study of Contemporary
                                Society
                            University of Notre Dame

Timothy Smith   Interfaith Center on Corporate
                                Responsibility
                            National Council of Churches

Mark W. Stanton   Executive Director
                            Health Policy International

William A. Struck   Director of Adult Education
                          Second Reformed Church

Rev. Leon Sullivan   Director
                          International Council for Equality of
                              Opportunity Principles

George Suter   Vice President, Administration
                          Europe, Africa, Middle East
                          Pfizer International, Inc.

Lee A. Tavis   C. R. Smith Professor of Business
                              Administration
                          Department of Finance
                          University of Notre Dame

Eloise Thomas, B.V.M.   Staff Member
                          8th Day Center for Justice

John P. Thorp   Department Head, Social Sciences
                          Ferris State University

Kiichiro Tsutani, M.D.   Program in International Health
                          Harvard School of Public Health

John A. Weber   Department of Marketing
                          University of Notre Dame

Jean Wilkowski   Chairman of the Board
                          Volunteers in Technical Assistance

Oliver F. Williams, C.S.C.   Associate Provost
                          University of Notre Dame

Hans A. Wolf   Vice Chairman
                          Syntex Corporation

Michael M. Yoshitsu   Associate Director
                          Pfizer International, Inc.

Charles E. Ziegler   Senior Vice President, External Affairs
                          CIBA-GEIGY Corporation